TOP TAX SAVING IDEAS FOR TODAY'S SMALL BUSINESS

THOMAS J. STEMMY

Edited by Camille Akin

The Oasis Press® / PSI Research
Central Point, Oregon

100198

Published by The Oasis Press®
© 1999 by Thomas J. Stemmy

This publication is designed to provide accurate and authoritative information in regard to the subject matter covered. It is sold with the understanding that the publisher is not engaged in rendering legal, accounting, or other professional service. If legal advice or other expert assistance is required, the services of a competent professional person should be sought.

> *— from a declaration of principles jointly adopted by a committee of the American Bar Association and a committee of publishers.*

Editor: Camille Akin

Please direct any comments, questions, or suggestions regarding this book to The Oasis Press®/ PSI Research:

Editorial Department
P.O. Box 3727
Central Point, OR 97502
(541) 479-9464

The Oasis Press® is a Registered Trademark of Publishing Services, Inc., an Oregon corporation doing business as PSI Research.

Library of Congress Cataloging-in-Publication Data
Stemmy, Thomas J.
  Top tax saving ideas for today's small business / Thomas J. Stemmy
  ;edited by Camille Akin. -- 4th ed.
    p.   cm. -- (PSI successful business library)
  Includes index.
  ISBN 1-55571-463-3
  1.   Small Business -- Taxation -- Law and legislation -- United States-
- Popular works.   2. Tax planning -- United States.   I. Akin, Camille.
II. Title.   III. Series.
KF6491.Z9S74 1998
343.7305 ' 268--dc21   98-33915
                                                              CIP

Printed in the United States of America
Fourth edition 10 9 8 7 6 5 4 3 2 1 0

 Printed on recycled paper when available.

To Jean and Tom Stemmy — the kind of parents whose inspiration makes books like this happen; and to Linda and Lynn — the kind of family whose faithful and loving support provides the remaining ingredients.

CONTENTS

PREFACE

What is a tax shelter under today's new rules? Are so-called tax shelters and loopholes still viable planning options now that massive tax reform has redesigned the rules of the game? More importantly, if any creative solutions remain, how can the small business owner know how to survive without paying a small fortune to the accountants and lawyers who know how the game is played?

This reference book provides an easy-to-read summary of the key tax planning alternatives debated by the professionals behind closed doors. It also demonstrates that the very concept of the tax shelter, as we know it, has undergone a cataclysmic change over the past ten decades. Most notably, the new laws have eliminated the "quick fixes" for the creative tax planner in business.

Your quest to conquer your ever-increasing tax burden must now take a different approach. If you plan to make it as a small business owner in this environment, you must recognize that you can no longer buy tax shelter relief or employ quick accounting solutions. Instead, you must prepare to deal with new, methodical rules of the game.

Although this book has been written in a concise, easy-to-read format, it involves the interpretation of a highly complex tax code and many tax regulations. This book will help you better understand the concept behind these rules and the planning options that are now available. If nothing else, you should at least know the right questions to ask your professional advisers.

To make the study complete, I draw on my experience as a tax practitioner, a university teacher, and a financial adviser to small businesses. I have reached back to the earliest days of my career when I first experienced the federal tax system in action. Those were the days when I served on the other side of the tax shelter fence as a fear-inspiring IRS agent!

Tom Stemmy
November, 1998

ABOUT THE AUTHOR

Thomas J. Stemmy has more than 30 years of experience as a tax specialist and consultant. He began his career in 1960 as a field agent for the Internal Revenue Service in Washington, D.C., and since then, he has been in private practice as a CPA. Mr. Stemmy is a partner in the law firm Stemmy, Tidler, & Morris, P.A. in Greenbelt, Maryland. In addition to his practice, he has taught federal taxation and business-related courses at the University of Maryland in College Park, Maryland.

Mr. Stemmy has authored numerous articles for professional publication. He has earned the coveted, nationally recognized Golden Quill Award from the National Society of Public Accountants. In addition, he is the author of *How to Slash the Cost, Time and Aggravation of a Tax Audit*, published by Prentice-Hall.

Mr. Stemmy holds a bachelor's degree in economics from Villanova University (Villanova, Pennsylvania), and a master's degree in management science from the National Graduate University (Alexandria, Virginia). He is licensed to practice as a CPA in Maryland and holds an enrolled agent (E.A.) designation that allows him to practice before the IRS.

ACKNOWLEDGMENTS

I am grateful to the CPA firm of Stemmy, Tidler & Morris, P.A., whose faithful support and organizational teamwork made this work possible. Particular credit is given to Vivian De Santis who gave considerable hours of her own time, while making certain that none of the controversial tax-planning issues got by without extensive research and debate.

For Christopher D. Morris, recognition is extended to his brilliance in helping settle the discussions involving the highly technical tax matters discussed in this book. To Rick Orazio Puglisi and Bob Jodoin there is appreciation for the endless support and inspiration emanating from their respective positions as true accounting professionals. Also, within the firm, equal gratitude is extended to Judy McCool whose usual administrative efficiency saw to it that the job got mailed, faxed, and delivered in timely fashion.

Special thanks go to William H. Sager, Legal Counsel to the National Society of Public Accountants, for his perceptive ideas and insight. And, to Dr. Walter Boek, President of the National Graduate University, I extend my gratitude for his interest and support in this writing.

Deepest appreciation goes out for the suggestions and commentary provided by John Parker and Stanley Pickett, the most qualified "business lawyers" I have known during all my years of practice. And, to John Dillon, of Legg Mason Wood Walker, I give thanks to an investment adviser whose creative insight and energy bring a new meaning to the term stockbroker. And, to Kelly Griffifth of Merrill Lynch & Co., I am grateful that she has extended to me the same kind of professionalism and loyalty that she extends each of her clients.

Finally, this book could not have taken shape without the vision of Emmett Ramey of PSI Research who knows, best of all, what kind of reference works are needed by the small business owner in America. He is the one that planted the seed and through the skillful editing of Camille Akin, that seed quickly took root.

INTRODUCTION

For many decades, America's small business owners have faced overwhelming odds against their long-term survival. Many have been quick to point the finger of blame at an oppressive tax system which, they contend, continues to stand in the way of a profitable business operation. More specifically, it is the Internal Revenue Service that is often singled out as the one powerful agency that can most quickly break the small business owner.

The IRS, with its enormously complex tax code and its army of enforcement officers, is arguably the most prominent force that you must contend with if you want to survive as a small business owner. Incidentally, the fact that you have this book — and have otherwise taken the first step toward legitimately reducing your potentially oppressive tax burden — suggests that you just might be one of the survivors.

In recent times, there has been a systematic, albeit slow, attempt by lawmakers to help the "little guy" make it. The layperson may not agree with this and many will hasten to point out that the ever-changing tax code today is nothing but a formulation designed to ultimately help the rich get richer. The professional adviser, on the other hand, sees a systematic thrust that has been doing the exact opposite in terms of showing preference. With one tax reform after another, you will see a trend toward creating more new tax breaks for the "little guy" while the wealthy get cut out by an array of threshold formulas that tend to stack the cards against high earnings.

And so, the good news is that as a small business owner, you probably have a lot to look forward to — as long as the legislative momentum continues to favor your survival. However, if you want to stay in the game, you must stay alert to the changing rules. That means you should try to keep apprised of every new loophole, tax deduction, or tax deferral that could help your cause. Above all, don't be ashamed to admit it if you are utterly in the dark as to the rules of the game. You are far from being alone. Just remember that there is an immense amount of literature and Internet data out there that can help you identify the tax benefits that are available to you as a small business owner. And, if you don't have the time or the inclination to seek out this material yourself, make sure you seek out a knowledgeable accountant or tax adviser. A short consultation could prove to be one of the best investments that you will ever make.

Chapter 1

GET TO KNOW THE CURRENT TAX ENVIRONMENT

When President Bill Clinton signed the Budget Reconciliation Act on August 10, 1993, a nation of taxpayers had seen the reinforcement of a tax policy that surprised no one. Flirtations with a "flat tax" scenario had been sounding good back in those days, at least in theory. But who really thought that our political forces would have created a tax code that would promote the notion that "everyone should pay at the same rate." Even in this age of complete fairness and equality for all, there exists a relentless undercurrent that demands "the more you make, the more you pay."

Whether you are for or against a policy that provides for a fair, flat, across-the-board tax rate, you may as well resign yourself to the fact that you won't see it any time soon. The 1993 tax act signed by the president sent a clear message that progressive tax rates are here to stay.

This chapter will focus on the provisions of the current, progressive tax structure and the impact that it has on small business owners. It also discusses the recent capital gains tax revisions and how these changes will affect your tax bracket. The main objective is to highlight the tax-saving opportunities in light of the marginal tax brackets that affect each and every one of us. Finally, you will learn how to deal effectively with the IRS should a problem arise.

Do You Know Your Own Tax Bracket?

It is interesting to note how few individuals have a real grasp of how much income tax they pay during the course of a year. In a recent seminar of aspiring entrepreneurs, the participants were asked to comment on their own personal income tax situation. The surprising response made it immediately clear that many had no idea how much taxes they paid last year, or how much they expected to pay at the end of the current year. And worse, the vast majority did not even have a clue as to their own personal income tax bracket. For any meaningful tax planning, you must be aware of your current and expected income tax bracket.

Individual Tax Rates Are Up for Higher Earners

Whether you operate as a corporation, a partnership, an LLC, or a sole proprietorship, you must plan on taking your profit out of the business sometime. This means that any change in the **individual** tax rates will be crucial as you try to keep your tax bill down. Ever since the 1993 act, most lower income individuals will experience minimal change in their tax liability. Higher earners, however, will pay the price. Individual tax rates remain at high levels for higher earners.

WATCH OUT FOR THOSE TAX BRACKET CUT-OFFS

Few taxpayers have been surprised as to how high the tax rates have crept during the past several years. Although the threshold for being taxed at these higher rates has been increased for inflation, the rates for many can be brutal.

For example, in the worst case scenario, you can be taxed as high as 39.6%. You will have reached the threshold to be taxed at this highest tax bracket if your taxable income exceeds the following:

- ◆ $278,450, if you're filing as married, single, or head of household; or

- ◆ $139,225, if you're filing as married, filing separately.

Illustration 1.1

- ◆ Pierre, filing as single, anticipates a taxable income in excess of $128,000 on his 1998 individual return.

- ◆ His taxable income for the following year is expected to drop below $100,000.

- ◆ He heard news that his sole proprietorship might receive an additional fee of $10,000 in late December because of a new contract.

- ◆ If the contract fee were to be deferred until January 1999, Pierre would save $500 in taxes. $10,000 would be taxed at 31% instead of 36%.

The same factors would apply if Pierre's anticipated taxable income for 1998 had been $278,450 instead of $128,000. Only the tax rates would be different. If received in the earlier year, the contract award would cause an additional tax liability of $860. This is because he would pay the 39.6% rate instead of the 31% rate (an additional 8.6%).

THE CORPORATE TAX RATES – ONE REASON TO BE INCORPORATED

Ever since 1994, some changes were made that affect the basic corporate tax rates. The lowest bracket of up to $50,000 remains the same at 15%. The highest bracket has been increased from 34% to 35%. However, this top rate only applies to those larger corporations with taxable incomes in excess of $10 million. For small business, the highest rate "tops out" at 34% — the same as under the old law. For professional corporations, however, the current rate is a flat 35%, regardless of what your income may be.

COMPARE CORPORATE RATES WITH INDIVIDUAL RATES

Smart business owner-operators never lose sight of their top marginal tax bracket. By so doing, you plan around paying at unnecessarily high rates. The key to getting the most under the current tax law is to observe the relative differences between individual and corporate rates.

You know that the top tax rate for an individual comes to 39.6% when adding on the surtax at the higher levels. At the same time, the corporate rate might be as low as 15% when you are at the very lowest levels. This fact, as observed in Chapter 2, prompts corporate owners to have their corporation pick up at least some of the income at the lower rates. If you are not operating as a corporation, you might think about the potential advantages for forming one.

Illustration 1.2

♦ From Illustration 1.1, assume that instead of a sole proprietorship Pierre operates as a corporation.

♦ Further, assume that he was personally in the top 39.6% bracket as an individual for 1998, but his corporation was at a break-even point.

♦ If Pierre were to let the $10,000 remain in the corporation where it would be put to work, he could save $2,460 in taxes for 1998 — paying $1,500 in taxes instead of $3,960.

CAPITAL GAINS TAX RELIEF HAS ARRIVED

A *capital asset* is recognized by a small business owner as investment property. It includes stocks, bonds, equipment, real estate, and the actual business entity itself. If you have ever tried to sell some stock or other investment property you may have dropped the whole idea, realizing the stifling capital gains tax makes selling a bad economic move. If you are among those who have held onto an investment for a particularly long period, you might wonder how you could ever justify paying the tax bite after inflation already took its toll from your profit.

⬚ *Special Note: The 1997 and 1998 tax acts have clarified the capital gains issue. Individuals should not have to pay one cent more that 20% of any capital asset held for a specified time period. Taxpayers in the lowest tax bracket can pay as little as 10%. The difference between the capital gains tax rate and the ordinary rate is significant indeed. All small business owners must be familiar with their message. (See Chapter 15 for more on capital gains.)*

A LOOK TO THE FUTURE: A KINDER, GENTLER SIDE OF THE IRS

It finally hit home that the need to shape up the IRS had been long overdue. In the Tax Reform Act of 1998 there had been a series of tax-saving benefits, many of which will be of interest to the readers of this book. The segment of the 1998 bill that favorably affects the small business owner is direct and to the point. To set the tone, the new law begins by directing that the IRS change its three-tier geographic structure — national, regional, and district offices. Instead, the IRS will work to set up operating units that serve particular groups of taxpayers. It has been declared that the specific groups will include: individuals, tax-exempt organizations, big businesses, and, you guessed it, small business owners.

For those individuals who have had the courage to invest their time, money, and resources in a small business operation in America, there are five special taxpayer advantages in the 1998 act of which you should be aware, including:

♦ The new national taxpayer advocate;

♦ The new burden of proof rules;

♦ New rules on privileged communications with your tax adviser;

♦ New rules on due process on tax collection matters; and

♦ New restrictions imposed on the IRS on supposedly unreported income.

ADVANTAGE #1: THE NEW NATIONAL TAXPAYER ADVOCATE

In the new law there is an expanded role for the so-called taxpayer advocate whose job is to assist taxpayers that are involved in a tax dispute with the IRS. This can prove to be a godsend for small business owners who will now be able to receive assistance from an individual who will be given a role as a serious advocate, wholly independent from IRS oversight.

Special Note: Under the new law, the small business owners will find it much easier to obtain a so-called "Taxpayer Assistance Order," a procedure designed to provide intervention when they are suffering, or about to suffer, a significant hardship on account of some IRS action.

ADVANTAGE #2: THE NEW BURDEN OF PROOF RULES

Prior to 1998, tax professionals had long been familiar with the one-sided rule that presumed the IRS determination of tax liability was generally correct. This meant, of course, that the burden of proof was placed on the taxpayer who had to prove that the IRS was wrong.

For IRS examinations that begin after July 22, 1998, the thrust will be to throw the burden of proof, on any issue or fact, back to the IRS if you:

♦ Cooperate with the IRS;

♦ Comply with your substantiation requirements;

♦ Introduce creditable evidence;

♦ Maintain adequate records; and

♦ Are an individual (not a corporation) with a net worth that doesn't exceed $7 million.

ADVANTAGE #3: PRIVILEGED COMMUNICATIONS WITH YOUR TAX ADVISER

Under the new law the IRS will be forced to extend the attorney-client confidentiality privilege to communications between a client (taxpayer) and any individual authorized to practice before the IRS. In general, the privilege is to be applied in any non-criminal tax proceeding before the IRS or in the federal courts. This could be a matter of importance to many small business owners who often rely on professionals such as CPAs, enrolled agents, or enrolled actuaries.

ADVANTAGE #4: DUE PROCESS ON TAX COLLECTION MATTERS

After January 18, 1999, the IRS must follow stringent new guidelines for enforcing tax collection policy. Designed to protect the taxpayer, the new rules state that:

"The taxpayer has 30 days after the mailing of a notice or tax lien to demand a hearing before an appeals officer. (By the way, that officer must not have had any prior involvement with your case.)"

Generally, the IRS will be required to give you 30 days notice before levying on property, during which time you could demand a hearing.

Both of these rules can have a profoundly favorable impact on many small business owners who have been frequently and severely harmed by the aggressive collection policy of certain collection officers.

ADVANTAGE #5: IRS BARRED FROM MAKING CERTAIN PRESUMPTIONS ABOUT SUPPOSEDLY UNREPORTED INCOME

In the past, many small business owners have been plagued by IRS officials who had taken it upon themselves to calculate income based on certain observations about a taxpayer's supposed financial status. The procedure relied on was the so-called "economic reality" technique. It was a technique used by the examining agent who essentially relied on presumptions based on certain facts and circumstances observed about the taxpayer, such as lifestyle and spending habits.

Under the new law, the IRS will not be able to use this procedure and otherwise allege that certain income had been unreported — unless there is a reasonable indication that such income is likely to exist.

CHAPTER SUMMARY

Due to major tax reform, a nation of taxpayers has seen continued efforts by Congress and the President to alleviate some of Middle America's tax burden. In particular, the Taxpayer Relief Act of 1997 and the Small Business Job Protection Act of 1996 have helped pave the way for the small business community. With their numerous tax reforms, the benefits of these two acts may help aspiring entreprenuers and encourage existing business owners. To know how these changes will affect you and how you do business, you'll first want to:

♦ Be aware of your own tax bracket and keep this in mind as you make any business decision;

♦ Understand the new capital gains tax rates and plan your purchases and sales accordingly; and

♦ Familiarize yourself with the restructuring of the IRS so you can take advantage of the friendlier and easier-to-work-with tax environment.

As you better understand where you fall into your own particular tax bracket and the overall tax impact on your business, you can get a better picture of your operating entity, be it sole proprietorship, corporation, partnership, or limited liability company (LLC). Chapter 2 will introduce you to these legal forms of doing business.

1998 Tax Rate Schedules

1998 Tax Rate Schedules

Caution: *Do not use these Tax Rate Schedules to figure your 1997 taxes. Use only to figure your 1998 estimated taxes.*

Single – Schedule X

If line 5 is: Over–	But not over–	The tax is:		of the amount over–
$0	$25,350	....	15%	$0
25,350	61,400	$3,802.50 +	28%	25,350
61,400	128,100	13,896.50 +	31%	61,400
128,100	278,450	34,573.50 +	36%	128,100
278,450	....	88,699.50 + 39.6%		278,450

Head of household – Schedule Z

If line 5 is: Over–	But not over–	The tax is:		of the amount over–
$0	$33,950	....	15%	$0
33,950	87,700	$5,092.50 +	28%	33,950
87,700	142,000	20,142.50 +	31%	87,700
142,000	278,450	36,975.50 +	36%	142,000
278,450	....	86,097.50 + 39.6%		278,450

Married filing jointly or Qualifying widow(er) – Schedule Y-1

If line 5 is: Over–	But not over–	The tax is:		of the amount over–
$0	$42,350	....	15%	$0
42,350	102,300	$6,352.50 +	28%	42,350
102,300	155,950	23,138.50 +	31%	102,300
155,950	278,450	39,770.00 +	36%	155,950
278,450	....	83,870.00 + 39.6%		278,450

Married filing separately – Schedule Y-2

If line 5 is: Over–	But not over–	The tax is:		of the amount over–
$0	$21,175	....	15%	$0
21,175	51,150	$3,176.25 +	28%	21,175
51,150	77,975	11,569.25 +	31%	51,150
77,975	139,225	19,885.00 +	36%	77,975
139,225	....	41,935.00 + 39.6%		139,225

Chapter 2

CHOOSE THE RIGHT IDENTITY TO STRUCTURE YOUR BUSINESS

You, like every new business owner, must have asked yourself at one time or another, "What kind of business entity is best suited for my particular operation?" For most entrepreneurs, the answer lies behind two specific questions.

- ◆ **Legal liability.** How can I get the best protection from business liabilities that can threaten not only my business assets, but my family's assets as well?

- ◆ **Tax considerations.** How can I get the best tax breaks out of the business entity that I select?

It is the second question involving the search for shelter from high taxes that underscores the subject matter of this opening chapter and sets the overall theme for this entire book. But first take a brief look at legal liability.

You have probably considered the question of legal liability first because of its ominous overtones that you might one day be a victim of a devastating lawsuit. Because of our litigious society you might have been told that you should always protect your personal assets by forming a corporation whenever you start any kind of business. Perhaps, you have also been told that multiple corporations, in some cases, provide further insulation for the business assets themselves. You might have been told that a limited partnership could provide shelter from liability for investors in certain situations. And, like many start-up business owners, you've probably heard some of the clamor regarding operating as an S corporation or a limited liability company (LLC). These two options have become fashionable as tax savers and should not be overlooked.

Whichever entity you have chosen or will choose, you may be wondering if you are still facing some element of risk to your assets and the assets of your family. Since this is a book about tax-saving ideas, it does not analyze issues like legal liability and exposure to lawsuits. Suffice it to say that no two business operations are identical; nor are the juxtapositions of any two owners of a business operation. What may be a smart way for your competitor to do business may very well prove to be a costly mistake for you. You might find yourself spending unnecessary time, energy, and money just to provide some overkill protection. When in reality, you have nothing but a scant exposure to legal liability.

If you are left with the slightest concern about exposure to legal liability in your prospective venture, confer with an attorney who has the right kind of credentials. In short, find an attorney who specializes in matters pertaining to business.

HOW TO SAVE TAXES WITH YOUR BUSINESS ENTITY

New business owners are quick to learn that confiscatory tax laws have a profound influence on the success or failure of all small business operations. As a small business owner, you want to get every break available under the law and you don't want to see the results of all your hard work get eaten up by the IRS and the tough tax laws. The problem, however, is that those tax laws have become so painfully complex that new business owners automatically assume they could never make the best of their available options without conceding the strategy planning to the tax professionals. Interestingly, the tax professionals themselves are often at odds with each other as to the **best** tax saving options in this ever-changing environment.

In the following chapters you will learn the fundamental **tax advantages and disadvantages** that attach to each type of business entity. You will have a working knowledge of the key tax questions that are raised every time an entrepreneur decides to go into business. This will equip you to play an active role in selecting the entity that best suits your own personal circumstances. At the very least, you will learn what kinds of tax shelter options are available for each type of entity when you finally sit down with your professional tax adviser. After all, you know best all the facets and idiosyncrasies of your own business operation. Additionally, you are better equipped to ensure that your personal financial planning objectives are met.

UNDERSTAND THE DIFFERENCES BETWEEN THE ENTITIES

Before we discuss the specific tax advantages and disadvantages of the various business entities, it is important that you know some fundamental tax considerations between a:

♦ Sole proprietorship

♦ General partnership

- Limited partnership

- Corporation

- Limited liability company

THE SOLE PROPRIETORSHIP

The sole proprietorship is thought of as the quickest and easiest way to set up a business operation. There are no blanket prerequisites nor are there any specific costs in starting a sole proprietorship. There may be some minor formalities, however, that will need attention depending on your state or your jurisdiction. These formalities, which of course apply to all business entities, mean that you will probably have to:

- Obtain an occupancy permit for your place of business;

- Secure a business license; and

- Apply for a franchise or registration number for your operation. This registration number will be used by the state agency to monitor the collection of sales tax and other regulatory matters.

All of these procedures are simple and can be done without the assistance of an attorney or accountant regardless of the state in which you are doing business. Once you start a sole proprietorship, you are the sole owner. Unless you are in a community property state in which your spouse is vested with a one-half interest, you alone have full control and responsibility for the operation.

THE GENERAL PARTNERSHIP

Like the sole proprietorship, starting up the general partnership could be a relatively easy process. No costs or formalities are required. Wise counsel, however, will give you about a dozen reasons why you should have a detailed partnership agreement drafted whenever you put yourself on the line with any other individual. A few items that you would be best advised to spell out in writing are:

◆ The amount of capital each partner is expected to contribute up front;

◆ The rights and duties of the partners;

◆ The method for sharing profits and losses;

◆ The salaries to be authorized;

◆ The methods for resolving disputes or taking in new partners; and

◆ The method for dissolving the partnership should dissolution become necessary. Remember, this is often the case.

☐ *Special Note: Although a written partnership agreement is highly recommended, tens of thousands of informal partnerships are carrying on quite well even though they are based on nothing more than a handshake and a pat on the back. You might also find it interesting to note that partnerships can vary immensely in size and type of operation. One partnership might hold out its shingle as a small service company owned by two, while another boasts a ranking among national conglomerates grossing millions of dollars.*

THE LIMITED PARTNERSHIP

A limited partnership is much like a general partnership except for one important fundamental difference. The limited partner is protected by law, in that this person's legal liability in the business is limited to the amount of his or her investment. It enables this special type of investor to share in the partnership profits without being exposed to its debts, in the event the company goes out of business. This protection exists as long as the limited partner **does not play an active role** in the partnership operation.

☞ KEY OBSERVATION

The limited partnership is more tightly regulated than the ordinary general partnership because of the protective provisions extended to limited partner investors. The laws of each state dictate certain registration requirements, which usually include filing a certificate of limited partnership with the respective state agency. A written partnership agreement is necessary when forming a limited partnership.

THE CORPORATION

Unlike the partnerships described above, the corporation is considered an artificially created legal entity that exists separate and apart from those individuals who created it and carry on its operations. With as little as one incorporator, a corporation can be formed by simply filing an application for a charter with the respective state. By filing this application, the incorporator will put on record facts, such as:

♦ The purpose of the intended corporation;

♦ The names and addresses of the incorporators;

♦ The amount and types of capital stock that the corporation will be authorized to issue; and

♦ The rights and privileges of the holders of each class of stock.

Remember, aside from tax reasons, the most common motivation for incurring the cost of setting up a corporation is the recognition that the shareholder is not legally liable for the actions of the corporation. This is because the corporation has its own separate existence wholly apart from those who run it. However, there are three other reasons why the corporation proves to be an attractive vehicle for carrying on a business.

UNLIMITED LIFE

Unlike proprietorships and partnerships, the life of the corporation is not dependent on the life of a particular individual or individuals. It can continue indefinitely until it accomplishes its objective, merges with another business, or goes bankrupt. Unless stated otherwise, it could go on indefinitely.

TRANSFERABILITY OF SHARES

It is always nice to know that the ownership interest that you have in a business can be readily sold, transferred, or given away to another family member. The process of divesting yourself of ownership in proprietorships and partnerships can be cumbersome and costly. Property has to be re-titled, new deeds drawn, and other administrative steps taken any time the slightest change of ownership occurs. With corporations, all of the individual owners' rights and privileges are represented by the shares of stock that they hold. The key to a quick and efficient transfer of ownership of the business is found on the back of each stock certificate. On the back of the stock certificate there is usually a place indicated where the shareholder can endorse and sign over any shares that are to be sold or otherwise disposed of.

ABILITY TO RAISE INVESTMENT CAPITAL

It is usually much easier to attract new investors into a corporate entity because of limited liability and the easy transferability of shares. Shares of stock can be transferred directly to new investors, or when larger offerings to the public are involved, the services of brokerage firms and stock exchanges are called upon.

There are pros and cons to operating your business as a corporation as you will learn in the following two chapters. One of the biggest tax disadvantages for the ordinary C corporation is the dreaded double taxation. Many business owners opt for electing to operate their corporations under subchapter S of the Internal Code. Also known as an S corporation, this entity allows income to pass through to the individual shareholders. Chapter 4 covers the ins and outs of operating as an S corporation.

GET EXPERT ADVICE

Your best bet is to get sound legal advice regarding your decision. Before you approach your attorney or tax adviser, you may want to educate yourself regarding your operating options. One way you can learn more about operating as a corporation is to read *The Essential Corporation Handbook* by Carl R. J. Sniffen. In addition, many business owners are going the do-it-yourself incorporating route. *InstaCorp: Incorporating in Any State* by Corporate Agents, Inc., one of the nation's leading incorporating specialists, details how you can incorporate without costly attorney fees. To learn about these helpful resources, contact The Oasis Press at the phone number listed in the front of this book.

THE LIMITED LIABILITY COMPANY

The last decade brought a new option to the repertoire of entities available to the new business owner — the limited liability company (LLC). The LLC has been viewed by some as the long-awaited answer to the small business operator who feels the need to secure protection from legal liability, but would rather not go through the expense of forming a corporation.

It is true that operating as a corporation has its share of drawbacks in certain situations. For example, as a business owner you would be responsible for additional recordkeeping requirements and administrative details. More important, operating as a corporation, at times, can create an additional tax burden. This is the last thing a business owner needs in the early stages of operation.

⌕ ***Special Note:*** *Prior to the current tax reform legislation, ordinary corporations were long thought of as one of the best ways for a small business owner to secure tax relief and advantageous perks. Tax reforms, however, have greatly diminished this advantage, and for some small business owners, the corporation has proven to be a veritable tax trap.*

In 1988, the IRS made planning alternatives available when it issued some unique rulings. What it did was offer certain nonincorporated businesses (with two or more individual owners) a low-cost opportunity to:

◆ Avoid some of the tax problems faced by regular corporations; and

◆ Enjoy the limited liability protection of duly qualified corporations.

Hence, the birth of the LLC. You can form an LLC for any lawful business as long as the nature of the business is not banking, insurance, and certain professional service operations. By simply filing articles of organization with the respective state agency, an LLC takes on a separate identity. Similar to a corporation, but without the tax problems of the corporation, it will be taxed like a partnership.

☞ KEY OBSERVATION

Although the LLC may sound like a miracle to many small business operators, it should be pointed out that many tax professionals are still leery about this attractive-sounding and relatively new entity. Some feel that more time is needed to test the uncharted waters. During this time, general laws and court cases will be handed down, clearing the air with its many unanswered questions. Until that happens, everyone is advised to proceed with caution. Each state has its own LLC laws. Make sure you contact your tax adviser or the secretary of state for the state in which you will do business.

CHAPTER SUMMARY

Before you consider starting a business, you should first give thought to the entity that best makes sense for your circumstances. Most important, remember that there are two major factors that you must consider: 1) legal liability and its related costs; and 2) tax considerations. Success or failure could very well depend on the time you take to explore both of these factors and secure advice regarding the multitude of questions that will arise.

One helpful way to learn about the state-specific laws and regulations that affect the business entities in your state is to get a copy of *SmartStart Your Business.* Published by The Oasis Press, the *SmartStart* series gives you all you need to know for filing as a sole proprietorship, corporation, partnership, or LLC in the state of your choice. For more information on this series, contact the toll-free number listed in the front of this book.

KEY CHARACTERISTICS OF EACH LEGAL ENTITY

Type of Business Entity	Formation	Legal Liability for Business Debts	How Profits Are Taxed by the IRS
Sole Proprietorship	Easiest of all entities to set up and operate. May require a license or permit, depending on your state of operation.	The owner has complete unlimited personal liability.	Owners are taxed individually at their own particular tax rate which could be as high as 39.6%.
General Partnership	Relatively simple to form and operate. A written partnership agreement is highly recommended.	All partners have unlimited liability.	Each partner is taxed individually at his or her own tax rate.
Limited Partnership	A bit more complex than a general partnership. States require a formal filing of a certificate of the limited partnership. Limited partners cannot play an active role in partnership operations.	Only general partners have unlimited liability. Limited partners are protected from liability except to the extent of their investment.	All partners are taxed individually at their own tax rates.
Corporation	Most complex and, in most cases, the most costly to form and operate. A charter must be filed with the state spelling out the purpose of the corporation, the kind of stock to be issued, and the rights of the shareholders.	Shareholder-owners are protected from liability from corporate obligations, unless they agree to guarantee same for borrowing purposes.	Corporation is taxed separately at the corporate rates. Rates effectively reach a maximum of 35%.
Limited Liability Company	Relatively easy to form, however articles of organization must be filed with the state.	Owners are protected from liability from business obligations unless they personally agree to guarantee same. Limited liability statutes differ from state to state.	Individual owners are taxed like partners; that is, at their own individual tax rates.

Chapter 3

DECIDE WHETHER INCORPORATION IS RIGHT FOR YOU

To help you decide whether or not incorporation is right for your business situation, turn your focus toward the tax advantages of the ordinary corporation — also known as a subchapter C corporation under the tax code. For tax purposes, the ordinary corporation is identified as a business entity that is separate and apart from its shareholders. That is, it pays a separate corporate tax on its profits without giving regard to the financial circumstances of its shareholder-owners. On the other hand, an S corporation (listed as subchapter S of the tax code) generally pays no corporate taxes. Instead, it passes its profits and losses to its shareholder-owners just as if it was a simple partnership. See Chapter 4 for a detailed study of the S corporation.

As you might expect, there could be significant tax **disadvantages** for some business operators when they elect to be treated as an ordinary C corporation. In fact, it is these disadvantages that force you to know the difference between the ordinary corporation and the S corporation. The right choice between S and C status could save you considerable tax dollars in the long run management of your business. The wrong choice could be an economic nightmare.

The question of whether or not you should incorporate your small business is an elusive one. Pick up any modern textbook or business manual for your answer and be prepared to get a dozen arguments explaining why any one of those entities described in Chapter 2 might be best for you.

Why are there no easy-to-follow guidelines? Some authorities reason that there are too many variables, making it exceedingly difficult for a small business owner to obtain a simplified set of rules. For example, in deciding whether or not you should incorporate, you might need to confer with your attorney and tax adviser about matters like:

♦ Federal regulations;

♦ State laws;

♦ Investors' rights;

♦ Legal liability; and

♦ Extra costs required to form and operate a corporation.

These issues highlight some of the more important nontax matters that need to be considered when starting your business operation. When you add **tax planning issues**, you are suddenly overwhelmed by the vast amount of criteria that require your attention.

To decide if a corporation is right for your operation, you can begin by completely segregating the **tax issues**. Many argue that the tax issues have as much economic importance as all the other issues combined. Since this book is about tax planning for small businesses, the book's messages should get you well on your way.

THE IRS AND ITS EVER-CHANGING PLAYING FIELD

Before we identify the specific tax advantages for doing business as a small corporation, it is important to take a brief look at the old rules. In so doing, a small business owner should gain a better sense of how the game is played on today's playing field.

Not too long ago, the ordinary corporation was regarded as the only smart option for operating a small business, especially if you didn't want to be eaten alive by endless taxes on your earnings. Congress argued that too many loopholes existed, as it set out to attack all corporations thought to be enjoying too many privileges under the tax code. The smaller corporations, however, were the ones getting the real edge, because loose interpretations of the rules allowed escape from taxes or deferment of taxes year after year.

Accountants and lawyers would take pride in showing their small corporate clients how they could legally and systematically:

◆ Juggle business profits at will and pay taxes at a corporate rate that was significantly lower than the individual rates;

◆ Deduct bonuses to key shareholders by merely accruing them on the books;

◆ Write off vast arrays of fringe benefits and perks to controlling shareholders while discriminating against other employees;

◆ Break up a business into multiple corporations and make it possible to split the profits among lower tax bracket companies; and

◆ Push retirement plans to the limit with few restrictions.

Then, after a series of tax reform movements, Congress finally took action. These allegedly outrageous tax advantages were destined to come to a screeching halt. With the stroke of a pen, Congress informed the small corporation owners that they would now have to share a level playing field with other nonincorporated business operators.

Despite a series of tax law changes, several tax shelter maneuvers for the small business corporation survived. It is up to you to determine whether or not these remaining maneuvers can still save you money in this high tax atmosphere.

THE TAX ADVANTAGES AVAILABLE TO TODAY'S ORDINARY BUSINESS CORPORATION

After you and your attorney agree that a corporation is your best bet from a legal standpoint, your next step should be to check out the **tax** standpoint with your tax adviser. To do this, specifically look at all the tax advantages available to operators of ordinary corporations. The most popular tax advantages available to the ordinary corporation are:

♦ Income splitting;

♦ Medical insurance;

♦ Disability insurance;

♦ Group-term life insurance;

♦ Deduction for dividends received; and

♦ Capital gains benefits.

INCOME SPLITTING

The tax law hits many individuals with a tax rate as high as 36%. For corporations, the highest rate is 35%. (Refer to the 1998 Corporation Tax Rate Schedule at the end of this chapter.) In short, the tide changes as the top individual rate surpasses the top corporate rate. How does this law affect you with a relatively small-sized business operation?

Your first question should be, who will actually pay those notoriously high tax rates anyway? According to the tables at the end of this chapter, if you were incorporated, your business would need to net as much as $10 million, after paying your salary, before that 35% corporate tax rate becomes effective. At the same time, you as an individual wouldn't be subject to the 36% rate in 1998 until your taxable income reaches $128,100 — or $155,950 for married couples.

◻ *Special Note: The current super rate, with the surtax included, can actually bring your top individual rate up to 39.6% — and even beyond that in some cases. However, this level of taxation only applies to most individuals having more than $278,450 in taxable income.*

The bottom line here is that most small business owners fall below those top (high income) rates. Thus, the best advice is to start taking a close look at the marginal rates in between. Accordingly, if yours is a moderate sized income, like most of America's business owners, you may find that there is room to save a large amount in taxes by income splitting. Put simply, this is done whenever you allocate your profit among **two** entities to take advantage of the lower tax brackets for each of those entities.

✎ PLANNING TIP

Although it may not fit your current way of doing business, paying a little corporate tax now and then may benefit you.

For example, suppose your small business corporation was getting ready to end its current business year with a modest profit from operations. Under the pre-tax reform environment, you might have drawn out those earnings as a bonus to keep from paying unnecessary corporate taxes. However, in light of tax law changes you might have a different viewpoint.

Suppose your bonus was facing the 39.6% tax bite applicable to individuals. You might decide that this is the year you should elect to pay a little corporate tax, assuming you were in the lowest corporate bracket.

A few years ago, an issue of *Money* magazine called attention to an increasingly popular solution for dealing with the "Biggest Tax Hike Ever" cast upon the American people. "Consider Incorporating," the author declared and proffered advice to those nonincorporated business owners who survive in this era of high taxation. In one example the author portrayed a business owner who was looking at a $25,000 profit to be reinvested back into the business. The author calculated that the business owner would have been left with $21,250 ". . . if he had bitten the bullet and left the money with his corporation which would pay only a 15% tax."[1] If the bonus was drawn after paying 39.6%, the owner would have ended up with only $15,100. The result speaks for itself. A $6,150 tax savings was available by using an ordinary corporation.

✎ PLANNING TIP

Before you take pains to begin the necessary paperwork to form an ordinary corporation, remember to look at the long-term when planning your tax strategies. Don't think only of the short-term as you try to beat the system by income splitting and paying those taxes at the lower corporate rates. You might need to pull some of those profits out for yourself some time soon. When you do, you are going to wind up paying an income tax all over again — this time at the individual rates.

The best advice is to get a competent professional to help you crunch the numbers to see if, and when, income splitting is for you.

SPECIAL CASE FOR PERSONAL SERVICE CORPORATIONS

Certain corporations are not entitled to take advantage of the lower graduated rates that start at 15%. Specifically, the personal service corporation is required to use a flat rate of 35% on all taxable income. The corporations that are in this category provide services in the fields of health, law, engineering, architecture, accounting, actuarial science, performing arts, or consulting. Also, to fit this personal service category, all the stock must be substantially held by employees, retired employees, or their estates, if they are deceased.

MEDICAL INSURANCE

Probably the most significant tax saving benefit still available to the ordinary corporation is the medical benefit plan for its employees. The law has become quite complex in this area, which is carried over from the old health and accident benefit rules embodied in the tax code. These rules cover a wide variety of insurance plans and arrangements that have left many professional advisers in a quandary as to the application of the rules.

One thing known for certain, however, is that payments you make for health insurance and medical reimbursements to employees get special tax sheltered treatment. That is, as long as the employer is an ordinary C corporation and a few basic rules are understood. This shelter is of particular interest to most small business operators as they are now threatened by one of the most uncontrolled living costs facing America today — the cost of health care.

The IRS no longer shows compassion to individual taxpayers who have to dip into their pockets to pay the increasing costs of doctors, dentists, therapists and the like. Furthermore, medical insurance premiums have now reached unheard of levels. With the tough 7.5% medical limitation, the only people who can get any real break on their individual tax returns are those who have either paid a small fortune in medical costs or have such small amounts of income that the limitation has no significance.

Small business owners of America take heed! Through the use of an ordinary corporation, there may be a way out of the dilemma that you face with rising health care costs. For example, if you and your spouse earn an adjusted gross income (AGI) of $80,000, and your children's orthodontic bills bring your total medical costs to $5,500, you're out of luck. There are no tax breaks from the IRS until your expenses reach $6,000 (your AGI of $80,000 multiplied by 7.5%). On the other hand, if those costs were paid through your closely held corporation, you might be allowed a full tax deduction for your expense.

Q. How can I get full tax shelter treatment out of medical expenses in my business operation?

A. To get full tax shelter treatment out of medical expenses in your business operation, you can offer a health and accident plan. With this kind of plan made available, your corporation can enjoy the benefit of a full tax deduction for those staggering health costs and health insurance premiums. The real bonanza is that employees who are covered do not have to report these paid benefits as income on their tax return; thus, no tax at either end.

Illustration 3.1

- Norbert is about to take a job with Galaxy, Incorporated.

- The company plans to pay Norbert $40,000 annually.

- Norbert needs medical insurance for himself and his family which is expected to run about $300 monthly.

- What if arrangements could be made to bring Norbert under the company's group plan? $3,600 in annual premiums would be picked up by the corporation, and Norbert's salary would be adjusted to $36,400.

- The result is advantageous to both parties.

- Norbert saves both income taxes and FICA taxes on the $3,600.

- Galaxy still gets a full tax deduction for $40,000, and also saves FICA taxes on $3,600.

Norbert's arrangement may sound attractive. However, a few simple rules must be followed. (Refer to the text below entitled Make Your Health and Accident Plans Pass the Test.)

DISABILITY INSURANCE

Disability insurance is another key area involving special tax breaks.

♦ As with most self-employed business owners, you will find it is imperative to buy income protection for yourselves because of the possibility that an accident or sickness can take you out of the operation for an extended period.

♦ As with medical insurance, disability premiums have grown to prohibitive levels.

♦ The only way that you're going to get any tax relief from your premium payments is by using an ordinary corporation.

Similar to medical benefits, there is a significant tax break for having an ordinary corporation pay the premiums for employee disability insurance plans. A full business deduction is allowed, while the employee does not pay taxes on the value of that fringe benefit. It makes no difference even if you, as the owner, are one of the employees.

Although disability insurance plans are a definite plus in every small business owner's tax planning program, there are three points that should be kept in mind.

♦ Group plans typically cover no more than 60% of salary.

- The disability benefits that you may one day receive as an employee will be taxable in those cases where the employer-paid premiums were not reported as income at the time of payment.

- To take advantage of the full tax shelter benefits, you must be aware of certain discrimination rules.

○ *Special Note: If your plan discriminates on behalf of the owners and higher compensated employees, those individuals may be taxed on the value of the excess coverage not received by those other employees. You must make your health and accident plans pass the test.*

MAKE YOUR HEALTH AND ACCIDENT PLANS PASS THE TEST

Whether you have a medical insurance plan, a disability plan or some combination of self-insurance, there are a few basic rules to follow to get the full tax shelter for your costs.

Most importantly, you must have an actual plan set up for the benefit of the employees, not just the owners of the business. The key word here is employee, and to be an employee for these purposes you must operate as an ordinary C corporation.

It is interesting to note that the health and accident plan can cover businesses that have just one employee — even if that employee is you, the owner of the business. For example, the IRS ruled that certain medical insurance premiums paid by a corporate employer for the benefit of the one key employee were free of tax to that employee, provided there was continued employment with the corporation. Again, the language in the plan addressed the benefits of **employees** — not the benefits of owners. It didn't make any difference that the one key employee was also the **only** employee in the entire business, or that tax saving was the true motive.

☞ KEY OBSERVATION

Look for a different test if you have a self-insured health and accident plan. With this kind of plan, discrimination toward owner-managers will cause the benefits to be taxed at the level of those owner-employees, if tax saving is the sole or primary motive.

BE AWARE OF NEW MEDICAL SAVINGS ACCOUNT OPTION (MSA)

Starting in 1997, certain small employers, including sole proprietorships, can get a deduction for contributions to a medical saving account. As with the health and accident plan, the employee is not required to pick up his or her share of the contribution as income. Although this new option has certain limitations and, in general, has not yet caught on in popularity, you should look at it as a possible option. Although it is still in a testing stage, there may be new developments at future dates.

Technically, a health and accident plan does not have to be in writing, nor must it be a formal arrangement to take advantage of the plan's tax sheltered benefits. However, if there is no written plan, be prepared to demonstrate that a plan actually exists either by prior practice or by prior agreement to make the medical payments. Regardless, make sure you notify your employees about the existence of the plan.

Illustration 3.2

♦ In a well-known tax court case, it was ruled that a plan did not exist where a corporation, without a prior history of employee reimbursement for medical costs, paid the medical expenses of a $10 dollar per week former employee.

♦ The employee was the aged mother of the corporation's four shareholders.

♦ The tax court would not accept the contention that the corporation was prepared to assist any faithful and long-term employee who suffered from a lack of funds. This arrangement, it pointed out, did not constitute an acceptable plan.

✎ PLANNING TIP

Get rid of the guesswork in your plans, whether they involve medical, disability, or some form of a self-insured arrangement. To ensure the plan's workability, put it in writing and see that all your employees get a copy.

GROUP-TERM LIFE INSURANCE

A corporate employer is still permitted to provide its employees up to $50,000 of group-term life insurance protection without a tax cost to those employees. The group-term insurance must be provided under a policy carried by the corporate employer which complies with the following conditions:

♦ It provides for the benefit of a group of employees as compensation for services rendered to the corporation; and

◆ It does not discriminate in favor of key employees in eligibility to participate, or to receive benefits.

Although group-term life insurance plans generally involve ten full-time employees, there are special rules to qualify group plans for smaller organizations with fewer than ten employees. To qualify for the death benefit exclusion, you must show that the insurance:

◆ Is available for all full-time employees; and

◆ Provides protection that is based on a uniform percentage of compensation, or else is set on the basis of coverage brackets set by the insurer, not the corporation.

Corporations with fewer than ten employees will not be disqualified from the tax shelter benefits of group-term life insurance if they do not provide coverage for:

◆ Part-time personnel who normally do not work more than 20 hours per week, or five months, in any calendar year;

◆ Those employed less than six months; and

◆ Those employees who are 65 years or older.

DEDUCTION FOR DIVIDENDS RECEIVED

The deduction for dividends received is one of the most overlooked tax breaks by owners of small business corporations. If you have an ordinary C corporation that owns shares of stock in another unrelated corporation, the dividends that you receive from your investment will, to a large extent, get tax free treatment. That is, as much as 70% of those dividends received will be free from tax by virtue of a special deduction.

For the most part, all that is required to qualify for this deduction is to show that the dividends received were, in fact, paid by another domestic corporation that is subject to income tax. That probably includes that great stock tip recommended by your investment adviser.

Illustration 3.3

◆ Long's Home Improvement Corporation, a small family owned-operated business, had started to accumulate some additional capital that it needed to retain for operating reserves and some possible future expansion.

◆ Joe Long had become disenchanted with the meager interest rates being generated by the corporation's money market funds and CDs at the bank. Looking ahead to some better yields and some future growth, Joe started to invest about $15,000 each year into attractive public utility funds and several stocks that touted generous dividend yields.

◆ The corporation, over a period of time, enhanced its financial position measurably as its stock portfolio outdistanced the more conservative fixed income investments. The real bonanza to Long's Corporation was found in the attractive cash flow being generated by those high dividend distributions which were paid by other domestic corporations. Joe found this to be 70% tax free.

Joe thought that his option was similar to tax free bonds, but these investments would grow in value over time. Take heed that the special dividend deduction does **not** apply to the following types of dividends:

◆ Dividends from deposits on withdrawal accounts in building and loans associations, mutual savings banks, and cooperatives;

◆ Capital gain dividends and returns of capital; and

♦ Dividends received from debt-financed stock when debt is incurred to purchase the stock.

🗀 *Special Note: The total amount of dividends that you may claim is generally limited to 70% of your corporation's taxable income.*

Capital Gains Benefit

Many investors agree that any capital gains tax has for too long stifled the incentive of those who would dare to invest in a small business. A common feeling is that when the time comes for the small business owner to sell out, a confiscatory capital gains tax will be assessed. Oftentimes, when you couple that tax with a persistent inflation factor for the years in business, little remains for the entrepreneur's risk and hard work.

The capital gains tax is a special, recently reduced tax reserved for those who sell special investment property. That special property would include certain business property, including stock in a corporation that was held for investment purposes, usually more than one year. Accordingly, when you sell your small business, expect to have the capital gains rules apply to your profits.

Q. How much capital gains tax will I have to pay under the new law if I sell the stock in my corporation?

A. In most cases, this tax rate is the same as the investor's marginal tax bracket; however, the maximum charge is 20%. For many years, there had been no concessions or tax benefits given by the government no matter how long you held onto your investment. Also, it should be noted that the lowered 20% rate is in addition to any state taxes whenever applicable.

☐ *Special Note: For those in the lowest tax bracket, the maximum capital gains tax rate may be an attractive 10%. Congress is considering a further reduction.*

Be reminded about a fairly recent tax law change that provides additional tax relief to certain business owners who look to sell their business interests. In simple term this is how it works: Fifty percent of any gain realized on the sale of stock in a small business corporation will be excludable from income.

Clearly, this provides an enormous tax-sheltering advantage to small business owners who one day expect to sell off their business interests. However, there are a few requirements to make this special 50% capital gains exclusion work.

♦ The stock that is sold must have been issued after August 10, 1993. Older corporations do not qualify.

♦ The corporation must be a qualified small business. Aside from certain dollar limitations, this generally means that you must be an ordinary corporation to qualify. S corporations are not eligible.

♦ At least 80% of the corporation's assets must be used in the active conduct of the business. That is, if you are involved in a business whose principal source of revenue is from services, such as a hotel or restaurant, you will not be eligible. Also, in view of this provision, doctors, lawyers, and accountants need not apply for the exclusion benefits.

To better understand the effects of the capital gains tax on your estate planning strategies, refer to Chapter 13.

CHAPTER SUMMARY

In addition to the general tax benefits of incorporating covered in this chapter, you must understand the term fringe benefits as it relates to the tax law. In Chapter 6, you will receive a full explanation, including:

♦ A list of the various fringe benefits that are available to all business entities under the current law; and

♦ Suggestions on how those benefits can be used to your tax advantage.

As a business owner who operates as an ordinary C corporation, take note of two specific fringe benefits whose full tax sheltered advantage only comes about when the employer is an ordinary corporation. Those two fringe benefits detailed in Chapter 6 are medical care and meals and lodging.

You will observe that both of these special benefits — medical care, and meals and lodging — involve a two-fold tax advantage.

♦ The employer (the corporation) will get a full tax deduction for the benefit paid.

♦ The employee will be permitted to exclude that benefit from their taxable income.

ENDNOTES

1. Lohse, Deborah, "The Biggest Tax Hike Ever," *Money*, August 1993, 58-63.

1998 Corporation Tax Rate Schedule

Corporation Tax Rate Schedule

If taxable income (line
30, Form 1120, or line
26, Form 1120-A) on
page 1 is:

Over —	But not over —	Tax is:	Of the amount over —
$0	$50,000	15%	$0
50,000	75,000	$7,500 + 25%	50,000
75,000	100,000	13,750 + 34%	75,000
100,000	335,000	22,250 + 39%	100,000
335,000	10,000,000	113,900 + 35%	335,000
10,000,000	15,000,000	3,400,000 + 38%	10,000,000
15,000,000	18,333,333	5,150,000 + 38%	15,000,000
16,333,333	——	35%	0

Chapter 4

BECOME FAMILIAR WITH THE S CORPORATION ALTERNATIVE

An S corporation is one that has all the legal protection and economic benefits of an ordinary corporation. There is, however, one significant characteristic that it doesn't share. It doesn't pay taxes like the ordinary corporation. In fact, except in isolated cases, it doesn't pay any taxes at all. Thus, the S corporation is more akin to a partnership or a sole proprietorship. Accordingly, its profits and losses are passed off to its owners just as if a corporation never existed.

Since 1958, the use of the S corporation has been a valuable planning tool for the small business owner. In recent years, that interest has suddenly grown to immense proportions. This chapter will give the reasons for the renewed S corporation popularity; this will benefit not only new business owners, but also those owners of ordinary corporations who are looking to make changes to get tax relief.

In this regard, you are reminded that a major reason for the interest in S corporation status is the disenchantment with some of the tax disadvantages that accompany the ordinary C corporation. Those disadvantages are identified throughout this chapter as you learn about the advantages of the S corporation as the likely alternative for deciding which type of corporation you will use.

✎ PLANNING TIP

When you examine the following criteria extolling the benefits of S corporations, remember to consider the trade-off. Try to evaluate the dollar savings that will be lost when you concede the tax benefits — health and accident plans and other fringe benefits — that are ordinarily allowed only to the C corporation. Only by observing the entire picture can you be assured of attaining the best tax breaks possible.

For information about applying for S corporation status, see the end of this chapter for forms and guidelines.

NO CORPORATE INCOME TAXES TO PAY ON PROFITS

No taxes for S corporations? The inexperienced business owner might be puzzled over this advantage. If the corporation doesn't pay taxes, that means the **shareholders** will be required to pay as they go. In other words, a tax bill at the individual rates rather than at the corporate level. Remember, it was pointed out earlier that there were distinct advantages to paying a corporate tax, at least periodically.

In Chapter 3 you learned how the technique of income splitting enables you to move income out of the high individual brackets into the lower tiered corporate rates. Income splitting, you are reminded, has become especially popular in recent years now that the changing tax law has raised the prior individual tax rates higher than they have been in decades. So, in light of this tax shelter, why elect S status and forego the benefits of income splitting available with an ordinary corporation?

☞ KEY OBSERVATION

Income splitting is sometimes not a workable solution, because most small corporation owners tend to pull out their profits in salaries and bonuses, as they are earned. There is usually little, if any corporate taxes left to pay at those low marginal rates when an ordinary corporation is used.

Income splitting with the ordinary corporation only makes sense when the corporate owner can afford to leave the profits in the corporation for future growth and development. If you are not in that enviable position, you need to be aware that there are certain risks when you have to pull out your profits intermittently throughout the year.

WHAT ARE THE RISKS?

There is a risk because the periodic draws that you make (bonuses, fringe benefits) may not be allowed as a deduction to the corporation. While you may think that all those special draws taken from the corporation are legitimate business deductions, the government might think otherwise. As it has done so often in the past, the IRS may try to characterize those payments as nondeductible dividends.

Accordingly, you could actually be required to pay a double tax as an ordinary corporation. This is because the corporation will have to pay a tax on those profits, and you, the shareholder, will pay a tax once again on the distribution.

◻ *Special Note: This so-called double tax might be called the worst tax case scenario for the small business owner. (See Chapter 5 for details and possible solutions.) One way to ensure that a double tax will not occur is to elect S corporation status, because S corporations don't pay taxes in the first place.*

Finally, the advantage of not having to pay corporate income taxes by choosing S status is one of simplicity, in an otherwise complicated process. When you don't have to pay a corporate income tax, there is no guesswork between corporate tax rules and individual rules, not to mention the difference in the rates. There is one tax only. The corporation merely acts as a conduit and passes the income to the owners — one time only.

Avoid Reasonable Compensation Problems

As noted above, one of the constant problems facing the ordinary C corporation is the potential threat by the IRS to disallow, as business deductions, the salaries and bonus payments to shareholders. To protect your corporation from this costly scenario, you need to take continuing steps each year to prove the legitimacy of these payments made to you.

Many feel that it is unfair that the IRS rarely challenges the compensation paid to nonstockholders and to other unrelated parties. After all, salaries and wages are supposed to be just one more category on the accepted list of *ordinary and necessary* business expenses. But when those wages are paid to a shareholder-owner, a whole different set of standards is applied.

The special standards for shareholder compensation will be explained in Chapter 5; however, for the purpose of this segment, you should be aware of the following facts.

♦ For the corporation to deduct salary payments to a shareholder, a *reasonable test* must be met.

♦ You may need to prove that the amount of the salary payment was justified in view of the hours you worked, your experience, your education, and the complexity of the job.

Q. Since owners of ordinary corporations have to worry about justifying their actions to the IRS every time they take money out of their businesses, is it better to switch to S status and eliminate these potential problems entirely?

A. No, not because of this issue alone. The IRS has shown a pattern of auditing closely held corporations and challenging the amounts paid to the shareholder-owners. The courts, however, have sided more with the business owner in recent years. This implies that there has been a growing intolerance of government trying to dictate reasonable standards by telling hard-working business owners how much their services are worth.

In conclusion, the risk of having your own personal draws and special payments disallowed as business expenses still exists. You need to weigh this fact and decide if those tax-sheltering benefits offered by the ordinary corporation (outlined in Chapter 3) will only lead to major tax problems down the road. Remember, as your profit margins and cash distributions increase, so does the risk of an IRS challenge to the money that you take out.

AVOID THE PERSONAL HOLDING COMPANY TAX

Personal holding company tax implications can be avoided by electing S corporation status. The personal holding company tax might be called a special *penalty tax*, which is imposed on ordinary corporations that generate too much personal holding company income. Put another way, the penalty tax is imposed on those **ordinary** corporations that might be defined as "a personal holding company."

☞ KEY OBSERVATION

The prime target of this penalty tax is the so-called incorporated pocketbook; that is, a corporation that idly stands by and holds investment income for the shareholder-owners.

What is the personal holding company income that is subject to the penalty tax? In general terms, personal holding company income consists of items like:

♦ Dividends, interest, royalties and annuities;

♦ Rents and royalties (with certain adjustments); and

♦ Amounts received for contracts for personal services if the corporation doesn't dictate who will perform the services.

Q. When will the personal holding company tax be applied?

A. This penalty is applied when personal holding company income makes up at least 60% of the adjusted gross income of the corporation. Also, the tax will only apply when 50% of the corporation's stock is owned by no more than five individuals.

You can be prepared! If it appears that your ordinary corporation is proportionately generating too much of those personal holding company income items as previously defined, pay as much money as possible to the shareholder-employees so that no profit is left to be taxed. However, if you can't justify making extra payments to the shareholder-employees as reasonable compensation, discontinue ordinary C corporation status as soon as possible. Remember, S corporations are not subject to the personal holding company penalty tax.

AVOID THE ACCUMULATED EARNINGS TAX

S corporation election is, once more, another way to avoid accumulated earnings tax, a penalty tax that often catches the unwary small business owner off guard. The tax is imposed on ordinary corporations when they are deemed to have improperly accumulated income. Under this subjective test, the IRS looks over the corporate owner's shoulder and tries to decide if the corporation has been retaining too much of its profits. The insinuation is that if those profits had been properly distributed to the shareholders, an additional income tax would have been paid by those shareholders as individuals.

The rate of tax on so-called improper accumulations had long been accepted at a flat 28% on accumulated taxable income. As a result of the 1993 tax act, the penalty tax has been raised to 39.6% for corporate tax years after 1992. Consult with your tax adviser about utilizing the consent dividend as a means of eliminating the potentially egregious tax liability.

The penalty tax will not apply until the accumulated earnings and profits of the corporation exceed $250,000. (For certain **service** corporations, the allowance is $150,000.)

✎ PLANNING TIP

If it appears that your corporation will tend to accumulate substantial profits, rather than paying them all out as you go, you should consider an election under subchapter S. An S corporation is not subject to this tough penalty tax as long as the S election is in force. Keep in mind, corporations that were formerly ordinary C corporations can still be exposed to IRS attack.

Below you will find a checklist of reasons that may, in individual cases, give justifiable reason for accumulating profits beyond the prescribed allowances.

CHECKLIST OF ACCEPTABLE REASONS TO ACCUMULATE INCOME IN A CORPORATION BEYOND THE PRESCRIBED ALLOWANCE

Acceptable grounds for accumulation are:

✓ Business expansion and plant replacement.

✓ Acquisition of either stock or assets.

✓ Payment of debts.

✓ Working capital.

✓ Investments or loans to customers or suppliers on whom the corporation relies for its continuing business.

🗋 *Special Note: It has been determined that the self-insurance of product liability risks is also a qualifying business need for which earnings and profits may be accumulated without incurring the accumulated earnings tax penalty.*

AVOID THE ALTERNATIVE MINIMUM TAX (AMT)

One of the more subtle advantages for using an S corporation points to the impact of the so-called alternative minimum tax (AMT) which always casts a cloud over the ordinary C corporation.

When Congress introduced this penalty tax, it had but one thing in mind. It wanted to do something about the growing clamor that businesspeople, in general, were not paying their fair share of taxes. The easy remedy was to put the spotlight on certain tax breaks enjoyed by business entities and to cause them to pay a special **minimum** tax for the privilege. The revised taxing procedure, it was felt, would speed up the drive toward equity among all taxpayers.

The idea sounded fair at first, but over the past several years, more and more small business owners have become unexpectedly jolted by the harsh reality of the plan. Small corporation owners in particular are feeling the blow as they start to learn more about the unexpected tax traps with AMT that are waiting to gouge them out of extra tax dollars.

Q. Just how do these tax traps work?

A. These tax traps work by first identifying certain tax advantages that you may presently enjoy as "tax preferences." If you are an ordinary corporation, the requirement is that you are to **increase** your usual taxable income by these preferences and pay a flat tax rate on that adjusted amount. If, for example, your regular corporation would ordinarily pay no tax at all, the **additions** to income could change that in short order.

The amount of the penalty tax under prior law was 20%. Prior to 1998, there was an exemption available of up to $40,000 of the adjusted income for the smaller corporations.

GOOD NEWS FOR SMALL CORPORATIONS

Starting in 1998, the harsh AMT penalty tax will not apply to small corporations. For 1998, if your corporation has had average annual gross receipts of $5,000,000 or less during the three preceding years, you are considered a small corporation. This means you will be "off the hook" for paying the tax.

◻ *Special Note: Once you qualify as a "small corporation," you generally will continue to be exempt from the AMT tax provided that your average annual gross receipts for the prior three-year period do not exceed $7,500,000.*

To plan around the AMT penalty you need to have a sense of the kind of items that you could be accountable for when you operate as an ordinary corporation. Following is a general sampling of some of the additions or tax preferences to income that could cause your corporation to be liable for the penalty tax assessment:

◆ Adjustment for inventory for those who use preferred methods for tax purposes;

◆ If you make an installment sale, the installment method of reporting income can't be used;

◆ If you normally deduct expenses for depletion, you must use the very conservative cost depletion method;

◆ If your regular books and records show a different amount of income than that shown on your tax return, numerous adjustments must be made to get them closer in line; and

◆ Income received from a life insurance contract, although usually tax free, *must* be called into the equation for these purposes.

ENJOY SEVERAL LOSS PASS-THROUGH BENEFITS

Like many start-up business owners, you might expect to lose money in the first year or so. The loss pass-through benefit is of key interest to you.

The ordinary business corporation, you will recall, is a taxable entity wholly separate from its individual shareholders. When a profit is generated, the corporation pays the applicable income taxes.

When a loss is realized, it can only be used to offset corporate profits and cannot give immediate tax benefits to the shareholder-owner.

For newly organized ordinary corporations, the losses generated must be carried forward, up to 15 years, and can be used only when taxable income occurs.

Illustration 4.1

♦ Pat Brown, a retired engineer, invests $75,000 to form Brown Corporation, an ordinary C corporation. With his monthly retirement and income from investments, Pat is already in the highest tax bracket.

♦ During the first start-up year, Brown Corporation incurs a loss of $30,000.

♦ Although Pat desperately needs personal tax shelter during this period, he cannot write off one cent from the corporation loss.

♦ The loss, instead, must be carried forward to subsequent years when, hopefully, profits will begin.

♦ In retrospect, had Pat filed a timely election for S status, he would have been able to write off the full $30,000 on his individual tax return for that year.

Suppose Pat wants to take advantage of the tax sheltered breaks for medical plans that are only available to the ordinary C corporation.

Pat would **also** like to be able to write off those heavy start-up losses in the first year of business. What should he have done?

Pat should have filed an election to be taxed as an S corporation immediately at the start of business in that first year when he knew that a loss would occur. During a later period when it is determined that profits are to begin, a revocation of the election should be made.

◻ *Special Note: You should try to plan ahead for the year that a profit is projected and switch from S status to that of an ordinary corporation. For S status to be revoked and ordinary corporation treatment to begin during a particular taxable year, a deadline must be met. A majority of the shareholders must file a consent to terminate the election by the 15th day of the 3rd month of the taxable year.*

Remember, if that deadline is not met, the entire year will remain in S status unless an event occurs that would disqualify the corporation from continuing as an S corporation.

AVOID DOUBLE TAXATION WHEN LIQUIDATING A BUSINESS

Perhaps the biggest cause for the recent mass exodus from ordinary corporation status to subchapter S points to a new liquidation rule, which was written as part of the 1986 tax act. What that revision did was eliminate a long time tax shelter benefit allowed to those business owners who finally decided to call it quits.

What benefit was eliminated? Under the old rules, the corporation had a special privilege allowing it to exclude from income most of the gains that it made when it sold out its assets in a liquidation process. The purpose was to ensure that there would be one tax only, when the shareholders received their final payout. Under current law, that favorable tax incentive for investing in a business has come under serious threat. Instead of a reward for investing in an ordinary C corporation, the owners will find themselves penalized with a debilitating *double tax*. For example:

♦   When a corporation sells off its assets, it must now pay the applicable corporate rates on the gains; and

♦   When individual shareholders receive the payoff distribution for their stock shares, they are subject to another capital gains tax on their entire profit.

It is interesting to note that the new rule took this penalty provision a step further to make sure that no benefits remain. For example, if a corporation simply distributes property, other than cash, to its shareholders in the liquidation process, gain will *still* have to be recognized as taxable — just as if the assets had been sold by the corporation at fair market value. The following illustration demonstrates the impact of the new law on ordinary corporations.

Illustration 4.2

♦   Lena Roe owns all of the stock of Roe Corporation, an ordinary C corporation. Her cost basis of that stock was $10,000.

♦   Roe Corporation has one single asset originally purchased for $200,000

♦   In accordance with its liquidation plan, Roe sells the asset for $500,000 and the $500,000 proceeds are distributed to Lena.

♦	Roe Corporation has a taxable gain of $300,000. Roe pays a tax at 34% in the amount of $102,000.	
♦	In this scenario, Lena has the following gain from the liquidation.	
♦	Amount of proceeds received	$500,000
♦	minus corporate tax liability	102,000
♦	Net amount received	398,000
♦	minus cost basis of the stock	10,000
♦	Gain to be reported by Lena -	$388,000
♦	The overall tax bill is:	
♦	Lena's tax at 20% ($388,000 multiplied by .20)	$77,600
♦	The corporation's tax	102,000
♦	The total tax bill	$ 174,600

Had Lena elected to file under subchapter S at the beginning, the tax bill at liquidation might be as low as:

Corporate tax:	-0-
Lena's tax:	
Tax on the corporate sale	$60,000
($300,000 multiplied by 20%)	
Total tax	$60,000

☐ *Special Note: Because of the double tax provision under the current law, election to file for S corporation status might effectively save Lena $119,600 in taxes upon liquidation. Although this saving should be adjusted for prior taxes paid on S corporation earnings, the inference is clear. A double tax is a high price to pay for an ordinary C corporation.*

As we conclude with Chapter 4 and the tax advantages of the S corporation, take a moment to reflect upon the business owner's need to see the whole picture. The following illustration identifies some very typical concerns in a common scenario.

Illustration 4.3

♦ Terry prepares to start a small business with a modest amount of cash and some bank financing. Immediate profits are expected.

♦ Terry is advised by her attorney to form a corporation.

♦ The corporation status, she is told, will allow her more flexibility for raising additional capital, plus protection from personal liability in the event of lawsuits.

♦ The accountant observes that Terry has a need for medical and disability insurance. The cost, however, is a prohibitive $8,000 annually for two policies.

♦ Terry will have only one employee at first. However, that employee is already covered by outside insurance and will not come under the corporation's health and accident plan.

♦ Terry's advisers note a classic tax shelter scenario regarding *expected health and accident plans and other incidental fringe benefits.*

♦ In her 31% tax bracket, Terry can pocket up to $2,480 in tax savings annually for the insurance payments alone. Under a qualified health and accident plan, all premiums paid and deducted by the corporation would be tax free to Terry as an employee, or $8,000 multiplied by 31%.

Terry, reacts to the newfound tax bonanza. "It looks like an ordinary corporation is the way to go," she thinks. She tallies up all the tax shelter benefits, including the minor **fringe benefit** allowances that would not be allowed if the S corporation alternative was elected. She and her adviser explore the possible downsides. The accountant then explains the ordinary C corporation disadvantages. Except for some cautions about *reasonable compensation*, there doesn't appear to be any major risk to operate as an ordinary corporation. Her final question to her well-educated advisers..."What happens when I sell the business?"

This last question brought a new twist to the planning scenario.

♦ Terry planned to operate and develop the business for about eight years and then sell.

♦ Also, she projected the business would be sold for a profit in the $500,000 range.

Because of the double tax on liquidations, the final scenario is surprising.

♦ With an ordinary C corporation, the overall "double" tax on the liquidation may be close to 50% — or $250,000.

♦ With an S corporation, the federal tax may be as low as 20% — or $100,000.

With this, the matter was decided. Even with the relatively modest tax savings that would be enjoyed year after year, there was no plausible reason for Terry to subject herself to the double tax by operating as an ordinary corporation. The onerous penalty tax upon sale would not apply with a successful S corporation.

Your next step is to send *Form 2553, Election by a Small Business Corporation,* to the IRS to be treated as an S corporation. A sample copy of this form is located at the end of the chapter to give you an idea of what is required of you.

☐ ***Special Note:*** *In general, most domestic (United States) corporations with fewer than 75 shareholders that have only one class of stock can be eligible for S corporation status. However, you should check with your adviser for other eligibility requirements.*

CHAPTER SUMMARY

The S corporation has long become an increasingly popular vehicle for tax-planning purposes. In fact, many so-called regular corporations have been electing to switch to the S provisions in order to negate several burdensome (if not catastrophic) tax implications within the overall picture. For others, however, there are shorter-term tax benefits for operating as a regular corporation. As a small business owner, you need to know if (or when) it makes sense to consider S status.

Form 2553, Election by a Small Business Corporation

Form **2553** (Rev. September 1997) Department of the Treasury Internal Revenue Service	**Election by a Small Business Corporation** (Under section 1362 of the Internal Revenue Code) ► For Paperwork Reduction Act Notice, see page 2 of instructions. ► See separate instructions.	OMB No. 1545-0146

Notes: 1. This election to be an S corporation can be accepted only if all the tests are met under *Who May Elect* on page 1 of the instructions; all signatures in Parts I and III are originals (no photocopies); and the exact name and address of the corporation and other required form information are provided.

     2. Do not file Form 1120S, U.S. Income Tax Return for an S Corporation, for any tax year before the year the election takes effect.

     3. If the corporation was in existence before the effective date of this election, see *Taxes an S Corporation May Owe* on page 1 of the instructions.

Part I   **Election Information**

Please Type or Print	Name of corporation (see instructions) FRESH AIR CORP	A Employer identification number 12 3456 789
	Number, street, and room or suite no. (if a P.O. box, see instructions) 321 1st AVENUE	B Date incorporated 6/1/93
	City or town, state, and ZIP code SEASIDE, DELAWARE	C State of incorporation DELAWARE

D   Election is to be effective for tax year beginning (month, day, year) . . . . ► 1 / 1 / 94

E   Name and title of officer or legal representative who the IRS may call for more information   F Telephone number of officer or legal representative ( )

G   If the corporation changed its name or address after applying for the EIN shown in A above, check this box . . . . ► ☐

H   If this election takes effect for the first tax year the corporation exists, enter month, day, and year of the **earliest** of the following: (1) date the corporation first had shareholders, (2) date the corporation first had assets, or (3) date the corporation began doing business . . . . ► N/A /

I   Selected tax year: Annual return will be filed for tax year ending (month and day) ► . . . .
If the tax year ends on any date other than December 31, except for an automatic 52-53-week tax year ending with reference to the month of December, you must complete Part II on the back. If the date you enter is the ending date of an automatic 52-53-week tax year, write "52-53-week year" to the right of the date. See Temporary Regulations section 1.441-2T(e)(3).

J Name and address of each shareholder; shareholder's spouse having a community property interest in the corporation's stock; and each tenant in common, joint tenant, and tenant by the entirety. (A husband and wife (and their estates) are counted as one shareholder in determining the number of shareholders without regard to the manner in which the stock is owned.)	K Shareholders' Consent Statement. Under penalties of perjury, we declare that we consent to the election of the above-named corporation to be an S corporation under section 1362(a) and that we have examined this consent statement, including accompanying schedules and statements, and to the best of our knowledge and belief, it is true, correct, and complete. We understand our consent is binding and may not be withdrawn after the corporation has made a valid election. (Shareholders sign and date below.)		L Stock owned		M Social security number or employer identification number (see instructions)	N Shareholder's tax year ends (month and day)
	Signature	Date	Number of shares	Dates acquired		
MATILDA BAKER		1/1/94	500	6/1/93	234-56-7890	12/31
BORIS BAKER		1/1/94	500	6/1/93	123-45-6789	12/31

Under penalties of perjury, I declare that I have examined this election, including accompanying schedules and statements, and to the best of my knowledge and belief, it is true, correct, and complete.

Signature of officer ►   Title ►   Date ►

See Parts II and III on back.   Cat. No. 18629R   Form **2553** (Rev. 9-97)

Form 2553 (continued)

Form 2553 (Rev. 9-97)   Page **2**

Part II   Selection of Fiscal Tax Year (All corporations using this part must complete item O and item P, Q, or R.)

O   Check the applicable box to indicate whether the corporation is:

1. ☐ A new corporation adopting the tax year entered in item I, Part I.

2. ☐ An existing corporation retaining the tax year entered in item I, Part I.

3. ☐ An existing corporation changing to the tax year entered in item I, Part I.

P   Complete item P if the corporation is using the expeditious approval provisions of Rev. Proc. 87-32, 1987-2 C.B. 396, to request **(1)** a natural business year (as defined in section 4.01(1) of Rev. Proc. 87-32) or **(2)** a year that satisfies the ownership tax year test in section 4.01(2) of Rev. Proc. 87-32. Check the applicable box below to indicate the representation statement the corporation is making as required under section 4 of Rev. Proc. 87-32.

1. Natural Business Year ► ☐ I represent that the corporation is retaining or changing to a tax year that coincides with its natural business year (as defined in section 4.01(1) of Rev. Proc. 87-32 and as verified by its satisfaction of the requirements of section 4.02(1) of Rev. Proc. 87-32. In addition, if the corporation is changing to a natural business year as defined in section 4.01(1), I further represent that such tax year results in less deferral of income to the owners than the corporation s present tax year. I also represent that the corporation is not described in section 3.01(2) of Rev. Proc. 87-32. (See instructions for additional information that must be attached.)

2. Ownership Tax Year ► ☐ I represent that shareholders holding more than half of the shares of the stock (as of the first day of the tax year to which the request relates) of the corporation have the same tax year or are concurrently changing to the tax year that the corporation adopts, retains, or changes to per item I, Part I. I also represent that the corporation is not described in section 3.01(2) of Rev. Proc. 87-32.

Note: *If you do not use item P and the corporation wants a fiscal tax year, complete either item Q or R below. Item Q is used to request a fiscal tax year based on a business purpose and to make a back-up section 444 election. Item R is used to make a regular section 444 election.*

Q   Business Purpose—To request a fiscal tax year based on a business purpose, you must check box Q1 and pay a user fee. See instructions for details. You may also check box Q2 and/or box Q3.

1. Check here ► ☐ if the fiscal year entered in item I, Part I, is requested under the provisions of section 6.03 of Rev. Proc. 87-32. Attach to Form 2553 a statement showing the business purpose for the requested fiscal year. See instructions for additional information that must be attached.

2. Check here ► ☐ to show that the corporation intends to make a back-up section 444 election in the event the corporation's business purpose request is not approved by the IRS. (See instructions for more information.)

3. Check here ► ☐ to show that the corporation agrees to adopt or change to a tax year ending December 31 if necessary for the IRS to accept this election for S corporation status in the event (1) the corporation's business purpose request is not approved and the corporation makes a back-up section 444 election, but is ultimately not qualified to make a section 444 election, or (2) the corporation's business purpose request is not approved and the corporation did not make a back-up section 444 election.

R   Section 444 Election—To make a section 444 election, you must check box R1 and you may also check box R2.

1. Check here ► ☐ to show the corporation will make, if qualified, a section 444 election to have the fiscal tax year shown in item I, Part I. To make the election, you must complete Form 8716, Election To Have a Tax Year Other Than a Required Tax Year, and either attach it to Form 2553 or file it separately.

2. Check here ► ☐ to show that the corporation agrees to adopt or change to a tax year ending December 31 if necessary for the IRS to accept this election for S corporation status in the event the corporation is ultimately not qualified to make a section 444 election.

Part III   Qualified Subchapter S Trust (QSST) Election Under Section 1361(d)(2)*

Income beneficiary s name and address	Social security number
Trust's name and address	Employer identification number

Date on which stock of the corporation was transferred to the trust (month, day, year) . . . . . ► / /

In order for the trust named above to be a QSST and thus a qualifying shareholder of the S corporation for which this Form 2553 is filed, I hereby make the election under section 1361(d)(2). Under penalties of perjury, I certify that the trust meets the definitional requirements of section 1361(d)(3) and that all other information provided in Part III is true, correct, and complete.

Signature of income beneficiary or signature and title of legal representative or other qualified person making the elec: Date

*Use Part III to make the QSST election only if stock of the corporation has been transferred to the trust on or before the date on which the corporation makes its election to be an S corporation. The QSST election must be made and filed separately if stock of the corporation is transferred to the trust after the date on which the corporation makes the S election.

Chapter 5

FRINGE BENEFITS AND SPECIAL TAX WRITE-OFFS

If you were to ask your accountant or tax adviser what a fringe benefit is under the tax laws today, you might detect some uncertainty in their response. Chapter 6 will address a special type of fringe benefit that makes for an additional tax advantage under the current law. The term fringe benefit is not actually defined in the Internal Revenue Code. It is only by examples in the regulations that we are able to ascertain exactly what a fringe benefit is and how it can lower your tax bill.

As the owner of a small business, you are probably not interested in technical definitions or in any of the convoluted language that makes up the tax law today. Your only interest is to find out how you can claim every business deduction so that you can survive in this high tax atmosphere. This chapter will help you see how this works. If anything, it should help you better understand what it takes to get a legitimate tax write-off for your small business under the current law.

First, How to Make a Business Expense Deductible

To determine what kind of business expenses are allowed as deductions under the tax law, be aware of a catch-all section of the tax code that specifically states that **any** expense that is considered *ordinary and necessary* in the operation of your trade or business will qualify as a business deduction. Because this sounds so simple, some business owners accept the key phrase, *ordinary and necessary*, in the tax code as tacit approval to write off anything, as long as it has some connection with the business. After all, who is to argue over their interpretation of what is *ordinary and necessary*?

Whether an expense is *ordinary and necessary* depends upon the facts surrounding each particular expense.

♦ First, an expense may be considered *ordinary* if it is the type that would normally be expected in the situation at hand even if the situation would seldom arise.

♦ Second, an expense can be considered *necessary* if it was appropriate and helpful to your particular business, or if it was clearly and reasonably related to your business.

If you have incurred a questionable business expense that you feel has met these tests, hold firm to your position. Don't let your accountant or even an IRS agent, for that matter, tell you otherwise. Remember, the tax code and the courts are on your side.

✎ PLANNING TIP

It is important to keep these reference standards handy when questionable expenses arise in the course of your business.

TYPICAL EXPENSES READILY ACCEPTED BY THE IRS

Some may argue that this rule, authorizing you to write off anything *ordinary and necessary*, is one of the most pervasive sections of the entire tax code. It provides for an infinite number of tax deductions for anyone who engages in any kind of trade or business. Further, when dealing with the common everyday expenses of business, there is usually no problem in meeting the *ordinary and necessary* tests for the small business owner-operator.

The IRS will rarely raise a red flag when you take a deduction for the typical expense items found on most tax returns. These typical expenses include classifications like:

♦ Cost of goods sold

♦ Office supplies

♦ Employees salaries

♦ Business taxes

♦ Repairs and maintenance

♦ Legal and accounting

♦ Travel and entertainment

♦ Insurance

♦ Licenses and permits

♦ Professional dues and fees

♦ Depreciation

Classifiers in the IRS Service Centers will expect these deductions to show up on most business tax returns, and inquiries are not usually raised unless there is concern over the dollar amounts claimed.

BE AWARE OF THE RED FLAG ALERTS

Every return filed in an IRS Service Center is statistically graded to determine its potential for error. This procedure is referred to as the Discriminate Function System (DIF). From this scoring system, a DIF score is generated. With this, the IRS computer program is able to calculate the potential for error based on past audit experience. The DIF score identifies those returns that are more likely to contain errors and need an audit. Be aware of the two most common items that can raise your DIF score and your chances of an audit.

RED FLAG #1

Deduction amounts that are higher than prescribed norms will send up a red flag to the IRS. Say, for example, you were to write off $18,000 in entertainment expenses for your small retail business that grosses only $100,000 per year. Chances are your DIF score would necessitate an audit even though those expenses may be thoroughly appropriate.

RED FLAG #2

Unusual deductions, or those that are outside the typical expense categories. These deductions might include items like casualty losses or, perhaps, travel to the Caribbean to attend a planning seminar.

As a small business owner, you need to be aware and track expenses incurred outside the everyday expense categories. Even if you are challenged, you will have the edge if you can demonstrate that the expense was an *ordinary and necessary* cost of carrying on your business endeavor.

✎ PLANNING TIP

Aside from the typical expenses that you can incur in business, another way to get an attractive write-off that will be accepted by the IRS classifiers is to provide a so-called fringe benefit to employees.

FRINGE BENEFITS HELP ANSWER THE RED FLAG ALERT

In the IRS regulations, reference is made to a series of so-called fringe benefits. These are viewed as special tax write-offs that are automatically approved as *ordinary and necessary* costs of doing business. In short, unless they are unreasonable in amount, the IRS seldom raises a flag when they are spotted on your tax return. A partial summary of these fringe benefits is:

♦ An employer-provided ticket to a sporting event or other entertainment;

♦ Employer-provided discount on certain goods and services;

♦ An employer-provided automobile;

♦ A flight on an employer-provided aircraft;

♦ Employer-provided discounts on commercial airline flights, or free flights; and

♦ An employer-provided vacation.

In one sense, the fringe benefits are a valuable tax advantage to the small business owner. In many instances they often provide a handsome tax write-off to a business just when it is most needed. However, beware of an interesting twist in the law regarding these types of fringe benefits.

Under normal circumstances, the assortment of fringe benefits, similar to the ones listed above, will **probably be included in the income of the employee who receives the fringe benefit.** Further, if you are the owner of a corporation, as well as a working employee, and you have received the fringe benefit, you will end up paying personal income taxes on the fringe benefit windfall. The situation could get worse. You could be in that formidable 39.6% bracket under the most recent tax law if your combined fringe benefits and your personal income exceed $278,450.

Q. What should I do before taking any fringe benefits from my corporation?

A. You should evaluate your own personal tax situation every time you take **any** kind of taxable benefit out of your business, whether it's a cash bonus or a certain fringe benefit. As shown in Chapter 1, your current tax bracket should help you decide if you want that benefit showing up on your tax return for that particular year.

One of the most common complaints of accountants and tax advisers is that small business clients all too often deviate from their planning regimen and pull out benefits from their corporations without considering their **personal** tax consequences. Whether it is a fringe benefit or an ordinary salary bonus, they overlook that the day of reckoning is soon to appear — the often dreaded April 15th!

Many small business owner-operators are simply trying to be cost conscious during these economic times. Rationally, they simply can't afford to pay their advisers to do a professional analysis every time they need to take a few dollars out of the company.

How should you, as the owner-operator, handle your fringe benefits and special payments? It is increasingly imperative that you, as a small business owner get a firm hold on your personal tax bracket for each operating year. This is especially important during these times of rising tax rates and a tax code that seems to be continually revised.

Find out what federal tax bracket you are in and add Social Security and the state tax, if applicable. To do this, you will need to first make a current projection of your personal income for the year. Then, ask your accountant for a schedule of the individual tax rates set in the tax code at that particular time.

If you are paying at the 39.6% marginal tax rate for that year and you could arrange to keep your income down to a minimum for the following year, your action could help you push a bonus or a fringe benefit into a year with perhaps a 15% rate. This would amount to a personal tax savings of 24.6%. Note: The following chapter discusses a special class of fringe benefits that allows for an extra tax benefit. This is because the employee recipients may be fully relieved from paying any tax whatever on the fringe benefit received.

BEWARE OF PENALTIES AND INTEREST FOR FAILURE TO PAY

A secondary problem arises when, as a small corporation owner, you use bad timing in paying yourself fringe benefits and other special allowances. Penalties and interest may occur if taxes on those benefits are not paid on a timely basis.

With personal tax rates on the rise, small business owners are taking a closer look at their personal tax bill. If they don't pay accordingly, the IRS computers will assess some tough interest penalties without failure.

⬜ *Special Note: As a general rule, a penalty situation arises when 90% of the tax is not paid up front by withholding or estimating payments.*

Below are some guidelines to avoid penalties and interest.

♦ Start paying estimated taxes at the end of the very next quarter following any of the special payments or fringe benefits that you received from your business.

♦ Take a close look at the special exceptions that still apply to those who underestimate their tax liability. For example, even though there has been some tightening of the rules, many could avoid penalties by simply making estimated tax payments that match last year's tax bill. (See *Form 2210* at the end of this chapter to see which exceptions may apply to you.)

✎ PLANNING TIP

Suppose you determine that you are going to be in a penalty situation because you will owe taxes on certain payments that you had received from the business earlier in the year. You should be aware that you cannot avoid the penalty by simply making an extra estimated payment in the last quarter. All payments must be made on time. Consider having your employer or corporation withhold additional amounts from your last paychecks during the remainder of the year. This will help you take advantage of a provision in the law that treats income tax withholding as if it had been paid equally throughout the entire year.

Remember, increasing your withholding at the very end of the year can spare you from penalty for not paying estimated taxes beforehand. In fact, many business owners treat this quirk in the law as a gaping loophole. To make the loophole work, however, you should apply a common sense standard.

Illustration 5.1

◆ Mort draws $60,000 in taxable fringe benefits at different intervals during the year from his wholly owned corporation.

◆ Although there was no tax paid in advance, Mort reasons that he could beat the system by simply waiting until December 31, and taking a paycheck with a big enough withholding amount to cover his federal tax bill for the entire year.

◆ For Mort, this seems like the perfect interest-free loan.

Some aggressive business owners have used this tactic to hold onto their entire withholding tax dollars for the entire year — interest free. The only reason it has worked is that the IRS has insufficient enforcement capability and human resources available to monitor this activity. There is word, however, that this activity will be looked at in the future, and some believe the chronic abusers will be subject to a host of other penalties for their action. For example, a false *W-4* form filing might become the subject of debate.

✎ PLANNING TIP

Proceed to take advantage of the provision that allows you to treat withholding as if it had been paid equally throughout the entire year. But use this loophole for what it was apparently designed. In simple terms, take care of unpaid taxes on occasional income items for which there is no withholding. Most importantly, don't apply the procedure if the dollar amount of the late withholding payment appears to be excessive or beyond that which is reasonable.

DEDUCTIONS FOR SPECIAL PAYMENTS TO SHAREHOLDERS TO ELIMINATE DOUBLE TAXATION

For many owners of small business corporations, there is one other situation that needs special attention. This is the costly potential double tax. The IRS loves to assess the double tax when ordinary corporations pay out periodic bonuses and fringe benefits to the shareholder-owners, especially at the end of the year.

○ **Special Note:** *As pointed out in Chapter 4, one way to eliminate the problem of the double tax is to forego the advantages of the ordinary C corporation and elect treatment as an S corporation.*

Illustration 5.2

♦ Jones Corporation, an ordinary C corporation, prepares to close out its year with a $50,000 profit.

♦ Mary Jones is in the 31% tax bracket and her corporation is at a lower 15% rate.

♦ Interestingly, Mary doesn't plan to leave the profit in the corporation and pay tax at the lower rate. Like many middle income business operators, Mary needs to pull out the cash accumulation for personal expenses.

One possible scenario could be:

Illustration 5.3

♦ The corporation pays $7,500 in taxes on the profit ($50,000 multiplied by 15%).

♦ The following year, the corporation takes the $42,500 remaining cash and makes a distribution to Mary.

♦ She then pays a tax of $13,175 on the distribution ($42,500 multiplied by 31%).

♦ The overall tax? $20,675 (a whopping 41.35% on the $50,000 profit).

Since no special steps were taken to show otherwise, the payment made to Mary was nothing more than an ordinary dividend.

Remember, the general rule is that dividends are not deductible by the corporation and will be subject to the double tax.

HOW TO GET AROUND THE CORPORATE DOUBLE TAX

In the real world, tax advisers for clients like Mary usually take steps to thwart this kind of onerous tax liability.

Q. How could Mary's corporate tax liability have been eliminated?

A. Mary could attempt to show that the $50,000 distribution is an authorized, authentic salary bonus that is deductible by the corporation. If so, Mary would succeed in wiping out the entire $7,500 corporate tax obligation.

With proper authorization for a legitimate deduction for a salary bonus, there would be no corporate tax liability. Instead, there would be a one time, individual tax that Mary would have to pay on the $50,000 distribution. The amount of that tax — $15,500 ($50,000 multiplied by 31%) — constitutes a savings of $5,175.

There are other steps to consider when making special payments to shareholders who work for the corporation. If there is **any** hint that the payments made are, in reality, an attempt to pull out the profits without paying a corporate tax, you can expect the IRS to see this as a dividend. You can easily see why examining agents like to raise an issue when a controlling shareholder waits until the very end of the year to make payments to the owners. Similar to Mary's case (illustrations 5.2 and 5.3), many opt to calculate the projected profit for the year and then turn around and make a bonus or other special payment to that shareholder. They usually end up paying just enough to eliminate the corporate tax bill.

The IRS and the small corporation continue to struggle over this issue. Each year, many corporation owners struggle just to survive and then they are faced with the task of having to prove that the money they took out was just recompense for all their hard work and effort.

THE REASONABLE TEST

It was shown earlier that all compensation paid for personal services must be reasonable to be deductible. When the payee is a shareholder, close scrutiny is sure to follow. What is reasonable is case specific and, thus, hard and fast rules don't exist. There are, however, guidelines set for the IRS by the courts which give some clues as to what the IRS will look for. There are five suggested factors for determining whether compensation paid to a shareholder is reasonable.

1. The role that the employee plays in the company;

2. Salaries paid by similar companies for comparable services;

3. The character and condition of the company;

4. Any conflicts of interest between the employee and the corporation. (This might make it easier for nondeductible dividends to be disguised as salaries or deductible fringe benefits.); and

5. Internal consistency. (Attention is directed to the past history of the corporation's compensation plan and whether or not it was reasonably and consistently followed.)

CHAPTER SUMMARY

It was shown earlier that all business expenses must meet certain guidelines before they will be deemed deductible under the current law. In general, they must be considered ordinary and necessary in the operation of your business. Certain commonly used expenses (including many fringe benefits) are expected to be found in small business, and normally, do not raise the DIF score and chances for audit scrutiny. Also, regular corporations be careful. To gain a full tax deduction for any salary or benefit to owner/shareholders, certain guidelines must be followed.

Form 2210, Underpayment of Estimated Tax

Form **2210**	**Underpayment of**	OMB No. 1545-0140
Department of the Treasury Internal Revenue Service	**Estimated Tax by Individuals, Estates, and Trusts** ▶ See separate instructions. ▶ Attach to Form 1040, 1040A, 1040NR, 1040NR-EZ, or 1041.	**1997** Attachment Sequence No. 06

Name(s) shown on tax return		Identifying number

Note: *In most cases, you do not need to file Form 2210. The IRS will figure any penalty you owe and send you a bill. File Form 2210 only if one or more boxes in Part I apply to you. If you do not need to file Form 2210, you still may use it to figure your penalty. Enter the amount from line 20 or line 32 on the penalty line of your return, but do not attach Form 2210.*

Part I	**Reasons for Filing** — If 1a, b, or c below applies to you, you may be able to lower or eliminate your penalty. But you MUST check the boxes that apply and file Form 2210 with your tax return. If 1d below applies to you, check that box and file Form 2210 with your tax return.

1 Check whichever boxes apply (if none apply, see the **Note** above):

  a ☐ You request a **waiver.** In certain circumstances, the IRS will waive all or part of the penalty. See **Waiver of Penalty** on page 1 of the instructions.

  b ☐ You use the **annualized income installment method.** If your income varied during the year, this method may reduce the amount of one or more required installments. See page 4 of the instructions.

  c ☐ You had Federal income tax withheld from wages and, for estimated tax purposes, you treat the withheld tax as paid on the dates it was actually withheld, instead of in equal amounts on the payment due dates. See the instructions for line 22 on page 3.

  d ☐ Your required annual payment (line 13 below) is based on your 1996 tax and you filed or are filing a joint return for either 1996 or 1997 but not for both years.

Part II	**Required Annual Payment**		
2	Enter your 1997 tax after credits (see page 2 of the instructions). **Caution:** *Also see page 2 for a special rule if claiming the research credit*	**2**	
3	Other taxes (see page 2 of the instructions)	**3**	
4	Add lines 2 and 3	**4**	
5	Earned income credit **5**		
6	Credit for Federal tax paid on fuels **6**		
7	Add lines 5 and 6	**7**	
8	Current year tax. Subtract line 7 from line 4	**8**	
9	Multiply line 8 by 90% (.90) **9**		
10	Withholding taxes. Do not include any estimated tax payments on this line (see page 2 of the instructions)	**10**	
11	Subtract line 10 from line 8. If less than $500, stop here; do not complete or file this form. You do not owe the penalty	**11**	
12	Enter the tax shown on your 1996 tax return (110% of that amount if the adjusted gross income shown on that return is more than $150,000, or if married filing separately for 1997, more than $75,000). **Caution:** *See page 2 of the instructions*	**12**	
13	Required annual payment. Enter the **smaller** of line 9 or line 12	**13**	

Note: *If line 10 is equal to or more than line 13, stop here; you do not owe the penalty. Do not file Form 2210 unless you checked box 1d above.*

Part III	**Short Method** (**Caution:** *See page 2 of the instructions to find out if you can use the short method. If you checked box 1b or c in Part I, skip this part and go to Part IV.*)		
14	Enter the amount, if any, from line 10 above **14**		
15	Enter the total amount, if any, of estimated tax payments you made ... **15**		
16	Add lines 14 and 15	**16**	
17	Total underpayment for year. Subtract line 16 from line 13. If zero or less, stop here; you do not owe the penalty. Do not file Form 2210 unless you checked box 1d above	**17**	
18	Multiply line 17 by .05986	**18**	

19	• If the amount on line 17 was paid on or after 4/15/98, enter -0-.
	• If the amount on line 17 was paid **before** 4/15/98, make the following computation to find the amount to enter on line 19.
	
	    Amount on Number of days paid
	    line 17 × before 4/15/98 × .00025 ....
		19	

20	**PENALTY. Subtract line 19 from line 18. Enter the result here and on Form 1040, line 65; Form 1040A, line 34; Form 1040NR, line 65; Form 1040NR-EZ, line 26; or Form 1041, line 27** ▶	**20**	

For Paperwork Reduction Act Notice, see page 1 of separate instructions.   Form **2210** (1997)

ISA
STF FED4435F.1

Form 2210 (continued)

Form 2210 (1997)   Page 2

Part IV | Regular Method (See page 2 of the instructions if you are filing Form 1040NR or 1040NR-EZ.)

Section A — Figure Your Underpayment

			Payment Due Dates			
			(a) 4/15/97	(b) 6/15/97	(c) 9/15/97	(d) 1/15/98
21	Required installments. If box 1b applies, enter the amounts from Schedule AI, line 26. Otherwise, enter ¼ of line 13, Form 2210, in each column	21				
22	Estimated tax paid and tax withheld (see page 3 of the instructions). For column (a) only, also enter the amount from line 22 on line 26. If line 22 is equal to or more than line 21 for all payment periods, stop here; you do not owe the penalty. Do not file Form 2210 unless you checked a box in Part I	22				
	Complete lines 23 through 29 of one column before going to the next column.					
23	Enter amount, if any, from line 29 of previous column	23				
24	Add lines 22 and 23	24				
25	Add amounts on lines 27 and 28 of the previous column.	25				
26	Subtract line 25 from line 24. If zero or less, enter -0-. For column (a) only, enter the amount from line 22 . .	26				
27	If the amount on line 26 is zero, subtract line 24 from line 25. Otherwise, enter -0-	27				
28	Underpayment. If line 21 is equal to or more than line 26, subtract line 26 from line 21. Then go to line 23 of next column. Otherwise, go to line 29 . . . . . . ▶	28				
29	Overpayment. If line 26 is more than line 21, subtract line 21 from line 26. Then go to line 23 of next column	29				

Section B — Figure the Penalty (Complete lines 30 and 31 of one column before going to the next column.)

			4/15/97	6/15/97	9/15/97	1/15/98
			Days:	Days:	Days:	Days:
30	Number of days FROM the date shown above line 30 TO the date the amount on line 28 was paid or 4/15/98, whichever is earlier	30				
31	Underpayment on line 28 (see page 3 of the instructions) × Number of days on line 30 / 365 × .09 ▶	31	$	$	$	$
32	PENALTY. Add the amounts in each column of line 31. Enter the total here and on Form 1040, line 65; Form 1040A, line 34; Form 1040NR, line 65; Form 1040NR-EZ, line 26; or Form 1041, line 27 . . . . . . ▶	32	$			

STF FED4435F 2

Form 2210 *(continued)*

Form 2210 (1997)					Page 3

Schedule AI — Annualized Income Installment Method (see pages 4 and 5 of the instructions)

Estates and trusts, do not use the period ending dates shown to the right. Instead, use the following: 2/28/97, 4/30/97, 7/31/97, and 11/30/97.		(a) 1/1/97 - 3/31/97	(b) 1/1/97 - 5/31/97	(c) 1/1/97 - 8/31/97	(d) 1/1/97 - 12/31/97

Part I Annualized Income Installments Caution: *Complete lines 20 - 26 of one column before going to the next column.*

1	Enter your adjusted gross income for each period (see instructions). (Estates and trusts, enter your taxable income without your exemption for each period.)	1				
2	Annualization amounts. (Estates and trusts, see instructions.) .	2	4	2.4	1.5	1
3	Annualized income. Multiply line 1 by line 2	3				
4	Enter your itemized deductions for the period shown in each column. If you do not itemize, enter -0- and skip to line 7. (Estates and trusts, enter -0-, skip to line 9, and enter the amount from line 3 on line 9.)	4				
5	Annualization amounts.	5	4	2.4	1.5	1
6	Multiply line 4 by line 5 (see instructions if line 3 is more than $60,600)	6				
7	In each column, enter the full amount of your standard deduction from Form 1040, line 35, or Form 1040A, line 19 (Form 1040NR or 1040NR-EZ filers, enter -0-. **Exception:** Indian students and business apprentices, enter standard deduction from Form 1040NR, line 34 or Form 1040NR-EZ, line 10.)	7				
8	Enter the larger of line 6 or line 7.	8				
9	Subtract line 8 from line 3	9				
10	In each column, multiply $2,650 by the total number of exemptions claimed (see instructions if line 3 is more than $90,900). (Estates and trusts and Form 1040NR or 1040NR-EZ filers, enter the exemption amount shown on your tax return.) .	10				
11	Subtract line 10 from line 9	11				
12	Figure your tax on the amount on line 11 (see instructions). . . .	12				
13	Form 1040 filers only, enter your self-employment tax from line 35 below	13				
14	Enter other taxes for each payment period (see instructions) . .	14				
15	Total tax. Add lines 12, 13, and 14	15				
16	For each period, enter the same type of credits as allowed on Form 2210, lines 2, 5, and 6 (see instructions)	16				
17	Subtract line 16 from line 15. If zero or less, enter -0-	17				
18	Applicable percentage	18	22.5%	45%	67.5%	90%
19	Multiply line 17 by line 18	19				
20	Add the amounts in all preceding columns of line 26	20				
21	Subtract line 20 from line 19. If zero or less, enter -0-	21				
22	Enter ¼ of line 13 on page 1 of Form 2210 in each column . . .	22				
23	Enter amount from line 25 of the preceding column of this schedule	23				
24	Add lines 22 and 23 and enter the total	24				
25	Subtract line 21 from line 24. If zero or less, enter -0-	25				
26	Enter the smaller of line 21 or line 24 here and on Form 2210, line 21 . . . . ▶	26				

Part II Annualized Self-Employment Tax

27a	Net earnings from self-employment for the period (see instructions)	27a				
b	Annualization amounts.	27b	4	2.4	1.5	1
c	Multiply line 27a by line 27b	27c				
28	Social security tax limit.	28	$65,400	$65,400	$65,400	$65,400
29	Enter actual wages subject to social security tax or the 6.2% portion of the 7.65% railroad retirement (tier 1) tax	29				
30	Annualization amounts.	30	4	2.4	1.5	1
31	Multiply line 29 by line 30	31				
32	Subtract line 31 from line 28. If zero or less, enter -0-	32				
33	Multiply the smaller of line 27c or line 32 by .124	33				
34	Multiply line 27c by .029.	34				
35	Add lines 33 and 34. Enter the result here and on line 13 above . . . . ▶	35				

STF FED4435F 3

Chapter 6

TAX-SHELTERED EMPLOYER-PROVIDED FRINGE BENEFITS

As was pointed out in the previous chapter, certain fringe benefits make for nice tax deductions in a business operation. In fact, as long as they are reasonable in amount, there are seldom any questions raised by the IRS when they are deducted on a business tax return. The one downside, however, is that this class of fringe benefits usually ends up on the employee's tax return and is fully taxed at the ordinary rates.

The general rationale of the tax law is unless a fringe benefit is excluded from income by some special provision in the tax code, it must be included in the employee's income.

There is a class of fringe benefits that is specifically exempted from income because of certain language in the tax code. Chapter 3 shows how the special tax break applies to benefits like health and accident plans. This chapter will focus on other fringe benefits and will provide you with guidelines on how to qualify for tax-sheltered treatment. If you are a small business owner, you will find these provisions particularly appealing. The benefits will not be denied to you just because you are the owner and employee.

On the one hand your business gets a full tax write-off for the fringe benefit made available. On the other hand, you, as the owner, may not have to pay one cent in taxes on the benefits paid. Take a look at the fringe benefits that are eligible for the tax-sheltered treatment.

MEALS AND LODGING FURNISHED BY THE EMPLOYER

An important tax-free windfall that extends to the employees of a business enterprise is that of meals and lodging that may be provided in the course of employment. Although this particular benefit only works with ordinary corporations when it involves owner-employees, all business operators should be aware of its existence.

With an ordinary corporation, employees can reap sizable tax savings if they receive meals and lodging on a continuing basis. What you need to do, however, is be able to show that the corporate employer gained some benefit in the process. In other words, you should be prepared to demonstrate that the employee isn't the only one getting value when this fringe benefit is made available.

What does the tax code say about meals? The value of meals furnished to the employee, his or her spouse, or dependents are tax free when:

♦ They are furnished for the employer's convenience; and

♦ They are furnished on the employer's business premises.

WHAT CONVENIENCE OF THE EMPLOYER MEANS

This implies that the employee's continued presence on the employer's premises is necessary to better perform duties properly or supervise others. Typically, this is the case when the employee is expected to handle emergency calls or special situations with short notice.

The meals are considered to be for the convenience of the employer if they are furnished for a "noncompensatory business reason" of the employer whether:

♦ They are free of charge, or

♦ They are for a flat fee, whether or not the employee accepts the meals.

✎ PLANNING TIP

Be prepared to show that there were sound business reasons for making the meals available that do not include compensatory reasons. If it appears that the employer was merely trying to pass off some extra benefits or compensation to the employee, it won't work.

Likewise, meals provided to promote goodwill, better morale, or merely to attract prospective employees will be considered compensatory and taxable.

WHAT THE TAX CODE SAYS ABOUT LODGING PROVIDED BY AN EMPLOYER

The rules for excludability are the same as for meals except one more tough requirement is added: the lodging must be accepted as a condition of employment.

☞ KEY OBSERVATION

It is important to note that meals and lodging made available to employees will not be disqualified for the special tax-free treatment just because those employees happen to be stockholder-owners.

Illustration 6.1

♦ Excel Corporation provided lodging to Fred, one of its major stockholders. Fred is a corporate officer and manager of the company farm.

♦ Because of the requirement that Fred be accessible at all times for the day-to-day management of the farm, the value of his lodging was excluded from his income.

♦ Additionally, since meals were furnished on the business premises and were for the convenience of the employer, they too were excluded from Fred's income as well as from the income of other employees.

DEPENDENT CARE ASSISTANCE PROGRAMS

This tax break may be of interest to employees who have dependent children that are physically challenged or are under age 13 that require day care during their parents' absence. The Dependent Care Assistance Program can also benefit you as an owner or principal shareholder as long as certain qualifications are met. The amount of dependent care assistance that you can exclude from income is generally up to $5,000. If you are married filing separately, the maximum is $2,500. Dependent care assistance can include the following:

- The cost of baby sitters, day camp, nursery schools, or other outside-the-home costs; and

- Employment-related household expenses — including domestic services in your home, such as laundry, cleaning, and cooking.

HOW DOES IT WORK?

A certain portion of the payments made by the employer for dependent care can be excluded from income whether they are paid to the caregiver directly or simply reimbursed to the employee. The special exclusion does not apply to employer-provided dependent care if payments are made to:

- Individuals for whom the employee is entitled to take a dependency exemption; or

- Children of the employee who are under age 19. There are certain restrictions against discrimination in favor of shareholder-owners and highly compensated employees.

☛ KEY OBSERVATION

A self-employed individual is recognized for these purposes as an employee. By definition, any self-employed individual who can be covered under a self-employed retirement plan may participate in dependent care assistance programs. They too can receive dependent care assistance that is excludable from income.

Another distinct advantage that must not be overlooked is that the self-employed individual receiving the benefits could also deduct the cost of providing the benefit.

✎ PLANNING TIP

It is important to put it in writing. Make sure you spell out the details of the dependent care plan. Remember, the employees must be notified of the existence of the plan, the eligibility to participate, and all the relevant terms.

EXCLUSION FOR NO-ADDITIONAL COST SERVICES

This tax-sheltered fringe benefit applies to the value of services provided to employees and their dependents for a reduced charge or no charge at all. Generally, it is free from tax to the employee if it can be shown that the employer sells the same service to nonemployee customers in the ordinary course of business in which the employee works. The key to making this benefit work lies in being able to demonstrate that:

♦ The employer incurs no substantial additional cost in providing such services to the employee; and

♦ The exclusion does not discriminate in favor of highly compensated employees.

One way to fit the definition of a no additional cost service is to understand the term *excess capacity services*. This refers to services that are available for use and would remain unused if the employees would not use them. For example:

♦ Hotel accommodations;

♦ Aircraft transportation;

♦ Train, bus, or cruise line transportation; and

♦ Telephone services.

Q. What does the phrase "the employer must have incurred no substantial additional costs" for the services rendered really mean?

A. The determination of substantial additional costs is handled on a case by case basis. Generally, it involves the cost of labor, materials, supplies, and other nonlabor costs.

When trying to determine if the employer has incurred a substantial additional cost, you should not confuse the definition with the fact that the employee might have reimbursed the employer for the cost of providing the service. Accordingly, any reimbursements made for the cost of the service has nothing to do with the question involving whether or not the employer has incurred a substantial additional cost.

Illustration 6.2

♦ Roadway Corporation is in the business of repairing computers and various types of electronic equipment. Roadway notified its employees that it would repair its employees' personal computer equipment at no charge.

♦ During the year, Roadway repairs Sue's personal computer but in the process incurs the substantial additional cost of $150 for materials. The total value of the repair service was $600.

♦ Sue offers to pay the additional cost of $150 with the expectation that this would make her eligible to exclude the entire benefit from income.

♦ Unfortunately, the amount of the $450 benefit ($600 minus $150) is fully taxable. It makes no difference if Sue reimburses Roadway for that portion of the cost. The fact is, a substantial additional cost was still incurred.

♦ However, if the additional cost incurred were for some minor supplies in the amount of $35, the value of the benefit would more than likely be fully excludable.

EXCLUSION FOR QUALIFIED EMPLOYEE DISCOUNTS

Discounts on qualified property or services that are taken by employees, their spouses, and children can turn into an attractive tax-free benefit in certain circumstances. The benefit refers to the right to exclude from income the discount savings as long as:

♦ The amount of the discount does not exceed certain limitations; and

♦ There is not discrimination among the higher paid employees.

What is the definition of *qualified property or services? Qualified property or services* refers to property and services, which are normally offered for sale to outside customers in the ordinary course of business. Certain specific property, however, is not eligible by definition and includes real property (residential real estate) and personal property commonly held for investment. In other words, this includes any kind of tangible or nontangible property commonly held for investment.

Illustration 6.3

♦ Chester is a consultant for a small stock brokerage firm for which he receives a discount for: commissions on security transactions; and stocks and bonds that he buys directly from the firm for his own account.

♦ Chester can exclude the discount on the commissions from his income, which is also subject to the limitations for discounts on services.

♦ Chester cannot exclude the discount on the purchase of securities for his own account since the securities do not meet the definition of *qualified property.*

☞ KEY OBSERVATION

Determine the limitations on the tax-free exclusions for property and services. The amount that can be excluded from income as a qualified employee discount on property sold to the employee is limited to the *gross profit percentage.* This means the *gross profit percentage* of the price that the merchandise would have been offered to outside customers is tax free. Of course, if the employee discount is in excess of this amount, that excess must be included in the employee's gross income and taxed accordingly.

EXCLUSION FOR WORKING CONDITION

There are instances when certain items of property or services are provided to an employee and will not be charged to that employee's income. There are general conditions that need to be met for this tax-sheltered provision.

♦ First, the cost of property or services would have ordinarily been deductible by the employee, had the employee paid for them.

♦ Second, the deduction would have been allowable as an *ordinary and necessary* business deduction for the employee in connection with the trade or business.

This may be easier to understand by just observing some examples of the business expense items that fit in this category. These include:

♦ Employer-paid subscriptions for business journals and periodicals;

♦ Use of employer-provided vehicles for business purposes;

♦ Employer-payment for on-the-job training;

♦ Employer-paid business travel for employees; and

♦ Educational assistance programs.

The requirement that the expense would have to be deductible as an expense in connection with that trade or business is important to understand. For example, consider the following fringe benefit arrangement.

Illustration 6.4

- ♦ Donald allows for physical examinations under a special program for his employees, Maria and Harold.

- ♦ The cost of the examinations *is not tax free* and must be included in both Maria's and Harold's income.

- ♦ Even though the cost of medical examinations would ordinarily be deductible as a medical expense, such costs would not have been deductible as an *ordinary and necessary* business expense of the employees involved.

- ♦ Had Donald provided for payment of the employees' professional dues or subscriptions to business journals, the employees would have been able to exclude the same as a *working condition* fringe benefit.

The nondiscrimination rules do not apply except in the unusual circumstances, such as with product testing programs. For example, if you provide personal computers for the business use of certain officers and managers in the company, the officers and managers can exclude the cost from their income, even though the other employees are not entitled to this fringe benefit.

EMPLOYER-PROVIDED TRANSPORTATION

You will recall that one of the ground rules for a working condition fringe to be nontaxable to the employee is that the expense must pass a deductibility test. More specifically, the expense must be ordinarily deductible had it been incurred by that employee in the course of that employee's trade or business. In spite of all the changes in the tax law in recent years, travel expense and automobile expenses are still deductible when incurred in business.

The definition of *employer-provided* transportation is all-inclusive; thus tax free treatment as a **working condition** fringe can extend to items like:

♦ Automobiles made available to employees

♦ Air flights

♦ Chauffeur services

♦ Taxis

♦ Miscellaneous local transportation

Note that the employee can receive these benefits tax free only when used on employer business. Commuting and personal use render the value of the services taxable.

Q. How do the working condition fringe benefit rules apply to an ordinary automobile that is made available for an employee's use?

A. It is clear from reading the tax rules that the use of an automobile qualifies for tax-free treatment under the working condition fringe rules. This is because automobile expense is one of the most typical trade or business expenses that an employee can incur.

Illustration 6.5

♦ Bold Company purchases a new automobile, which it makes available to its major shareholder, Herb.

♦ Herb uses the car solely for business, as he needs to travel along a particular sales route.

♦ The value of the car is totally tax free to Herb since he would ordinarily have been allowed to deduct the cost of an automobile in his particular work.

♦ Suppose Bold Company actually provides *two* cars to Herb, but one is used solely by his wife who did not participate in the business. In that case, Herb will be taxed only on the value of the second car.

♦ In real life circumstances, a situation like Herb's, involving 100% business use of an automobile, is somewhat far fetched.

♦ It is only in the most unique circumstances that a working employee could demonstrate that the automobile is solely driven for business.

☞ KEY OBSERVATION

IRS auditors may have become a bit more tolerant of the tough recordkeeping rules imposed on the operators of business autos. In almost all cases, however, they still make some analyses during an audit, separating business from personal mileage. Unless you have a meticulous log of your business miles, kept on a contemporaneous basis, it is likely that you will incur an adjustment resulting in additional tax liability.

As an employer, you may be able to eliminate this burdensome recordkeeping requirement. If you have a written policy that generally prohibits personal employees from using a car for personal use or if you include the full annual value of the car in an employee's wages, then you will not have to keep the meticulous log of business miles.

⬚ *Special Note: The toughest cases are the ones involving commuting expenses that are never deductible as a business expense. In almost all cases, there is some element of commuting for an employee who leaves his or her home to begin a workday.*

VEHICLES USED PARTIALLY FOR NONBUSINESS PURPOSES

If you, like most employees, use your employer-provided automobile for personal use from time to time, you need to refer to a simple formula to determine the tax consequences. The formula is:

---

the value of the vehicle's availability

Multiplied by

the ratio(*) between business and personal miles

(*ratio = business miles divided by total miles)

the working condition

Equals

fringe benefit (tax free)

Illustration 6.6

♦ Sharp Company provides a car for its employee, Rose.

♦ The value of the car for the year is $3,000 to Rose if she were to use it 100% of the time.

♦ During the year, Rose drives the car 7,000 business miles for the company and 3,000 personal miles. 10,000 total miles were driven during the year.

♦ By applying the formula, the tax-free working condition fringe is calculated.

$3,000 (the value of the vehicle's availability)

Multiplied by

.70 or 70% (the ratio of business car use)

Equals

$2,100 (the working condition fringe benefit)

See Chapter 10 for more information on the use of business automobiles.

✎ PLANNING TIP

Even if you happen to generate a tax liability because of the personal use of a company-provided vehicle, you should be aware that the cost would still be less than if you leased the car. It would also, more than likely, be cheaper than if you bought and financed the car on your own.

In the event the employer is a corporation of which the employee is a major shareholder, take caution when cars are provided with little or no business purpose. The extra compensation might be viewed as a dividend to the shareholder if the overall compensation is deemed to be unreasonable. Don't forget the tough, double tax problems associated with dividends to shareholders.

EMPLOYER-PAID TRIPS

Many employees, including officers of companies, often receive expense-paid trips that combine elements of business with pleasure. To determine whether or not the cost of these trips is a taxable event to the employee, you need to evaluate the primary purpose for taking the trip.

Determine if an employer-paid trip is primarily business in nature. In reviewing the relevant facts for determining the business or personal nature of employer-paid trips, you begin to readily appreciate the value of keeping written records in business. Some of the factors that are brought into the equation are:

♦ The amount of actual time spent on business, as opposed to pleasure;

♦ The geographic considerations; and

♦ The general attitude and position of the employer.

For example, if a business meeting is held at a luxury resort, a nonbusiness tone already exists. If that employer looks to the occasion as primarily a pleasurable event while passing out written memos regarding this issue, then a nonbusiness purpose probably will be inferred. Remember, no factor is conclusive by itself. Training and professional development for the business is a strong indication that a trip is primarily business-related.

THE KEY TEST

No income will result to the employee if, from the employee's point of view:

♦ The trip was primarily business in nature; and

♦ The employee does not spend a significant amount of time pursuing personal benefit and enjoyment.

If you can demonstrate that the primary purpose of the trip was personal, then the value of the trip will be taxable income. Each case is judged by its own facts and circumstances.

Illustration 6.7

♦ ARC Employees Monte and Oscar went to Miami to observe a new software program related to their business operations.

♦ The trip lasted four days and a major portion of their time was devoted to sharing technical ideas at business sessions and dinner meetings.

♦ Even though ARC emphasized a holiday-like tone when it tried to stimulate employee participation, the trip will probably be deemed primarily business and tax free to Monte and Oscar.

Illustration 6.8

♦ Later that year, ARC paid for its business manager, Victoria, a 33% shareholder, to go to London to learn about a manufacturing process that they planned to introduce.

♦ During Victoria's stay, she meets with several business owners and potential suppliers. She failed to keep records thereof.

♦ After she returned, neither she nor ARC could produce minutes of business meetings, business reports or even a corporate resolution authorizing her to go on the fact finding mission.

♦ Unfortunately, this required Victoria to report the entire trip as income.

EMPLOYER-PROVIDED PARKING

If you provide your employees with free parking, you might just find that they can exclude that allowance from their income. As long as you meet the definition of *qualified parking*, the payments for such can be treated as a nontaxable transportation fringe.

◻ *Special Note: After 1997, new restrictions will disqualify this benefit if it is provided "in lieu of taxable compensation" and cash is taken.*

WHAT IS QUALIFIED PARKING?

Qualified parking refers to parking that is provided to an employee. Qualified parking does not include parking at a facility that is located on or near the employee's personal residence. This means that a self-employed individual cannot qualify under this definition. It also means that the actual parking facility must be located either on or near the employer's business premises; or at a location, or near a location, from which the employee commutes to work, when that person commutes by mass transit or hired commuter vehicle.

Illustration 6.9

♦ Road Corporation provides a parking allowance for its managing officers Ed and Jill.

♦ Ed parks his car in a lot located directly across the street from the office.

♦ Jill's parking location is at an old lot next to a train station located two blocks from her home.

♦ Ed can treat his parking fringe as a tax-free benefit, however Jill will be taxed on the allowance, since the facility is near her personal residence.

♦ It is important to remember that Road does not have to satisfy any nondiscrimination rules to qualify parking for the tax-free treatment as a working condition fringe benefit.

EMPLOYER-PROVIDED COMMUTER TRANSPORTATION

Transportation that is provided to an employee for commuting may, in certain cases, be considered a nontaxable transportation fringe. To qualify for this tax-free benefit the transportation must be provided in a *commuter highway vehicle* and it must involve transportation between the employee's residence and the place of employment only.

WHAT IS A COMMUTER HIGHWAY VEHICLE?

A *commuter highway vehicle* is any highway vehicle that has the following characteristics:

♦ A seating capacity of at least six adults, not including the driver;

♦ The vehicle will incur 80% of its mileage in transporting employees between their residences and the place of employment; and

♦ Eighty percent of the mileage on the *commuter highway vehicle* can reasonably be expected to be on commuting trips in which the vehicle is filled to at least one-half capacity.

For example, if your company uses a highway vehicle with a seating capacity of eight, not including the driver, it must be reasonably expected that 80% of the total mileage of the vehicle, for a particular period, will be devoted to transporting at least four employees between their residences and the place of employment.

EMPLOYER-PROVIDED TRANSIT PASSES

Still another way to provide an employee with a fringe benefit for transportation to and from work is to provide a *transit pass*. Up to certain limits, these fringes are excludable from income by the employee. A transit pass is any of the following:

♦ A pass;

♦ A token or fare card; or

♦ A voucher, or any other item that is used for transportation or for a reduced transportation rate.

Further, the transportation must be on mass transit facilities such as by rail, bus, or ferry.

☛ KEY OBSERVATION

Cash reimbursements to employees for transit passes do not generally qualify for the same tax-free treatment, unless it can be shown that such passes were not readily available for distribution by the employer.

THE DOLLAR LIMITATION OF TRANSPORTATION FRINGE BENEFITS

There is a dollar limitation on the amount of qualified transportation fringe benefits that can be considered tax free. The amount of qualified fringe benefits that an employee can exclude from income is based on the type of benefits provided.

- For qualified parking the maximum tax-free amount is limited to $170 per month.

- The tax-free amount for employer-provided transit passes and commuter transportation in commuter highway vehicles (combined) is $65 per month.

- The dollar amounts of these limitations are to be increased each and every year based on a prescribed index reflecting cost of living adjustments.

◻ *Special Note: An employer can elect to pay for and deduct transportation fringes in excess of these limitations, even though the tax-free portion to the employee is limited to these amounts.*

THE *DE MINIMIS* FRINGE BENEFIT

Just like it sounds, a *De Minimis* fringe is an insignificantly small benefit made available to an employee. In fact, it is small enough in dollar value that the IRS will not bother to require the employee to report it. After considering the frequency with which these benefits are made available, the *De Minimis* rule suggests that it wouldn't be worth the effort for IRS to try and account for them.

Special tax-free treatment can apply to *any* property item or service that an employer might make available to employees during their course of employment. The following are some common examples of tax-free *De Minimis* fringes as spelled out in the tax regulations:

♦ Occasional typing of personal letters by a company secretary;

♦ Occasional personal use of an employer's copying machine. (The regulations for copy machines specifically require the employer to maintain sufficient restrictions and don't allow more than 15% personal use by employees.);

♦ Occasional cocktail parties or theater or sporting event tickets;

♦ Group meals or picnics for employees and their guests;

♦ Traditional birthday or holiday gifts with a low fair market value, not including cash;

♦ Coffee, doughnuts, and soft drinks;

♦ Local telephone calls; and

♦ Flowers, fruit, books, or similar property provided to employees under special circumstances. (For example, this may be on account of illness, outstanding performance, or family crisis.)

The tax law spells out certain specific benefits that **do not** meet the definition of *De Minimis* fringes and thus, are fully taxable. These are:

♦ Season tickets to sporting or theatrical events;

♦ Commuter usage of an employer-provided automobile more than one day a month;

♦ Membership in a private country club or athletic facility, regardless of the frequency with which the employee uses the facility;

♦ Employer-provided group term life insurance on the life of the spouse or child of an employee; and

♦ Use of an employer-owned or leased facility for a weekend.

☛ KEY OBSERVATION

Although the above items are normally taxable, some may enjoy tax-free exclusion as a fringe benefit under some other provision of the law, such as a *working condition* fringe.

You must evaluate the frequency with which fringe benefits are made so that you can determine if the benefits are truly *De Minimis* in amount. You need to look at the frequency that you, as the employer, provide the fringe benefit to each of your employees. Accordingly, the rule states that if an employer provides a free meal every day to one particular employee only, the value of those meals is not *De Minimis* with respect to that employee — even if the meals are provided infrequently or occasionally to the entire workforce.

Q. Do cash payments and cash payment equivalents qualify for tax-free treatment under *De Minimis* fringe benefit rules?

A. Generally, neither cash payments nor gift certificates qualify as *De Minimis* fringes. For example, if you provide one of your employees a single ticket to a popular new theater event, the employee can exclude the ticket as a *De Minimis* fringe. If you give the employee cash to purchase the ticket, it is **not** tax free.

There are essentially **two** exceptions in which an employee can receive a cash payment or allowance and have it treated as a *De Minimis* tax-free benefit, which include:

♦ Meal money, and

♦ Local transportation fare.

For meal money or local transportation fare to be excludable as *De Minimis* fringe, they must not only be reasonable, but they must meet the following conditions:

♦ They are provided on an occasional basis, not regularly or routinely;

♦ They are due to overtime work; and

♦ They are for meals and meal money that enable the employee to work overtime.

HOW TO QUALIFY PAYMENTS FOR LOCAL TRANSPORTATION AS A *DE MINIMIS* FRINGE

The tax-free benefit for local transportation is only available when the transportation is provided because of *unusual* or *unsafe* conditions for the employee.

Unusual circumstances are determined on a case by case basis to determine if the employee is entitled to exclude the benefit from income. Some examples that qualify are:

♦ A normally nine-to-five employee is called in for a special project at 8:00 P.M.; or

♦ An employee is asked to temporarily change a day shift routine to a night shift for a one-week period.

The amount of paid transportation that is excluded from income is the excess of the value of a one-way trip over $1.50.

LOBBYING EXPENSE DEDUCTION MAY PROMPT LOBBYING EFFORTS FOR SMALLER PARTICIPANTS

Under old law, a taxpayer was entitled to deduct lobbying expenses when it involved attempts to influence legislation concerning the taxpayer's trade or business, provided that it qualified as an *ordinary and necessary* expense of doing business. The old rules did not permit a deduction when the expense was related to participation in political campaigns or in attempts to influence voters or the general public.

A special *de minimis* rule exempts in-house lobbying efforts from the general rule. If the lobbying expenses incurred on your own do not exceed $2,000, they still may be deducted. Incidentally, this special benefit will not apply if the payments are made to professional lobbyists and trade associations.

The new law still denies deductions for campaign expenses and grass roots lobbying. Specifically, it now disallows deductions for costs of efforts to influence certain covered executive branch officials; that is, when those efforts are directed at influencing official actions or positions of that official.

A CAFETERIA PLAN

A cafeteria plan is the one employer sponsored plan in which the employee is actually given a choice between taking cash or certain specific tax-free fringe benefits. Under ordinary circumstances, whenever an employee has a right to choose between nontaxable and taxable benefits, like cash, that right causes a taxable event regardless of the decision.

However, under a cafeteria plan, no amount will be taxable to the employee who chooses among the fringe benefits in the plan. There will only be taxable income if the employee happens to choose the cash as payment.

With a little bit of planning, the employees can lower their taxable income while tax deductible contributions continue to be made by the employer.

Illustration 6.10

- ◆ BB Corporation pays Lois, an employee, $40,000 annually, plus $6,000 which she is free to take in cash or in qualified benefits.

- ◆ If Lois takes the cash, the full $46,000 will be taxed to her as salary.

- ◆ If the $6,000 was offered as a choice between cash and benefits under a cafeteria plan, Lois could elect to take the fringe benefits tax free.

- ◆ For example, Lois might elect to take medical insurance coverage.

- ◆ The portion of Lois' salary that is applied toward the medical insurance premiums is excluded from her income. If an employee, like Lois, later receives insurance reimbursements under the policy, those reimbursements are also tax free.

To qualify as a cafeteria plan, follow these criteria.

- ◆ All participants must be regular employees. If only one participant is a nonemployee, then the entire plan would be disqualified and all benefits would be fully taxable to everyone.

- ◆ The participants can choose between two or more benefits consisting of cash and qualified fringe benefits.

- ◆ Participants must first make an election among the benefits offered under the plan.

- ◆ A cafeteria plan must be in writing and contain certain minimum information.

- ◆ A cafeteria plan may not provide for deferred compensation arrangements for the participants, except for certain 401(k) plans.

☞ KEY OBSERVATION

The purpose of requiring the plan to be in writing is to formalize the plan and eliminate any questions as to its scope and qualifications as a cafeteria plan. The written document must contain data such as 1) a specific description of each of the benefits available; 2) eligibility rules for participation; 3) procedures governing the elections of the employees; and 4) other data on how employees can make contributions under the plan.

Qualified benefits that may be offered to employees under a cafeteria plan include:

♦ Coverage under a health and accident plan, including long-term disability and accidental death and dismemberment;

♦ Group term life insurance;

♦ Dependent care assistance programs; and

♦ Certain vacation plan allowances.

Caution! Benefits are also subject to discrimination testing.

CHAPTER SUMMARY

There are numerous tax-free benefits to expenses you incur as the employer. As long as you follow the IRS rules, a definite tax advantage could emanate from employer-provided:

♦ Meals and lodging;

♦ Dependent care assistance;

♦ Services that would be no additional cost to either party;

♦ Transportation;

♦ Trips;

♦ Parking; and

♦ Commuting expenses.

In addition, today's small business owner-employers can use the De Minimis fringe and cafeteria plan to benefit themselves and their employees while at the same time providing a nice tax shelter for their business expenses.

As with any other business deduction, the IRS will hold you accountable for proper documentation. And, unless you follow these rules, the IRS will place a stringent limitation on these deductions based on a percentage of their adjusted gross incomes.

The key, then, is to set in motion tax-saving strategies that will provide a tax benefit for both you and your employees. The next chapter will provide the techniques for making your employees' business expenses deductible.

Chapter 7

STEPS TO ENSURE EMPLOYEE BUSINESS EXPENSE DEDUCTIBILITY

Since 1986, Congress' quest to take away employees' rights to claim tax deductions for business expenses has been relentless. It began with a technique called the *2% floor,* **originally** introduced to the *1040 Tax Return* preparer. The average taxpayer discovered the sudden disappearance of the familiar *miscellaneous deductions* category. *Miscellaneous deductions* is the general category used when writing off employee business expenses. Illustration 7.1 demonstrates the financial limitations imposed on the business professional.

Illustration 7.1

♦ Reedy, an executive with Family Business Corporation is paid $80,000 annually — his adjusted gross income (AGI). Reedy incurs business travel expenses totaling $1,500, which he pays out of his own pocket.

♦ By applying the 2% limitation rule, the first $1,600 of business expense is not deductible.

♦ Although only $100 short of the minimum requirement, Reedy is allowed no business deduction. All of his out-of-pocket costs are wasted for tax purposes.

Now, as business professionals advance to higher income levels, **another** limitation has been imposed on employee deductions. This limitation places a *3% floor* on *all* of the itemized deductions that can be claimed on a tax return.

◻ *Special Note: Under current law, any taxpayer whose 1997 adjusted gross income reaches $121,200, or $60,600 if married but filing separately will lose an additional 3% of his or her deductions. These threshold amounts, however, are to be adjusted for inflation.*

To understand the importance of getting around the limitations, the employer and the employee both need to reflect on the breadth and variety of the business deductions that are lost when they are paid out of the employee's pocket.

Some examples of employees' business deductions that generally are wasted as tax write-offs because of the limitations on miscellaneous deductions are:

♦ Business transportation costs;

♦ Commercial travel;

♦ Lodging while away from home;

♦ Business meals and entertainment;

♦ Continuing education courses;

♦ Subscriptions to professional journals;

♦ Union or professional dues;

♦ Professional uniforms;

♦ Job hunting expenses; and

♦ Investment expenses.

You can take steps to keep these valuable business expenses.

THE FIRST STEP: SET UP A REIMBURSEMENT PLAN

Q. What can be done to remove these tough limitations on legitimate business expenses?

A. To remove these tough limitations on legitimate business expenses, consider setting up a reimbursement plan. If you pay business expenses out of your pocket from time to time, and the company cannot afford to reimburse those extra costs, consider reducing your salary. The result could be a 100% tax deduction for expenses that would otherwise be **lost**.

Accordingly, if the appropriate procedures are followed, the otherwise wasted business expenses paid for out of the employee's pocket may become fully deductible.

Illustration 7.2

♦ Mark has an adjusted gross income of $100,000. He spends $600 for professional books and supplies and $1,200 for business entertainment.

♦ Mark will get no deduction, because his business expenses do not exceed the 2% limitation of $2,000, or $100,000 multiplied by 2%.

♦ However, suppose Mark arranges for the *company* to reimburse him for the business expenses of $1,800, while reducing his salary for the same amount.

♦ The expense, thus, is passed off to the company and Mark will succeed in gaining a 100% tax deduction.

There are a few rules that have to be followed to get the tax advantage. Specifically, the company needs to follow the requirements of a qualified reimbursement arrangement. If this is done, any reimbursements or expense account allowances received by Mark need not be reported on his tax return.

The idea is that, with qualified reimbursement arrangements, any reimbursements or expense allowances simply do not have to be included in the employee's income. When this occurs, there is no concern about deductions or limitations because the employee doesn't report any income in the first place.

☞ KEY OBSERVATION

In the event that the employer erroneously includes the nonreportable expense reimbursement on an employee's *Form W-2*, then the employee is permitted to take a special step to remedy the problem. In this case, the deduction can be taken directly off the top, rather than as an itemized deduction on his tax return.

In the next section, examine another, more subtle benefit for using a reimbursement arrangement with your employer.

THE SECOND STEP: MINIMIZE IRS SCRUTINY

In setting up a reimbursement arrangement, the function of taking tax deductions is shifted from the employee to the employer. Many see this as a clear advantage for the business professional because there will probably be less scrutiny under IRS enforcement policy.

Every time you decide to write off your out-of-pocket business expenses on your own personal return, you are making a tactical decision that might trigger something more than a reduction in your tax bill. You were made aware in Chapter 5 that if you include any special deductions on your **personal** *1040 Tax Return*, you may be raising your DIF scores. When those deductions are high enough so that you get a worthwhile tax savings, your chances of being called in for an audit are raised measurably.

It is a well-accepted fact that an IRS audit will create an additional cost to you as a taxpayer. You may be the most honest taxpayer around, as well as the best record keeper, but if you are called in for an audit it will invariably cost:

♦ Time to organize your records for the auditor; and

♦ Money to secure professional representation.

When the function of taking legitimate tax deductions for everyday business expenses is the employer's responsibility, there is little reason for the IRS to take issue. On the other hand, if the deductions for the various out-of-pocket business expenses would show up on the **individual** tax return, chances are that the red flags will be raised.

Illustration 7.3

- Tess was paid a salary of $60,000 from Tessco, a company that she manages and partly owns.

- She paid, out of her own pocket, $1,500 for auto expense and $500 for continuing education.

- Tess lost $1,200 of her business deductions when she filed her tax return because of the 2% limitation, or $60,000 multiplied by 2%. Tess also lost some sleep because she feared possible IRS scrutiny. It happened that she had some trouble locating all of her backup records for the expenses claimed and, with her raised DIF scores, she thought a tax audit would be highly likely. If an audit *did* occur, she was fearful that there might be questions about certain personal "gifts" that she received from outside parties. Although her accountant had convinced her that the gifts were totally tax free, she was convinced that an audit could only lead to embarrassment and a no-win situation.

- Her chances of an audit would be greatly reduced if she had participated in a reimbursement plan.

- Tessco, for instance, could reimburse Tess for her out-of-pocket expenses.

- Tessco would proceed to write off the auto and education expense along with the rest of its ordinary business expenses.

In Tess' situation, there are no raised DIF scores, and no returns filed in an unusual manner; thus, very little chance exists of Tess' return being pulled for an audit. Additionally, the $2,000 in business expenses is fully deductible.

THE THIRD STEP: CHOOSE BETWEEN AN ACCOUNTABLE PLAN OR A NONACCOUNTABLE PLAN

As noted earlier, a reimbursement arrangement needs to meet certain criteria before you can be assured that the payments that you receive as an employee are tax free. You have probably guessed by now, the **primary** criteria for a reimbursement arrangement must involve some kind of requirement of accountability.

☐ **Special Note:** *The key to getting approval of your employee expenses arrangement from the IRS is to show that you have an accountable plan with your employer.*

In an *accountable plan*, the tax benefits are automatic. However, with a *nonaccountable plan*, the employee will:

♦ Be required to report any reimbursements as income;

♦ Have to deduct the expenses on personal returns which will be subject to closer IRS scrutiny; and

♦ Be subject to the tough *floor limitations.*

☞ KEY OBSERVATION

With nonaccountable plans, reimbursement payments must be reported as wages on the *Form W-2* and be subject to withholding.

There are no particular formalities for setting up a proper accountable plan and making it work. However, many employers have hastened to draft official policy statements and employment agreements so as to show good faith that the following three specific requirements have been met. The three requirements to qualify an expense reimbursement plan as *accountable:*

♦ There must be a **business connection** for the expenses.

♦ The employee must adequately **substantiate** those expenses to the employer.

♦ The employee must **return to the employer**, within a reasonable time, any amount paid under the arrangement that exceeds the expenses substantiated.

THE FIRST CONDITION OF ACCOUNTABILITY: THE BUSINESS CONNECTION

The first condition of accountability is an easy one to satisfy when trying to render the reimbursement plan as accountable. Illustration 7.4 shows that the expenses have been incurred in connection with the performance of services as an employee.

Illustration 7.4

♦ Richard is a sales agent for Company Z and he incurs expenses for business lunches with prospective customers.

♦ Since business promotion is expected in his position as a sales representative, Richard is performing a specific business function, which is directly connected, with his business position.

♦ Thus, the first condition of being *the business connection* is easily satisfied and Richard should qualify for the deduction.

⬭ **Special Note:** *If advance payments are made to the employee, they need to be made within a **reasonable time** of the date on which it is expected that the expense will occur. Otherwise that advance will not be treated as meeting the business connection requirement.*

THE SECOND CONDITION OF ACCOUNTABILITY: SUBSTANTIATION

Whether you plan to have an expense reimbursement arrangement with your employees or not, be aware of the substantiation rules.

☛ KEY OBSERVATION

If a current expense *reimbursement arrangement* exists, an agent will look again to your business records. An IRS auditor will require substantiating evidence that the employee provided you, the employer, with the backup data.

An accountable plan is when the employee accounts to the employer for business expenses. In an *accountable plan*, when an employee incurs a business expense and seeks a tax-free reimbursement from the employer, sufficient information is needed.

♦ First, the employer must be able to identify the specific nature of the expense item.

♦ Second, it must be shown that the expense is attributable to the employer's activities.

There is a slightly different twist for applying the substantiation rules when an employee expense reimbursement plan is in effect. With such a plan, the employee deals directly with the employer. The plan provides the employer with the prescribed documentation in support of the business expenses incurred.

Working on the "honor system," both parties make a record of the documentation without IRS involvement. The unique twist is that the employer unwittingly takes over the task of tracking the authenticity of the business expenses paid by staff employees directly, and alleviates much of the IRS's work.

Like it or not, the employer now has the responsibility of verifying that the substantiation rules have been properly followed before a tax-free reimbursement is made.

The positive side is that once the employer is satisfied with the substantiation, the employee could walk away with the reimbursement with absolutely no hassles from the IRS.

Remember, each element of expense must be individually substantiated. It is unacceptable for an employee to combine a batch of expenses in general categories like "miscellaneous expense" or "entertainment." Individual details must be directly spelled out by the employee just as if dealing with the IRS directly. Individual substantiation is seen in Illustration 7.5.

Illustration 7.5

♦ Faye pays out of her own pocket a printing fee for a company newsletter.

♦ Faye provides her employer with a paid invoice, a written voucher describing the specific business purpose of the newsletter, and a memo showing that the expense was attributable to Faye's employment activities.

♦ Faye has properly substantiated the expense, and thus, the reimbursement is properly excluded from her income and her *W-2* reporting.

☞ KEY OBSERVATION

There are special substantiation rules when the reimbursement is for travel, entertainment, gifts, or use of an auto or other listed property.

If the plan reimburses the employee for *travel, entertainment, gifts, auto expenses or listed property items,* there must be **extra** proof provided to pass the substantiation requirements. It is important for the small business owner to be familiar with these special substantiation rules for two reasons:

♦ First, employers will need this more detailed backup data whether they are reimbursing an employee or simply incurring the expenses on their own.

♦ Second, this special category of business write-offs is always subject to special scrutiny by IRS examiners because of the frequent abuse with these specific deductions.

☐ *Special Note: Because of the IRS's major interest in these special expense areas, the substantiation rules are outlined separately in Chapter 8.*

THE THIRD CONDITION OF ACCOUNTABILITY: RETURN EXCESS REIMBURSEMENTS TO THE EMPLOYER

When the IRS set up this final condition for an accountable plan, it wanted to make certain that excess reimbursements were promptly returned to the employer. For example, if the employee receives a reimbursement in excess of the amount that was substantiated, it must be paid back within a reasonable period. If not, that excess amount will be treated as paid under a nonaccountable plan.

Remember, with a nonaccountable plan, any such reimbursement would be fully taxable to the employee, unless the employee could beat the tough floor limitations, he or she could lose the entire tax deduction.

Q. What is the reasonable period of time that the employee has to return the excess amount of reimbursement or provide the substantiation?

A. The prescribed reasonable period of time depends on the method of payment of the expense reimbursement. Generally, the time period runs from 30 to 120 days.

Illustration 7.6

♦ On June 1, Roy paid out-of-pocket expenses totaling $1,900 for professional tools in connection with his job with Fry Corporation.

♦ On the same day Fry reimbursed $1,900 to Roy.

♦ Roy had lost part of his records — receipts and paid invoices — and was unable to substantiate $700 of the $1,900 in expenses.

♦ By December 1, Roy did not repay the excess payment, nor did he come up with the lost records.

♦ The $700 excess payment is deemed to be a reimbursement in connection with a *nonaccountable* plan.

♦ Roy is required to report the $700 payment as income for the year. He would be entitled to take a corresponding personal deduction for the expense only if he found the missing records and was able to exceed the floor limitations.

CHAPTER SUMMARY

In summary, there are two distinct advantages for setting up an employee expense arrangement.

♦ First, valuable tax deductions that would otherwise have been lost due to tough limitations on the individual's tax return are saved.

♦ Second, attention is shifted away from the individual taxpayer to the employer — the business entity. Thus, there is less likelihood for a confrontation with the IRS.

Since this book is directed to small business owners, many are probably wondering if there are any special risks when the employee and the employer are one and the same. It seems illogical, for example, that the IRS would be disinterested in an arrangement whereby small business owners are themselves accountable for all of their own travel and entertainment expenses.

There is a special provision in the law that deals with employees who happen to have an interest in the business. The employee may still be accountable for personally incurred business expenses when the employee owns more than 10% of the business. What this means is that the owner-employee needs to be prepared to produce the backup records for the IRS in an audit situation.

As a practical matter, however, this requirement should create no significant additional burden for you. As with **any** employee who renders an accounting to the employer, it is commonly expected that the employee would keep a photocopy of the substantiation records turned over to the employer. After all, if an IRS agent started investigating the employer's books, and found a poorly kept recordkeeping system, the employee would be held accountable for the expenses anyway.

☞ KEY OBSERVATION

Since the new *reimbursement* rules, the IRS has rarely challenged their tax-saving benefits. As long as the reimbursement amounts are reasonable in amount, examining agents will usually not quarrel with a company for taking business deductions for expense reimbursements to any employee. The added advantage is that the employee's personal tax return is left alone, when a reimbursement plan is in proper working order.

Chapter 8

LEARN HOW TO BEAT THE RECORDKEEPING GAME

In the previous chapter you learned that, since 1986, the playing field has been changed for individual employees who incur business or professional expenses of any kind. Nowadays, if employees incur costs for such expenses, the tough new floor limitations will eliminate most of the tax benefits.

Through a special plan known as a *reimbursement arrangement*, employee business expenses become the employer's responsibility; this permits the employee to secure the full value of the tax deductions. By properly accounting to the employer for an expense, the reimbursement doesn't have to appear on the employee's *W-2* or tax return.

The warning, however, is the procedure doesn't let you off the hook for keeping records of the expenses. The only difference is that the records are usually presented only to the employer rather than to the IRS — a more palatable requirement indeed.

In this chapter, you will learn the rules of the recordkeeping game, also known as substantiation rules.

THE BURDEN OF PROOF COULD VERY WELL BE ON YOU

At one time or another, business owners can expect that they will be challenged by the IRS about their deductions. If you have your business deductions challenged, you should be prepared to show that:

♦ You are the one entitled to take the deduction in question;

♦ The year for which the deduction is claimed is the correct year; and

♦ The amount claimed is deductible under the new law.

Unless you take certain specific steps (identified in Chapter 1) you'll find that the burden of proof is on you for proving your deductions. **Don't take business deductions for granted.** The arguments "everybody is doing it" or "it's commonplace for a certain expense to be claimed" are not sufficient. Business deductions are a matter of ·legislative grace; therefore, as a business owner you must establish your right to claim them. If your day of reckoning comes, be prepared to prove that you are entitled to the write-off.

On the other hand, the IRS examiners and the courts have been known to allow some leeway for deductions even when the taxpayer has not maintained a sophisticated recordkeeping system. As a business owner, you are given the opportunity to provide corroborating evidence or testimony to support the burden of proving that the expense was in fact a true business expense.

Remember, when no reliable testimony or evidence is presented by taxpayers, the IRS has consistently denied the authenticity of the business expense claimed.

Illustration 8.1

♦ Ned owns a small design company, Nedco. Last year he failed to keep records for the cost of its materials and tools.

♦ Upon IRS audit, Ned managed to produce a detailed schedule for many of the materials and tools by using trade catalogs as guides for description and pricing.

♦ The catalogs, however, were not identified or brought into evidence. He did not present data about the alleged suppliers or other outside testimony either.

♦ Nedco was prohibited by the IRS from deducting the cost of the materials and tools. If outside testimony or objective evidence had been provided, the deduction would have been allowed.

🗂 *Special Note: It is up to you, the taxpayer, to take the initiative and provide **all necessary documentation to support a claim**. Contemporaneously written notations, statements from witnesses, and any reliable reference material all have major relevance when taken as a whole.*

✎ PLANNING TIP

If you incur occasional out-of-pocket cash expenses in your business, keep a detailed daily log. Even if the expenses are for minor items like telephone calls, tips, or tolls. Keep a written record detailing the amount, date, and purpose.

CLAIM YOUR DEDUCTIONS IN THE RIGHT YEAR

One common problem that faces taxpayers results from the failure to claim business deductions in the proper year. Each tax year is handled separate and apart from other years. The IRS is very scientific in ensuring that no income or expenses are pushed in a year that they were not incurred.

Illustration 8.2

♦ Joann, a management consultant, paid for the lease of computer equipment during her first year of business.

♦ Since her income was negligible that year, she didn't claim the rental expense.

♦ She did, however, take the deduction in the following year when her tax bracket was much higher.

♦ Joann is not entitled to the deduction in the second year. In the event of an IRS audit she could be subject to a tax assessment including interest and penalties.

✎ PLANNING TIP

If you have a business deduction and it is uncertain as to which of the two consecutive years that it belongs, choose the earlier year. If the IRS takes issue, you can move the deduction to the following year. If you start by taking it in the following year, and it is not approved, then you may be prohibited by the statute of limitations from claiming it in the earlier year.

PAY BY CHECK

Oftentimes small business owner-operators are unable to produce canceled checks in support of the expenses claimed in their business operations. The best way to prove the existence of a business expense is to *pay by check.*

There are many excuses why check writing is not always practical. You might reason that the $5 purchase of some cleaning materials, or the occasional $2 parking meter fee is easier to pay by cash. Truly, not everything can be paid directly by check in business.

The solution is to use your checkbook as an ultimate backup weapon anyway. When you have occasional out-of-pocket cash expenditures, jot down the details on a petty cash voucher. At least once a month, write a business check to reimburse yourself for those monthly cash expenditures. This provides a formal basis for the simple entries that you enter on your books. This procedure provides timely corroboration and evidence for the expenses, and gives a more business-like appearance for the management of your overall accounting records. (Refer to Chapter 7 for the rules on expense reimbursement arrangements.)

As expected, IRS agents become particularly inquisitive when observing that there are significant cash transactions in a business enterprise. Whenever they find owner-operators not making their business expenditures in the normal check writing fashion, they always begin to broaden their investigation and ask more questions.

✎ PLANNING TIP

On the other hand, there is no law that states you can't pay your bills in cash. If you must pay a bill with cash, be prepared to take a few extra steps to prove the existence of the business expenditure.

PROVE THE LEGITIMACY OF CASH EXPENDITURES

It is quite common for an IRS examining officer to blatantly disallow certain business deductions, because the taxpayer did not have a typical accounting system. It is even more common to challenge deductions when expenditures are not supported by the usual canceled checks. In the appeals process, there are numerous cases where IRS findings have been overturned and the record set straight for the taxpayer. This means the IRS cannot dictate that the canceled check is the only documentation available to prove the authenticity of a business expenditure.

Q. What are some typical problems for a taxpayer who is trying to prove that certain business expenditures have, in fact, been made?

A. This is best explained in the following illustrations.

Illustration 8.3

♦ Rick is a business owner who made cash purchases of inventory. Rick produced detailed invoices signed by the sellers.

♦ The IRS auditor disallowed *all* the purchase deductions, because he was unable to locate any of the sellers.

♦ The court, however, overturned the IRS's insinuation that Rick had fabricated the cash purchases. As a credible witness, the company bookkeeper supported the reliability of the expense claim. Also, the books and records were clear, complete, and kept in a business-like manner.

Illustration 8.4

♦ Rick's brother, Tony is a business consultant. When the IRS asked for proof that he made the payments for office rental claimed on his return, he could not produce canceled checks. Tony did produce some receipts for the payments, which were signed by the building manager.

♦ Tony was criticized by the court, which was concerned that a professional business consultant would fail to keep canceled checks.

♦ Fortunately for Tony, the signed receipts were deemed to be adequate by the IRS. Tony was ultimately allowed the claim for the rental deductions.

Each case is based on its own merit. When checks are not available, no specific guidelines exist as to what the IRS or the courts will accept as adequate corroborating evidence.

TRACK ALL BUSINESS MILEAGE AND TELEPHONE USAGE

Probably one of the most common recordkeeping problems of business taxpayers is substantiation of *business mileage.*

In one well-publicized case, an Amway® distributor's mileage record could not be tied to the daily business calendar and other activity records. Further, the taxpayer could not even identify the non-deductible commuting mileage from his residence to the place of employment. **No substantiation, no deduction** was the final message to the frustrated taxpayer.

Remember, travel and transportation are among a special category of business expenses that require a prescribed format of recordkeeping procedures spelled out in the tax law.

Another common problem area involves the business use of your telephone. In another high profile case, a sales representative failed to meet certain common sense rules of substantiation. As others have tried, this taxpayer came up with a round estimate of the business usage on his home phone. With a probably conservative, good faith estimate, his tax return showed 80% of phone calls were exclusively for business activity.

The IRS disagreed. The taxpayer had done nothing to adequately identify on his telephone records the specific nature of **any** of the individual business calls, and thus, no deduction was allowed.

Remember, a contemporaneous record detailing the purpose of the telephone calls would have salvaged the deduction.

🗋 *Special Note: A recent tax law revision stipulates that if you have a single phone line in your home, then the presumption is that all local calls are personal in nature and not deductible.*

PAY CLOSE ATTENTION TO DETAIL

As most professional tax advisers will attest, poor recordkeeping is one of the biggest roadblocks in the way of successfully representing a client before the IRS. Even if you have canceled checks and have a normal bookkeeping system, extra backup data may sometimes be required to ensure your business deduction.

☞ KEY OBSERVATION

Oftentimes, an expense is contested by an examining agent because the taxpayer didn't take a moment to make a brief notation at the time the expense was incurred. IRS auditors are trained to look well beyond formal journal entries and the standard accounting books for supporting evidence. The following illustration provides a typical example.

Illustration 8.5

♦ Valerie is a property manager who purchased large quantities of business materials. As a responsible business owner, she seemed to do everything in line with correct general bookkeeping procedures.

♦ When Valerie makes a payment it is reflected on credit card statements, canceled checks, or both.

♦ The payments are neatly organized in a cash disbursements journal.

♦ A formal general ledger exists giving a concise summary of all operation expenses.

♦ Thus, Valerie's business materials appear to be readily identifiable to the IRS.

If Valerie were pulled for an audit by the IRS, at first she would be looked at favorably, in terms of general credibility and accuracy, by the examining officer. The examining agent, however, might ask to see some additional backup data for the unusually large quantities of business supplies.

Without additional explanatory data, how is the agent supposed to know, for example, that some of the plumbing or electrical supplies weren't actually used in Valerie's own kitchen? How would the agent know if some of those check payments to the hardware store were nothing more than the purchase of Christmas presents? If a reference file were readily available to provide written details for each expense item, the examining officer would be able to make a positive acknowledgment and be able to close the case without raising costly challenges about the tax deduction.

Illustration 8.6

♦ Henry, an actor, deducted so-called business supplies on his tax return. He kept a logbook to note that the supplies were for skin care, hair care, and makeup.

♦ He did not, however, provide any details as evidence to prove the supplies were for business rather than personal use.

♦ The tax court did not want to be in the position of making the choice, and thus, the deduction was denied.

Illustration 8.7

♦ Julia owned numerous rental properties.

♦ Under audit, she claimed that her personal gardener also took care of her rental units and that a portion of his cost should be deductible.

♦ The IRS disagreed. There was no evidence to support the actual time spent by the gardener on each project.

Once again, the absence of supportive written detail cost a taxpayer the right to make what appears to have been a legitimate claim.

WHEN ALL ELSE FAILS, GET OUTSIDE TESTIMONY

Obviously, a businessperson who has complete books and records, and additional backup will have little difficulty in proving the deductibility of business expenses. Unfortunately, successful businesspeople can't spend **all** their time playing bookkeeper. There will be times when they don't have all written records, and they will need alternative ways to substantiate expenses for the IRS.

Q. How far can I go without standard accounting records and detailed memos?

A. The answer usually depends on the amount of evidence presented by your outside witnesses, their general credibility, and any contradictions in the given testimony. Illustration 8.8 demonstrates the importance of witness testimony.

Illustration 8.8

- ◆ Miles, a freelance movie producer, spent two years in Africa on an assignment.

- ◆ His responsibilities required him to hire a staff to perform a variety of duties, including photography, sound functions, cooking, and automobile driving.

- ◆ All Miles' books and records were destroyed by fire.

> ◆ After the credible testimony of his staff members, the tax court was satisfied that the deductions Miles claimed were valid. Even though the back-up records were not particularly sophisticated, the testimony proved that they did seem to tie into the books.

An Exception to the Rules: The Famous Cohan Case

Named for the famous entertainer, George M. Cohan, this case is often relied on by taxpayers who, for one reason or another simply cannot prove certain deductions claimed on their tax return. The principle is based upon the **court's authority** to make a deal with the taxpayer, when there is evidence to show that the IRS is probably wrong in denying a deduction.

Herein, a reasonable estimate is made of an expense based on the facts that are available. This subjective approximation is only made when:

◆ The IRS denies the **entire** business deduction; and

◆ The amount allowed by the IRS was arbitrarily **low**.

The Cohan method of estimating expenses will only be used when it can be shown that:

◆ A business expense must have existed in view of the income that was reported by the business; and

◆ It can be demonstrated that the taxpayer is entitled to the deduction and is able to come up with a plausible basis for making the estimate.

Remember, taxpayers should be aware of the many risks with this approach when trying to secure tax deductions, as explained in Illustration 8.9.

Illustration 8.9

♦ Candice owns a janitorial business. Her accountant lost all of her business records.

♦ Without any documentation, the IRS denied the entire deduction for cleaning supplies she had requested.

♦ The court overturned the decision and allowed Candice her deduction. It stated that the IRS acted arbitrarily in view of the reported income of the business.

In other words, it was pointed out that the taxpayer:

♦ Could not have earned the amount of income that she did without incurring some expenses for cleaning supplies; and

♦ Was able to help put together a reasonable estimate based on the facts of the case.

Special Note: There is a common situation, however, in which the courts will readily refuse to give the taxpayer a break by granting any estimated deduction for business expenses. This occurs when the taxpayer was able to obtain duplicate records or other evidence, but did not.

Small business operators are expected to provide the IRS with whatever books and records were maintained. If the records could be introduced as evidence at a trial, but they are not, every single operating expense of the business could be denied.

Finally, there is a special group of business expenses for which the Cohan rule will not apply under any circumstances. For this particular group of expenses, estimates are simply not permitted and the taxpayer must come up with specific proof as detailed in the law.

Without this specific proof, no deduction is allowed. The expenses that require special substantiation procedures are:

♦ Travel expenses;

♦ Entertainment;

♦ Business gifts; and

♦ A special class of deductions referred to as listed property items.

Specific guidelines for deducting this special class of business expenses are outlined in Chapter 9.

CHAPTER SUMMARY

Shortcuts in recordkeeping never pay off for the small business owner. Although recent concessions have made it easier to deduct legitimate business expenses, it is a significant advantage to make a record of as much detail as possible.

Chapter 9

DIFFERENT RULES FOR A SPECIAL CLASS OF DEDUCTIONS

Everyone in business today, in one way or another, incurs costs that involve travel, entertainment, business gifts, or some form of a listed property deduction, like computers and automobiles. These particular write-offs can generate enormous tax savings for a wide variety of small business owners.

On the other hand, many small business owners fear taking full advantage of these deductions since the IRS closely scrutinizes them. It is easily understood why some owners could be intimidated by the recordkeeping requirements for this special class of expenses.

It is tough to survive in today's environment, under the juggernaut of rules, regulations, and bureaucratic policies. The last thing a small business owner has time for is more bookkeeping and administrative headaches.

What you can do is learn and adhere to the IRS's substantiation guidelines when you try to claim a deduction for the following special class of expenses:

♦ Travel;

♦ Entertainment and business gifts; and

♦ Listed property deductions — some elements of a special class of business property deductions such as, computers and automobiles.

This special grouping of expenses, as pointed out earlier, requires strict substantiation guidelines to validate a tax deduction. The Cohan Case in Chapter 8, and any other methods of estimating deductions, won't work when these particular expenses are involved. Keep in mind, if your small business has an expense *reimbursement arrangement*, there is a different twist on the substantiation rules.

As pointed out in the previous chapter, the *reimbursement arrangement* has shifted the substantiation requirements for business expenses from the employee to the employer. When there are strict substantiation guidelines, as with this special class of expenses, those guidelines must be met. Only this time, the employee accounts directly to the employer instead of to the IRS.

This chapter spells out the substantiation requirements in the simplest language possible. It will spell out how you could qualify your special class deductions with minimum effort. You will learn your rights in the event that you cannot keep up with the strict laws as they apply to this special class of deductions. Refer to Chapter 15 for the latest tax law on expensing.

KNOW THE SPECIAL CLASS OF DEDUCTIONS: THE ELEMENTS OF DEDUCTIBILITY

No deduction will be permitted for this special class of expenses unless the taxpayer verifies all of the following items for each expenditure:

1. The **amount** of the expense, or item;

2. The **time and place** of the expense, whether it be travel or entertainment;

3. The **date and description** of business gifts;

4. The **business purpose** of the expense or item; and

5. The **business relationship** to the taxpayer of each person entertained or receiving a gift.

For this special class of expenses, the IRS is looking for solid proof that the expenses were actually incurred. Accordingly, the five specific substantiation requirements must accompany each expense included in these categories. That means some special written memorandums are required.

If you don't have a system to make simple explanatory notations, then purchase an inexpensive notebook to make memorandums. Remember, to take advantage of this special class of business deductions, you simply need to create some records. Even if it is an informal method, show that you have taken steps to provide the five specific details as listed above. For instance, a brief journal entry noting the **amount, time, place, date, purpose, and business relationship** must be made at, or near the time the expense was actually incurred.

Illustration 9.1

♦ Barbara entertained a significant number of prospective clients in a real estate development business, but feared meeting the tough substantiation tests by the IRS.

♦ Taking the advice of her attorney, she created a detailed information trail by charging *all* entertainment expenses on a business credit card. Under audit, Barbara confidently presented the IRS officer with the credit card statements which efficiently recorded 1) the <u>amount</u> of the expense; and 2) the <u>date and place</u> of the entertainment.

♦ The IRS disallowed her a full deduction. Two important elements were missing: 1) the <u>business purpose</u> of each lunch and dinner; and 2) the <u>business relationship</u> of each person she entertained.

♦ Barbara should have made separate contemporaneous notations in a book, or on the credit card vouchers. An informal memo identifying the client and the real estate transaction would have sufficed.

As seen from Illustration 9.1, **substantiating the business purpose for travel, entertainment, and business gifts** is probably the toughest requirement in the prescribed format. Cases abound where the taxpayer's accounting records were deemed inadequate, because they did not contain a simple written statement about **why** a business luncheon or a special trip took place.

☐ *Special Note: Lately, the IRS and the courts have become more reasonable in accepting that the degree of substantiation will vary based on the facts and circumstances in each case. The rules are bent in the substantiation of business purpose in some cases, as evidenced in the following.*

♦ A written explanation about the discussion that took place was not necessarily required for every business meal paid for by a salesperson who calls on customers in an established sales route.

♦ An explanation was self-evident in a case where a certain title company tried to substantiate a number of out-of-state business trips that the title company had sponsored. The company had invited a number of real estate attorneys and various real estate professionals in the community. The taxpayer prevailed because the out-of-state meetings were backed up by minutes of board meetings, advance notices, technical reports, and numerous supporting documents and testimony.

WHEN YOU'LL NEED ADDITIONAL DOCUMENTARY EVIDENCE

Clearly the best way to get a deduction for the special class of expenses is to keep some kind of account book, diary, or log. In these records you have a complete record of the expenditure at or near the time that it was incurred. There are times, however, when even extensive written memos won't satisfy and additional documentary evidence will be required to substantiate the expense.

Q. What kind of expenses specifically require that additional documentary evidence, such as receipts and paid bills, be provided?

A. Generally, documentary evidence is required when the expense is for: 1) lodging while traveling away from home; and 2) **any** other separate expenditure of $75 or more.

Interestingly, the requirement to identify in detail nominal amounts has been around for decades. As one more anachronism in the tax code, this floor limitation prompts today's business owner to ask, "Just what business expense wouldn't cost more than $75 in today's economy?"

⎙ *Special Note: In spite of the sparse $75 rule, all small business owners should get additional documentary evidence to substantiate **all** business expenditures in the special class of expenses. You probably will find it advantageous to have a **signed receipt or a paid bill** for all travel, entertainment, business gifts, and listed property items.*

Q. What information should the documentary evidence show to substantiate the special class of expenses?

A. All receipts and paid bills must indicate the amount, date, place, and essential character of the expense.

Indeed, the requirement to produce paid invoices and receipts for virtually every expense related to travel, entertainment, business gifts and listed property deductions is a stringent one. Remember, **anything over $75** requires additional documentary evidence.

OBTAIN A COLLECTIVE VOICE – USE CORROBORATED STATEMENTS AS BACK-UP

As previously stated, the tax law emphatically states that any special class of business expenses **must** be substantiated by adequate records. In that same section of law, you can observe that the deduction could also be substantiated by the employee's own statement if supported by **corroborating evidence.**

Accordingly, you can take steps to protect your deductions for which there are no records by obtaining back-up statements from outside parties. There are two words of caution. First, statements by outside parties must be precise. Second, the corroborative evidence must be either written or verbal statements by individuals with prior knowledge of the element of the expense. When you are trying to prove business purpose or the business relationship of a transaction, the IRS will accept circumstantial evidence.

Where substantiation records are missing or unavailable, the courts will accept verbal testimony from outside parties about the content of the records, provided that the testimony is credible.

☐ *Special Note: Self-serving testimony by the taxpayer that is not backed by corroborating evidence is not enough to prove the deduction.*

Illustration 9.2

♦ Dr. Eddington is a physician whose practice requires him to travel in and around three counties.

♦ Because of his stressful circumstances, he was unable to keep the required log of his business and personal mileage for last year.

♦ Upon audit by the IRS, Dr. Eddington produced some convincing corroborative evidence, including statements from both his secretary who kept the office records, and an emergency room supervisor. He testified on behalf of himself as well.

- He also showed that he had documentary evidence as he presented the IRS with office records of house calls, auto service records and mileage summaries.

- Dr. Eddington had proved his case with both written and verbal documentary evidence, even though he did not keep a contemporaneous log.

Illustration 9.3

- Mary, a real estate agent, incurred expenses for automobile use, meals, and lodging.

- The IRS determined that Mary's canceled checks, receipts, and entries in her daybook were not sufficiently detailed to constitute adequate records.

- However, she offered sufficient corroborating evidence from outside parties to establish the amount, time, place, description, and business purpose.

- This evidence, along with her own testimony about the importance of incurring travel and entertainment in her business was sufficient to prove the deduction.

On the other hand, there are numerous cases that have ended with negative results for the taxpayer. Consider the example below.

Illustration 9.4

♦ Hal presented various kinds of documents to back up business travel and meals with his clients.

♦ He kept checks, restaurant receipts, ticket stubs, and credit card statements.

♦ He did not, however, bring forth evidence of the <u>business purpose</u> of each encounter or other verification to substantiate that business discussions actually occurred.

♦ None of Hal's deductions were accepted as substantiated business expenses.

✎ PLANNING TIP

All small business owners should be careful not to rely on the idea that there are easy alternative methods for substantiating the special class of business expenses. IRS agents are sensitive to the five specific requirements for proving every element of these expenses.

TRAVEL EXPENSE

Travel expense is an important item to the small business owner, since it generally involves a substantial tax write-off and occasionally allows some mixture of recreation with business. To qualify for the deduction you must show the cost was incurred while traveling **away from home** in the conduct of your trade or business.

The broad definition of deductible travel expense includes all costs of travel, including meals and lodging while away from home. These can include:

♦ All transportation involved in a project worked on away from home — this means transportation to and from the location and any transportation costs while you are at that location;

♦ Telephone, telegraph and fax service;

♦ Computer rental fees;

♦ Baggage service;

♦ Personal laundry, cleaning, and pressing;

♦ Private airplane operation costs; and

♦ Maintenance and operating costs of an automobile.

IRS examining officers are quick to raise questions about the **away from home** requirement, because there is misinterpretation as individuals make various kinds of business trips.

As a business traveler, ask yourself, "How far do I have to travel before my expenses are deductible because they were incurred away from home?"

Remember, there is no set number of miles that need to be traveled. Instead, you must show that your duties required you to be away from the general area of your tax home for a period substantially longer than an ordinary workday. Furthermore, during your time away, you will require sleep or rest to meet the demand of your work. Put another way, your absence from your tax home must be of such a duration that you could not reasonably leave and return to that business location before and after each day's work.

✎ PLANNING TIP

Travel expenses for conventions, seminars and business trips are carefully scrutinized by the IRS to determine if they are merely disguised vacations. If the business or professional activity is only a small fraction of the sojourn, the major part of the deduction, including the cost to get there, will be disallowed.

Illustration 9.5

♦ Dr. Palmer attends a dental surgeon seminar in Bermuda. The primary reason for the trip is strictly professional.

♦ While in Bermuda, he includes reasonable costs for hotel, meals, tips, laundry, and telephone service.

♦ During his stay, he spent some time sightseeing and touring the city, unrelated to his professional work.

♦ Dr. Palmer can deduct all his costs except for the local sightseeing and touring, which is considered personal enjoyment.

IRS ATTEMPTS TO DEFINE TEMPORARY WORK ASSIGNMENT

If you have ever traveled away from home on business, you are surely aware of the significant tax advantage of writing off the cost of your travel-related expenses. Transportation, meals, lodging, and even laundry expenses are among the wide assortment of deductions available that can provide tax savings to a business traveler. The problem, however, lies in ascertaining which of your travel assignments qualifies for the deduction.

In basic terms, to qualify for a deduction, you must demonstrate that the business travel assignment was strictly for a temporary period. Anything beyond temporary travel infers that the travel period was in fact indefinite. In other words, when you don't know how long you will be away from home, you simply aren't entitled to any deduction for your travel-related costs.

In the past, the rules for defining temporary work assignments have been rather complex. The rules were even more complicated when your travel stay extended as much as one to two years. The IRS has tried to clear the air by providing three easier-to-follow guidelines for defining temporary, thus deductible, travel.

If your employment away from home at a single location is realistically expected to last, and does, in fact, last for one year or less, the employment is considered temporary and, thus, is deductible — unless facts and circumstances indicate otherwise. If that period of employment away from home is realistically expected to last for more than one year, the employment is indefinite and, thus, not deductible. This guideline applies whether or not the employment period exceeds one year. If employment away from home at a single location initially is realistically expected to last for one year or less, but at some later date it is then expected that the time period will probably go beyond a year, then two situations may result. All that time that it was realistically expected that the job assignment would be one year or less will be treated as temporary — thus, deductible. At the point in time that it looks like the job will go beyond a year, you will be then in the **indefinite** zone, which means no more deductibility. Take a closer look at this guideline as described in the following illustration.

Illustration 9.6

♦ Simon took a job assignment in Chicago that was expected to last nine months. Due to new circumstances that occurred after seven months, it became apparent that Simon would be required to stay in Chicago for six additional months — for a total of 13 months.

♦ Simon's employment in Chicago is temporary for seven months, and, thus, his travel expenses are deductible for that period.

♦ During the remaining six months, his stay in Chicago is considered indefinite and not allowable as a deduction.

Obviously, you should clarify job assignment time schedules for you and your employees to evaluate the effects of a potential tax trap.

In the event that you are unable to produce the required backup documents, don't necessarily be alarmed. IRS examining officers sometimes give the impression that there are no exceptions to the rules. Be aware that several tax court decisions disagreed with the IRS and allowed taxpayers to substantiate certain expenses with various types of corroborating evidence.

NEW RULES ON DEPENDENTS AND AMOUNTS

By and large, the general rules on the deductibility of travel expenses remain unchanged since the tax act of 1993. There are, however, two revisions that are worthy of note. The first refers to the cost of having your spouse or other family member accompany you on a business trip. The second has to do with a change in the amount of business meals that can be deducted after the change in the law.

The current law affects dependents' accompaniment during business travel. After 1993, no deduction is allowed for the travel expenses of a spouse, dependent, or other individual accompanying a person on business travel unless:

♦ The family member is an employee who works for the person paying the expenses;

♦ The accompanying individual has a bona fide business purpose; and

♦ The expenses would otherwise be deductible.

Under the old rules, the accompanying individual didn't have to be an employee.

Illustration 9.7

♦ Mr. Thomas, an employee of Tee Company, is accompanied on a business trip by his wife Mrs. Thomas, who is not an employee of the company.

♦ Mrs. Thomas served a bona fide business purpose with her presence as she assisted her husband. For example, she arranged all of the business meetings and entertaining of clients after hours.

♦ None of the expenses paid by Tee Company are deductible under the letter of the new law, because Mrs. Thomas is not an employee of the one paying the expenses.

✎ PLANNING TIP

The new law does not offer a definition of bona fide employee, nor does it define what is meant by business purpose. Accordingly, whether there is a bona fide employee or a bona fide business purpose will have to be determined on a case by case basis.

THE LAW AFFECTS BUSINESS MEAL COSTS

Recent updates in the tax law regarding business meals do not change tax deduction policy or procedure. The change is related to the amount allowed to be written off for meals, whether they are for business travel or for entertainment.

Generally, if business meals are substantiated and are **not lavish or extravagant**, they can be deducted from income. Under the old law, the deduction was limited to 80% of the amount of the expense and **for any year after 1993, the deduction limit is 50%.**

As a result of the 1997 Tax Act, certain air transportation employees, certain interstate truck operators and interstate bus drivers, certain railroad employees, and certain merchant mariners will face an increased deductible percentage to be phased in according to the following table:

Taxable Years Beginning in...	Deductible Percentage
1998 and 1999	55%
2000 and 2001	60%
2002 and 2003	65%
2004 and 2005	70%
2006 and 2007	75%
2008 and thereafter	80%

To ensure a deduction for traveling expense, including meals and lodging, you need to substantiate four specific elements. To pass the test, keep a journal to record the items listed in the following table.

RECOMMENDED FORMAT FOR SUBSTANTIATING TRAVEL COSTS AWAY FROM HOME

Amount	Jot down the amount of each expenditure as you travel away from home. Include transportation, lodging and meals. For your own costs of travel, you can group the cost of breakfast, lunch, and dinner into a category called *meals*.
Time	Record the date of departure and return of each trip away from home. Show the number of days away from home on business.
Place	Record the destination or locality of each business trip. This simply means to make a note of the city, town, or other designation.
Business Purpose	This is the most confusing aspect to most business travelers. Be sure to take a few minutes to make a memo entry in your record describing your business reason for making the business trip. You might make a note of the business benefit expected as a result of the travel.

COMPUTE DEDUCTIONS WITH THE *OPTIONAL METHOD*

Many small business owners are not aware of a simplified method for computing the deductible amount of meals, lodging, and incidental expenses while on business travel away from home. Referred to as the *optional method*, this procedure spares the traveler from keeping an inordinate amount of detail on actual expenses while away from home on business. Generally, this special provision applies to regular employees — **not** to owners of 10% or more of a corporation.

The amount that is allowed to be deducted under this provision is set in a federal per diem rate table and is revised at different intervals. The table permits the taxpayer to use a flat amount for meals and incidentals without receipts. (Refer to Appendix B for Federal Per Diem Rate Table.)

Truly, the *optional method* spares the taxpayer from keeping the actual bills and receipts for every meal and incidental expense item while traveling. However, don't forget to record the three other specific elements — **time, place, and business purpose** of the travel.

Illustration 9.8

♦ Rick, a self-employed commercial mover, has traveled across two states to Mobile, Alabama. He stays there for ten days trying to develop new business clients.

♦ Unable to collect all the receipts for his meals and other incidental travel costs, he elects to use the *optional method.* He carefully keeps a diary identifying the whereabouts of each trip, the date, and a note about each prospective new client.

♦ Rick can substantiate $380 for meals and incidental expenses even though he does not have the actual receipts. This is calculated at $38 per day multiplied by 10 days. (Keep in mind, Rick's expenses are subject to the deduction limits set forth in the table presented earlier in this chapter. The 1998 deductible amount is 55%.)

⬜ ***Special Note:*** *The cost of virtually **all** meals, including beverages, is now subject to a 50% limit under the new law — whether those meals are for entertainment or business travel. So if you elect the short-cut version of the per diem method of recordkeeping, the lump sum allowance attributable to meals and incidental expenses will be subject to the tough new 50% limitation. For this reason many will want to consider foregoing the optional method and keep a record of the actual costs.*

If you have Internet access, you may access the federal per diem rates via the IRS Web site (*http:www.irs.gov*). In addition, to these rates you will find all the publications and forms for your business' tax-planning needs.

ENTERTAINMENT EXPENSES AND BUSINESS GIFTS

Deductions for business entertainment are a prime target for IRS agents and other examining officers. It is seen as the tax deduction most often abused by small business owner-operators looking for self-serving tax write-offs. Because of this assumption, over the years Congress has written some hard and fast qualifying rules that must be met before this unique deduction will be considered.

The qualifying rules for entertainment deductions are sometimes considered absurd in light of the additional demands that they place on business. Congress' attempt to react to the abuses of a few, has put more pressure on all small business owners already inundated by a sea of bureaucratic paperwork.

The tough requirements for entertainment deductions have reached diminishing returns; only a handful of business operators know exactly how the requirements work. In fact, many tax professionals don't bother wading through all the rules with their clients unless they try to claim an inordinate amount of entertainment expenses. Even highly trained IRS agents often refrain from getting involved with the murky fine points of the law, unless there are substantial dollar amounts involved.

☞ KEY OBSERVATION

Entertainment expense is still high on the list of deductions that raise a red flag on business tax returns. When the amount claimed is abnormally high for the type of business involved, there will be a rise in the DIF scores, and will increase the likelihood of that return getting caught up in the audit stream.

THE IMPACT OF THE CURRENT TAX LAW

Always looking for revenue raising sources, Congress has found a way to control business entertainment deductions without sending IRS auditors to do the work. In essence, Congress slashed the amount that could be deducted in a normal business setting. As we earlier learned, any approved entertainment deductions after 1993 will only be allowed to the extent of 50% of their full cost.

PASS THE ENTERTAINMENT EXPENSES DEDUCTIBILITY TEST

Whether you are in a business or an investment setting, you must meet a certain test for deductibility of entertainment expenses.

As with any cost of doing business, the taxpayer must show that the expense is an *ordinary and necessary* cost of doing business. (Refer to Chapter 5.) In addition, the cost must be directly related to the active conduct of the trade or business.

With this kind of language, small business owners, tax professionals, and IRS agents constantly debate over deductibility. The solution can only be settled by subjective negotiation.

The rule is: Entertainment is directly related to the taxpayer's business when it can be shown that there was an active discussion aimed at obtaining immediate revenue, or the entertainment occurred in a clear business setting.

Illustration 9.9

♦ Chip, a self-employed management consultant, held numerous cocktail parties and other social events for his business clients and associates.

♦ His daybook and canceled checks indicated that entertainment had taken place, but there were no detailed records identifying active business deductions. Nor did he show the existence of a clear business setting.

♦ No deduction was allowed.

Prepare to pass one more test if you want to assure locking in your entertainment deduction. The *associated with* test is your next step to save the deduction, should you fail the directly related test.

> ## ☞ KEY OBSERVATION
>
> The *associated with* test allows you a greater degree of flexibility for getting a deduction because it only requires that the entertainment be associated with the trade or business activity. It also states that the entertainment can take place before or after the business discussions.

There is a myriad of possibilities as to what can and cannot qualify as an entertainment expense when referencing the *associated with* test. A few observations can be made that might pique the interest of the small business owner as a potential tax-saving advantage with entertainment expenses. The entertainment that takes place before or after business discussions could include activities like:

♦ Business goodwill entertainment in night clubs,

♦ Sporting events,

♦ Theaters, and

♦ Fishing trips.

🗍 *Special Note: It is not necessary that you spend more time on business than on entertainment. It is not important that the entertainment and the business discussion take place on the same day, although it is helpful when the business discussion takes place **immediately** before or after the entertainment. Remember, each case is based on its own facts and circumstances.*

If IRS agents and tax professionals have problems with the strict interpretation of the entertainment expense rules, how are you supposed to know what to do? Clearly, the only way that you can survive the business entertainment test is to take aggressive action. Make sure that a detailed record is made each time an entertainment event occurs. Use the five specific elements — **amount, time, place, business purpose, and business relationship** — and win your case.

Just as you learned with travel expense, you need to create a simple chart that will force you, or your employees, to make a contemporaneous record of all the required details of the entertainment transaction.

🗌 *Special Note: A report document that looks official will command more respect than some scattered notes in the margin of a daybook. Hastily drawn memos identifying the details about entertainment expenses will come across to the IRS auditor as being noncontemporaneous and more importantly, inaccurate.*

In recent years, IRS auditors have begun to recognize that legitimate small business operators can't always pass these strict recordkeeping tests. They recognize, however, that they can still substantiate items like travel and entertainment by alternative methods often backed up by corroborating statements from outside parties. But even if you don't have corroborating statements on your side, remember that you have rights to substantiate your deductions by less orthodox means, however informal.

RECOMMENDED FORMAT TO PROVE YOUR ENTERTAINMENT EXPENSES

Item to be Proved	Substantiation Requirement
Amount	Record the amount of every expense as it is incurred. Incidental expenses, such as taxis and telephones may be totaled on a daily basis.
Time	The IRS wants to see a record on the date of the business meals or entertainment event. For meals or entertainment, show the date and duration of the business discussion, before and after a business deduction.
Business Purpose	Make a note of the business reason or the economic benefit gained, or to be gained. Also, be sure to comment on the nature of the business discussion.
Business Relationship	Make a memo about the party being entertained. Give the name, occupation, and other identifying data that shows that party's relationship to you. If the entertainment was a business meal, you must also prove that either you, or one of your employees, were at the meal.

Illustration 9.10

♦ John, a sales representative, incurred substantial amounts of entertainment expenses throughout the year.

♦ The IRS denied his deduction primarily because he did not keep an organized and contemporaneous log to prove the details surrounding every expense.

♦ <u>Upon appeal</u>, John was allowed the deduction, because it was determined that he had, in fact, taken enough steps.

♦ First, he produced canceled checks showing various restaurants and specific individuals who were involved. Second, an informal diary was produced containing the names of customers that he met on certain days and some of the restaurants where entertaining took place.

♦ Third, and most important, he made an effort to record in his diary certain facts stating that business-related issues were discussed.

On the other hand, there is an abundance of cases with the opposite ruling. Because IRS auditors are particularly inquisitive about entertainment deductions, you will be wise to keep a detailed record. (Refer to the table, Elements to Prove Certain Business Expenses, at the end of this chapter.)

KNOW THE RULES FOR CLUB DUES

For many years, the small business owner has enjoyed full tax deductions for dues paid to country clubs and social clubs. For example, use of the *Kiwanis Club* could be deductible provided the facility was used primarily for the furtherance of business.

Unfortunately, there had been some changes made under the 1993 tax act. For amounts paid after 1993, the new law went so far as to disallow deductions for all club dues. The disallowance applies to all types of clubs, whether they are business, athletic, social, luncheon, or sporting clubs.

☞ KEY OBSERVATION

Keep in mind, although the underlying club membership dues are no longer deductible, in certain cases, there may be significant tax write-offs available for club expenses. For example, business meals, drinks, and special functions are deductible if they are *directly related to* or *associated with* business or business discussions.

Under the current ruling, the IRS relented to public pressure over this tough law. The regulation now makes an allowance for dues paid to "professional" or "civic" or "public service" organizations. Accordingly, if you belong to such an organization for business reasons, you may now claim the cost of membership. Some examples of the allowable organizations cited in the new regulation are:

◆ Kiwanis

◆ Lions

◆ Rotary

◆ Civitan

This new regulation allows deductions for dues for professional organizations, such as:

- Business leagues

- Trade associations

- Chambers of commerce

- Boards of trade

- Real estate boards

Illustration 9.11

- Lorraine, a mortgage broker, paid $4,000 for her annual dues at a country club where she conducts a vast amount of business.

- The annual bar bill of $3,000 was the result of Lorraine's efforts to promote general goodwill for her business. There were also $5,000 in substantiated receipts for business luncheons for which Lorraine identified individual clients and the business discussions.

- Lorraine is permitted to deduct only the cost of the business luncheons, since they were directly related to the active conduct of her business.

☞ KEY OBSERVATION

Had Lorraine kept a detailed record of the business solicitation activities at the bar — **amount, time, place, business relationship, and business purpose** — the deduction probably would have been allowed. She would have demonstrated that her efforts involved something more than general goodwill.

WHEN GIVING GIFTS TO CLIENTS, KNOW YOUR LIMIT

Gifts to clients, customers and business associates are deductible if they are an *ordinary and necessary* cost of doing business. It is interesting to note, however, that deductions for such gifts are limited to an unrealistic **$25 per donee (recipient).** Because of the minimal dollar amount involved, IRS auditors are not particularly finicky when these deductions are claimed. Some examples of deductible business gifts, subject to the $25 limit are:

♦ The cost of gifts to customers at Christmas by a small manufacturing business;

♦ Gifts of flowers to customers whose family members were ill or had died; and

♦ The cost of magazine subscriptions to clients.

Remember, business gifts are subject to the tough $25 limitation no matter that they are made in connection with a good sound business purpose. The actual deduction is limited to $25 for each individual recipient each year. On the other hand, there is not a limitation on gifts that are made to other business entities, such as corporations or partnerships.

☐ *Special Note: Although there is usually no limit on the amount of business gifts made to business entities, the limitation will still apply if the gift is clearly intended for the benefit of a particular shareholder, owner, or employee.*

Illustration 9.12

♦ At Christmastime, Ace Printing Company sent a $30 fountain pen to each of its 40 best customers (all individuals).

♦ Ace can deduct a total of $1,000 ($25 per pen multiplied by 40 customers).

♦ Ace Printing also has a major corporate client to which it sent a season of professional baseball tickets costing $250.

♦ The tickets were to be made available to any of the large number of the corporation's employees.

♦ Since it was clear that none of the tickets were earmarked for the eventual use of any one individual, the entire cost of $250 is deductible

---

LISTED PROPERTY

For this last segment of special deductions, the same ground rules apply. In other words, do your best to record the details of each transaction. If those records are not available, you should start looking for someone outside to back up your claim.

Q. What specifically is this listed property for which I need special substantiation?

A. For the most part, listed property includes the following business property: automobiles and other transportation property; property used for entertainment, recreation and amusement; and computers or cellular phones.

If you plan to take a tax deduction for any one of these items, be prepared to substantiate the following, by adequate records or by outside testimony:

♦ The amount and date of each separate expenditure for each item of listed property;

♦ The amount and date of the use of that property for business; and

♦ The business purpose for using the property.

Without question, the vast majority of items in this listed property category involve business automobiles. In fact, the numbers of cars used in small business today are so great that the following chapter is dedicated entirely to the tax implications. Suffice it to say for now, that if you use any kind of business property that falls into the listed property category, keep a contemporaneous log and record the required details. For automobiles that means a continuing mileage record. (Refer to Chapter 10 for specific details on automobile usage.)

☛ KEY OBSERVATION

Whether the listed property item is an automobile, an airplane, or a cellular phone, as a small business owner you should keep not only the prescribed detail of its use, but also substantiate related costs, such as lease payments, repairs, and maintenance.

Illustration 9.13

♦ Amy, a country western singer, leased a computer in her home, which she only used to record songs and to correspond with radio stations.

♦ She failed to keep a running log of the dates and business use of the computer. However, she was able to produce outside testimony that the computer was *only* used for the furtherance of business as originally claimed.

♦ Amy was ultimately allowed the deduction. Even though she didn't have written records, her own statements were adequately substantiated by corroborating evidence.

Chapter Summary

The primary purpose of this chapter is to apprise the small business owner about a special class of business deductions that can be expected to come under special scrutiny by the IRS. The inference is that the expenses within this special grouping are so fraught with abuse that they can only be allowed as deductions if they meet certain specific substantiation requirements.

If you, as a business owner, incur costs for **travel, entertainment and business gifts**, you will be required to produce records to identify specifics like **amount, time, and business purpose** if called in for audit. You learned that if those records are for some reason unavailable, you may still assert your rights to use other alternatives — regardless of what the IRS examiner might suggest. In other words, the small business owner still has the right to secure the deduction by obtaining outside testimony and corroborating evidence.

Elements to Prove Certain Business Expenses

Table 4. How To Prove Certain Business Expenses

IF you have expenses for:	THEN you must keep records that show details of the following elements.			
	Amount	Time	Place or Description	Business Purpose and Business Relationship
Travel	Cost of each separate expense for travel, lodging, and meals. Incidental expenses may be totaled in reasonable categories such as taxis, daily meals for traveler, etc.	Dates you left and returned for each trip and number of days spent on business.	Destination or area of your travel (name of city, town, or other designation).	Purpose: Business purpose for the expense or the business benefit gained or expected to be gained. Relationship: N/A
Entertainment	Cost of each separate expense. Incidental expenses such as taxis, telephones, etc., may be totaled on a daily basis.	Date of entertainment. (Also see Business Purpose.)	Name and address or location of place of entertainment. Type of entertainment if not otherwise apparent. (Also see Business Purpose.)	Purpose: Business purpose for the expense or the business benefit gained or expected to be gained. For entertainment, the nature of the business discussion or activity. If the entertainment was directly before or after a business discussion: the date, place, nature, and duration of the business discussion, and the identities of the persons who took part in both the business discussion and the entertainment activity.
Gifts	Cost of the gift.	Date of the gift.	Description of the gift.	Relationship: Occupations or other information (such as names, titles, or other designations) about the recipients that shows their business relationship to you. For entertainment, you must also prove that you or your employee was present if the entertainment was a business meal.
Transportation (Car)	Cost of each separate expense. For car expenses, the cost of the car and any improvements, the date you started using it for business, the mileage for each business use, and the total miles for the year.	Date of the expense. For car expenses, the date of the use of the car.	Your business destination (name of city, town, or other designation).	Purpose: Business purpose for the expense. Relationship: N/A

Timely recordkeeping. You do not need to write down the elements of every expense at the time of the expense. However, a record of the elements of an expense or of a business use made at or near the time of the expense or use, and supported by sufficient documentary evidence, has more value than a statement prepared later when generally there is a lack of accurate recall.

A log maintained on a weekly basis, which accounts for use during the week, is considered a timely record. An expense account statement you give your employer, client, or customer can also be considered a timely record. This is true if it is copied from your account book, diary, statement of expense, or similar record.

Separating expenses. Each separate payment usually is considered a separate expense. For example, if you entertain a customer or client at dinner and then go to the theater, the dinner expense and the cost of the theater tickets are two separate expenses. You must record them separately in your records.

Season or series tickets. If you purchase season or series tickets for business use, you must treat each ticket in the series as a separate item. To determine the cost of individual tickets, divide the total cost (but not more than face value) by the number of

games or performances in the series. You must keep records to show whether you use each ticket as a gift or entertainment. Also, you must be able to prove the cost of non-luxury box seat tickets if you rent a skybox or other private luxury box for more than one event. See *Entertainment tickets* in chapter 2.

Allocating total cost. If you prove the total cost of travel or entertainment but you cannot prove how much it cost for each person, you must divide the cost among you and your guests to determine the business and nonbusiness cost. To do so, divide the total cost by the total number of persons. The result is the amount you use to figure your deductible expense for each qualifying person. See *Allocating between business and nonbusiness expenses* in chapter 2.

Combining items. You can make one daily entry for reasonable categories of expenses such as taxi fares, telephone calls, or other incidental travel costs. Meals should be in a separate category. You can include tips with the cost of the services you received.

Expenses of a similar nature occurring during the course of a single event are considered a single expense. For example, if during entertainment at a cocktail lounge, you pay separately for each serving of

refreshments, the total expense for the refreshments is treated as a single expense.

Car expenses. You can account for several uses of your car that can be considered part of a single use, such as a round trip or uninterrupted business use, by a single record. For example, you may make daily entries at several different locations on a route that begins and ends at your employer's business premises and that may include a stop at the business premises between two deliveries. You can account for these using a single record of business miles driven. Minimal personal use, such as a stop for lunch on the way between two business stops, is not an interruption of business use.

Gift recipients. You do not always have to record the name of each recipient of a business gift. A general listing will be enough if it is evident that you are not trying to avoid the $25 annual limit on the amount you can deduct for gifts to any one person. For example, if you buy a large number of tickets to local high school basketball games and give one or two tickets to many customers, it is usually enough to record a general description of the recipients.

Incomplete records. If you do not have complete records to prove an element of an expense, then you must prove the element by:

Chapter 10

AUTOMOBILE AND LOCAL TRANSPORTATION EXPENSES

The cost of buying and operating an automobile is one of the most common operating expenses of small businesses. Whether you are self-employed or on the payroll of your own business entity, the rules for deducting automobile expenses should be a prime concern to you. These rules, however, are so fraught with hedges and limitations that many business owners often don't know what they can write off. It is important to understand the variables involved with transportation; then plan ahead!

COMMUTING EXPENSES

Everyone is familiar with the general rule prohibiting a tax write-off for the cost of commuting between a taxpayer's residence and his or her place of business. Whether you use a bus, train, or taxi to travel to work, the IRS views the expense as strictly personal in nature, and no tax write-off is allowed.

The rules apply even if there is no public transportation available and commuting by auto is your only option. If you are an ordinary employee, the rules are even tougher.

Illustration 10.1

♦ Theresa, an employee, is legally deaf and unable to obtain a driver's license.

♦ Since there is no public transportation in her area, she incurs the expense of taxi service for travel to and from her job.

♦ Unfortunately, the court concluded that there could be no exceptions to the general rule. The deduction was denied.

LOCAL TRANSPORTATION

In light of the tough rules on commuting, there doesn't seem to be much hope for deducting local transportation costs that you incur with your personal car. There are some circumstances, however, that offer significant tax-saving advantages. If you closely look at these advantages, you'll see that the benefits favor the small business owner.

Small business owners need not be shy about claiming expenses for local transportation when they are so entitled. If the transportation is an *ordinary and necessary* cost of doing business, and it is not considered commuting, take it as a deduction. Further, if the amount claimed is not an unreasonable amount, the auto expense deduction should not raise your DIF scores nor the chance of subsequent audit risk.

WORK AT TWO DIFFERENT LOCATIONS

If your job, as an employee, takes you to two or more places during the course of a single day, you can deduct the cost of traveling from one job to another. Keep in mind, the initial commute and the final return are considered commuting and are not allowed.

Illustration 10.2

♦ Roger is an urban planner who is employed by a small consulting company.

♦ On one long-term engagement, he travels ten miles from home to job site A and gets no reimbursement for mileage.

♦ On the same day, he is required to incur the additional cost of getting to job site B, some sixty miles farther.

♦ Roger can deduct the transportation costs for the additional sixty miles to get from job site A to B.

WHEN THE OFFICE IS AT HOME

Because of the commuting factor, most taxpayers are denied the ability to claim most, if not all, of their expenses for local transportation in connection with their work. The cost of getting to and from the job simply doesn't come into the equation. For some, the mileage tacked onto their cars just for commuting often adds up to the majority of the total miles traveled for the year. Unfortunately, all those miles are wasted for tax purposes.

When your primary business residence is in your home, a different set of rules may apply. You may be able to deduct all transportation costs the moment you leave the house on business. (Refer to Chapter 11 for how to qualify for an office in your home.)

☞ **KEY OBSERVATION**

Many taxpayers operating out of their home automatically believe that the cost of transportation between their first and last stop of the day is, in fact, commuting and not deductible. The IRS held this position in the past, however, the tax courts have looked at it differently. As a result, many taxpayers with home offices have walked away with the full deduction.

Illustration 10.3

♦ Dr. Sprock, a psychiatrist, has an office in his home, which is the focal point of his practice.

♦ He incurs substantial mileage costs going from his home to several hospitals and clinics in the area where he sees patients.

♦ Since Dr. Sprock has established his home as his place of business, his transportation expenses to the various business locations are deductible. The trips are not regarded as commuting.

In an actual case, an attorney worked as a sub-contractor for a law firm. His office was in his home. It was ascertained that he performed 90% of his work outside the office of the law firm. In an interesting twist, the tax court concluded that his house was his principal place of business and auto travel between the home office and the law office was fully deductible.

TEMPORARY WORK LOCATIONS

In a ruling involving local transportation expense, the IRS has declared that travel between a taxpayer's house and a temporary work location could be allowed as a deduction.

⬚ *Special Note: If you can show that the temporary trips are to locations other than the usual place of business, they will be permitted regardless of the travel distance.*

Illustration 10.4

♦ O'Brien is a management consultant for Bongo Industries.

♦ He normally travels from his residence to any one of a number of client offices each day.

♦ His cost of traveling to those locations on a regular basis would be considered commuting and no tax write-off is allowed.

♦ If Bongo gives an irregular assignment that causes O'Brien to make some temporary trips to the location of the new project, then that travel expense would be fully deductible.

⬚ *Special Note: The IRS has warned against taxpayers abusing this liberalized rule by claiming deductions between home and an alleged temporary location, even when there is no proof of a valid business purpose. If this occurs, the deductions will be disallowed and penalties imposed.*

✎ PLANNING TIP

Before this ruling, the only time you could write off travel to a so-called temporary location was when that transportation involved travel to a location beyond the general area of the taxpayer's home. You will recall from Chapter 9 that with travel away from home, there is no allowable transportation deduction. The IRS's former position was in error. Transportation expenses to temporary job sites are now deductible even if it only involves **local** transportation.

If you have filed a tax return **that is not closed** by the statute of limitations (usually three years) and you could benefit from this new ruling on travel to temporary job locations, consider filing an amended return.

TRACK AUTOMOBILE MILEAGE

To avoid the chore of keeping details of all automobile expenses, the taxpayer is entitled to claim a deduction for a fixed mileage allowance — for 1997 it is set at 31.5 cents ($0.315) per mile; for 1998 it is set at 32.5 cents ($0.325). Regardless of which method is used, there is **no acceptable substantiation** without tracking the underlying miles traveled for business.

Before looking at the techniques for getting the biggest deduction for your automobile expenses, first focus on the job of determining business mileage.

One of the greatest challenges facing accountants and tax professionals is persuading their small business clients to properly track their business mileage. Too many ignore the responsibility with excuses like:

♦ It's not worth the bother because of the negligible amount involved;

♦ I'll keep my receipts for gas and maintenance; or

♦ We can easily reconstruct the mileage figure at the end of the year.

In response, you are reminded that automobile expense is within that special class of deductions requiring special substantiation requirements. The five basic elements — **amount, time, place, business purpose,** and **business relationship** — must be proved. In this case, the element most difficult to prove is the amount or, better yet, the amount of business use. In addition to mileage, you may also deduct for tolls and parking expenses when incurred for business purposes.

The IRS has flatly declared that the appropriate way to measure business use of an automobile is to prove the business mileage, unless you can come up with another method. In other words, you could have all the necessary gas tickets and repair bills, but if you can't identify the business miles, you haven't proved anything.

Q. What if I don't have any recorded details of my business auto expense, but I know that I used my car at least 50% of the time to visit clients?

A. As with any expense in the special deduction category, you do have an alternative. However, you would have to find corroborating evidence or outside testimony to back up your claim as to the business miles traveled.

If you are in a situation where you have absolutely no records to support your business miles claimed, you should try to reconstruct a mileage chart. Refer back to a travel itinerary, a daybook, or whatever sources you can find. Remember, you are entitled to use corroborating evidence even if it is your own testimony. If your testimony is not sufficient, then rely on the testimony of an unrelated party.

✎ PLANNING TIP

Keep a log to identify the location and purpose of all your business trips if you want to eliminate risk later on. If those records are unavailable, begin to reconstruct your business mileage with the best evidence you can find.

As a practical matter, IRS auditors and agents are fairly reasonable when examining the business mileage of the small business owner. They understand that it is quite difficult for everybody to keep a contemporaneous log recording each minute detail every time you use your car.

Further, they know that if you take the issue to court, the court will probably **allow at least some amount** of deduction based on the evidence made available — including your credibility.

If you appear credible and provide enough facts and details, your chances are good for a reasonable deduction for automobile expense even if your records are lost or unavailable.

Clearly, there are no set allowances and guidelines for *reasonable* amounts of business mileage for certain businesses or professions. Each case is looked at in terms of its own circumstances. Some interesting conclusions were reached in various court proceedings where the IRS and the taxpayer were in disagreement. Based on such proceedings, an average time usage per profession is highlighted in the following table.

PERCENTAGE OF BUSINESS MILEAGE PER TOTAL MILES*

Profession/Business	Business Use of Automobile Allowed
Anesthesiologist or businessperson	39%
Attorney (with two cars, but only used one car)	75%
Another Attorney	30%
Auto Dealer	70%
Cemetery Plot Salesperson	80%
Dentist (directed a clinic and made outside calls)	80%
Doctor	75%
Income Tax Preparer	15%
Owner of rental real estate	20%
Structural Engineer	70%
Wholesale Fruit and Vegetable Dealer	50%

These business use percentages have been allowed in certain cases. They are not meant to provide any generally accepted guidelines.

CALCULATE ACTUAL OPERATING EXPENSES

You may elect a deduction of the actual costs of operating the car for business instead of claiming the flat mileage allowance. The additional burden, of course, is that the owner-operator must produce additional records to substantiate those expenses.

Typical costs for operating a motor vehicle would include the following items:

♦ Gas and oil

♦ Lease or rental fees

♦ Repairs and maintenance

♦ Tires and supplies

♦ Insurance

♦ Depreciation

INTEREST PAID ON CAR LOANS

Generally, if you own a personal automobile, any interest paid on its purchase will be disallowed as a deduction. Under the current law, personal interest expense is simply no longer deductible. If you are self-employed, however, the business portion of the interest paid on your car will be deducted off the top on the business part of your tax return. This demonstrates yet another disadvantage as an ordinary employee.

✎ PLANNING TIP

If the owner of the car is your small corporation, then the interest is deductible as an *ordinary* business expense, similar to any interest paid for business property. For this reason, many prefer to purchase their business cars in the corporate name.

CHOOSE THE MILEAGE ALLOWANCE OR ACTUAL EXPENSES

Q. Is the rumor true that you'd be better off by simply forgetting the actual expenses and claiming the flat mileage allowance?

A. Since the government enacted the restrictive rules on auto depreciation, the difference between the mileage allowance and the actual expenses has been significantly minimized. For example, if you have an inexpensive car and your gasoline and maintenance expenses are minimal, your best option would be to take the mileage allowance. To be sure, calculate your options. Be aware of the allowable depreciation under the current rules.

Special Note: The IRS imposes stringent limits on the amount that could be deducted for depreciation. Because depreciation is severely limited, the actual expense option becomes much less attractive to the small business owner.

The maximum amount of depreciation for each year you own your car is set forth by the IRS and is subject to change each year.

Whether you own an $80,000 Mercedes Benz or a $25,000 Honda, the maximum amount that you could claim for depreciation is shown in the following table.

DEPRECIATION SCHEDULE FOR AUTOMOBILES PLACED IN SERVICE IN 1997

Period	Maximum Depreciation Allowed
First year	$3,160
Second year	$5,000
Third year	$3,000
Each succeeding year	$1,775

For example, suppose you purchase a $20,000 car in 1997 for business use only. You travel 10,000 total business miles that first year. By using the flat mileage allowance of $0.315, you would simply deduct $3,150 on your tax return. With the actual expense method, your depreciation deduction alone would be $3,160, which in itself, is about equal to the flat mileage allowance. Of course, any additional costs for gas, oil, or maintenance would be allowed as an additional tax write-off. Clearly, a major tax savings can be yours by using the actual method. The tax savings get better. For the second year your depreciation deduction is a hefty $5,000. Add this amount to your operating expenses and you will have a sizable business deduction.

❒ **Special Note:** *If you own a lower priced car, in the $16,000 range, be aware of a further reduction. This occurs when cars that are used less than 50% for business are limited to a depreciation deduction that is based on a conservative straight line method over five years. For some, this calculates a deduction as low as 10% of the business portion of the car for the first year.*

☞ KEY OBSERVATION

In the first year, if you decide to use the actual expense method, including accelerated depreciation, **you cannot use** the mileage allowance for that car in a later year. Conversely, if you claim the IRS allowance in the first year, you forfeit the right to use the special depreciation table shown above.

WHEN THE CAR IS USED FOR BUSINESS AND PERSONAL DRIVING

As a practical matter, very few individuals can actually substantiate 100% business use. By the time the taxpayer accounts for personal use of the car (particularly commuting) there is usually a sizable amount of the yearly expense that must be carved out. (See *Form 2106* at the end of this chapter.) Accordingly, you must be careful to claim only the allocable portion allowed.

Illustration 10.5

♦ Charley drove 16,000 miles last year.

♦ 12,000 miles were driven for business-related purposes, or 75%.

♦ His actual expenses for the year, including depreciation were $6,000.

♦ Charley is allowed to claim $4,500 ($6,000 multiplied by .75).

LEASING VS. PURCHASING

There was a time when auto leasing agents would pitch the fantastic tax benefits to be gained by leasing your car. The premise was that when you deduct lease payments for business property, there is usually no hassle from the IRS. Leasing agents used to claim:

♦ "You don't have to worry about making allocations for personal use."

♦ "Recordkeeping is a lot simpler."

♦ "All of your lease payments are fully deductible."

Today, the smart small business owner is aware that none of these claims have merit. Instead:

♦ You **do** have to keep mileage records and identify business and personal mileage.

♦ It is just as simple to make payments to a bank as to a leasing agency.

♦ By themselves, lease payments are not fully deductible.

HOW TO WRITE OFF YOUR LEASED CAR

First, determine your total mileage for the year — including personal miles. Then, apply the business percentage to the sum of:

♦ The total of your **actual** expenses for the year — including gas, oil, maintenance, and insurance — but excluding depreciation; and

♦ All of your lease payments for the year.

Remember, when you lease a business car, you should keep all your records for operating that car during the year. It is interesting to note that for 1998 you have a new option to use the 32.5 cents per mile allowance. However, you probably will be better off deducting the actual expenses.

Illustration 10.6

◆ Phyllis is a realtor who leases a $25,000 car on January 1, 1997.

◆ She travels 20,000 miles for the year and 15,000 miles, or 75%, is for business.

◆ Her records show that she spent $2,200 for operating the car and $4,800 in lease payments — a total of $7,000.

◆ Her deduction is 75% of her total outlay of expenses, or $5,250 ($7,000 multiplied by 0.75).

◻ *Special Note: You might argue that the limitation on depreciation makes for a distinct advantage for the leasing option, because depreciation is never a factor. After all, you **do** get a business deduction for the lease payment — at least for the business portion.*

The IRS settles this argument by setting specific and equal rates for both higher and lower value cars. The IRS provides a table that charges you with a dollar amount of extra income based on the value of your car. This amount from the table is added back to your income and simply offsets a portion of the deduction that you get for those hefty lease payments. (Refer to the table at end of this chapter.)

In Illustration 10.6, the value of Phyllis' automobile in the first year, was $25,000. The income adjustment table causes her to account for a $79 income adjustment for a car of that value. Phyllis must reduce the amount of her deduction for the lease expense by a modest $59 ($79 multiplied by 0.75). Since Phyllis only had to pick up $59 as an income adjustment in her leasing arrangement, this seems generous compared to the restrictive depreciation tables for purchased cars.

LEASING IS STILL A POPULAR OPTION

You may wonder why there still is a surge of interest in leasing and not purchasing business automobiles. The only tax advantage is seen in the IRS's income adjustment for leased cars table. Remember, however, Phyllis only had to pick up $79 as an income adjustment in her leasing arrangement in Illustration 10.6.

In earlier days, it was unimaginable how anyone could fare better by leasing his or her car rather than buying it. Administrative costs alone, built into the lease contracts, should surely outweigh any advantages of getting a vehicle without the problems of ownership. Recent studies show that this may not be the case. A small business owner looking to conserve up front cash, could drive away with a leased car and stay ahead financially at the same time.

What has happened during the past several years to make leasing a car advantageous? The automakers themselves have boosted the industry by:

♦ Lowering the internal rate of interest so that you could actually wind up paying less interest than if you financed the car yourself; and

♦ Giving you a higher residual value when the terms of your lease are up.

CHAPTER SUMMARY

Although auto expenses are a common and acceptable business deduction, there are numerous observations to make in order to qualify deductibility — particularly for local business transportation. The flat mileage allowance is arguably the easiest and most sensible option to use, however, it remains extremely important to track your mileage daily. The leasing business is a fast-growing industry that operates differently than the world of buying and selling. The uninitiated and uninformed will pay a price for their lack of awareness. At least be familiar with some of the language used in the leasing business. Know the following terms before talking to a leasing agent.

♦ **Capitalized cost.** The overall price agreed upon for the car.

♦ **Capitalized cost reduction.** The amount of your down payment.

♦ **Invoice.** The price that the dealer paid for the car. Remember, many customers are actually beating this price as the manufacturers offer their special rebates.

♦ **Depreciation.** Unlike depreciation for tax purposes, this refers to the difference between the capitalized cost and the value at the end of the lease term.

♦ **Subsidies.** Special benefits passed on by the automaker — either through a lower interest rate or a guarantee of a higher residual value at the end of the lease.

♦ **Option to purchase.** This is important if you lease a higher quality car that you will consider keeping. It gives you the right to purchase the car for the residual value at the end of the lease.

♦ **Residual Value.** The presupposed value at the end of the lease. You get to agree to this value **before** you sign the lease.

Remember, when in doubt, allow your attorney or accountant to look over the lease proposal.

FOUR IMPORTANT DON'TS

✓ **Don't** get caught up in the *monthly payment syndrome.* Remember, there are many facts to consider, such as the dealer's mileage allowance, sales taxes and property taxes. Read your contract in its entirety and make sure that every promise made is put in writing.

✓ **Don't** sign a lease for a period longer than you expect to keep the car. Your cost to get out could be prohibitive.

✓ **Don't** accept a proposal without comparing the deal with other leasing firms. Shop and compare with at least two or three independent agencies.

✓ **Don't** forget to focus on your purchase options and obligations at the end of the lease period. Insist on a closed-end lease, also known as a *walk away* lease. Your purchase option in a closed-end lease might give you a win-win situation. If the car, at the end of the term, is worth more than the fixed price option, you'll have a bargain. If it's worth less, you walk away.

Form 2106, Employee Business Expenses

Form **2106**	**Employee Business Expenses**	OMB No. 1545-0139
Department of the Treasury Internal Revenue Service (99)	▶ See separate instructions. ▶ Attach to Form 1040.	**1997** Attachment Sequence No. **54**

Your name JOE SALESPRO	Social security number 111-22-3333	Occupation in which you incurred expenses SALES REP

Part I   Employee Business Expenses and Reimbursements

STEP 1 Enter Your Expenses		**Column A** Other Than Meals and Entertainment	**Column B** Meals and Entertainment
1	Vehicle expense from line 22 or line 29	**1** 3,150	
2	Parking fees, tolls, and transportation, including train, bus, etc., that did not involve overnight travel or commuting to and from work . .	**2** 250	
3	Travel expense while away from home overnight, including lodging, airplane, car rental, etc. Do not include meals and entertainment	**3**	
4	Business expenses not included on lines 1 through 3. Do not include meals and entertainment	**4**	
5	Meals and entertainment expenses (see instructions)	**5**	– • –
6	**Total expenses.** In Column A, add lines 1 through 4 and enter the result. In Column B, enter the amount from line 5	**6** 3,400	– • –

Note: *If you were not reimbursed for any expenses in Step 1, skip line 7 and enter the amount from line 6 on line 8.*

STEP 2   Enter Reimbursements Received From Your Employer for Expenses Listed in STEP 1

7	Enter reimbursements received from your employer that were not reported to you in box 1 of Form W-2. Include any reimbursements reported under code "L" in box 13 of your Form W-2 (see instructions)	**7** – 0 –	– 0 –

STEP 3   Figure Expenses To Deduct on Schedule A (Form 1040)

8	Subtract line 7 from line 6	**8** 3,400	– • –
	Note: *If both columns of line 8 are zero, stop here. If Column A is less than zero, report the amount as income on Form 1040, line 7.*		
9	In Column A, enter the amount from line 8. In Column B, multiply the amount on line 8 by 50% (.50). If either column is zero or less, enter -0- in that column	**9** 3,400	– • –
10	Add the amounts on line 9 of both columns and enter the total here. Also, enter the total on **Schedule A (Form 1040), line 20.** (Fee-basis state or local government officials, qualified performing artists, and individuals with disabilities: See the instructions for special rules on where to enter the total.) . . . . ▶	**10** 3,400 –	

For Paperwork Reduction Act Notice, see instructions.   Form **2106** (1997)

ISA
STF FED4395F.1

Form 2106 (continued)

Form 2106 (1997)   Page 2

Part II   Vehicle Expenses (See instructions to find out which sections to complete.)

Section A — General Information

			(a) Vehicle 1	(b) Vehicle 2
11	Enter the date vehicle was placed in service	11	1/1/97	
12	Total miles vehicle was driven during 1997	12	15,000 miles	miles
13	Business miles included on line 12	13	12,300 miles	miles
14	Percent of business use. Divide line 13 by line 12	14	46.66 %	%
15	Average daily round trip commuting distance	15	10 miles	miles
16	Commuting miles included on line 12	16	2,500 miles	miles
17	Other miles. Add lines 13 and 16 and subtract the total from line 12	17	2,500 miles	miles
18	Do you (or your spouse) have another vehicle available for personal purposes?			☒ Yes ☐ No

19 If your employer provided you with a vehicle, is personal use during off-duty hours permitted? .... ☐ Yes ☐ No   ☐ Not applicable

20 Do you have evidence to support your deduction? .... ☒ Yes ☐ No

21 If "Yes," is the evidence written? .... ☒ Yes ☐ No

Section B — Standard Mileage Rate (Use this section only if you own the vehicle.)

22	Multiply line 13 by 31½ ¢ (.315). Enter the result here and on line 1. (Rural mail carriers, see instructions.)	22	3,150 —

Section C — Actual Expenses

			(a) Vehicle 1	(b) Vehicle 2
23	Gasoline, oil, repairs, vehicle insurance, etc.	23		
24a	Vehicle rentals	24a		
b	Inclusion amount (see instructions)	24b		
c	Subtract line 24b from line 24a	24c		
25	Value of employer-provided vehicle (applies only if 100% of annual lease value was included on Form W-2 — see instructions)	25		
26	Add lines 23, 24c, and 25	26		
27	Multiply line 26 by the percentage on line 14	27		
28	Depreciation. Enter amount from line 38 below	28		
29	Add lines 27 and 28. Enter total here and on line 1	29		

Section D — Depreciation of Vehicles (Use this section only if you own the vehicle.)

			(a) Vehicle 1	(b) Vehicle 2
30	Enter cost or other basis (see instructions)	30		
31	Enter amount of section 179 deduction (see instructions)	31		
32	Multiply line 30 by line 14 (see instructions if you elected the section 179 deduction)	32		
33	Enter depreciation method and percentage (see instructions)	33		
34	Multiply line 32 by the percentage on line 33 (see instructions)	34		
35	Add lines 31 and 34	35		
36	Enter the limit from the table in the line 36 instructions	36		
37	Multiply line 36 by the percentage on line 14	37		
38	Enter the smaller of line 35 or line 37. Also, enter this amount on line 28 above	38		

STF FED4395F 2

Dollar Amounts for Cars first Leased in 1997

Appendix B-1. Inclusion Amounts for Cars First Leased in 1997

Fair Market Value		Tax Year of Lease[1]				
Over	Not Over	1st	2nd	3rd	4th	5th and Later
$ 15,800	$ 16,100	$ 1	$ 5	$ 5	$ 8	$ 10
16,100	16,400	4	10	13	18	21
16,400	16,700	6	15	22	27	32
16,700	17,000	9	20	30	36	44
17,000	17,500	12	28	40	49	58
17,500	18,000	16	37	53	65	77
18,000	18,500	20	46	66	82	95
18,500	19,000	24	55	80	97	114
19,000	19,500	28	64	93	113	132
19,500	20,000	32	73	106	129	151
20,000	20,500	36	82	120	145	169
20,500	21,000	40	91	133	161	187
21,000	21,500	45	99	147	177	205
21,500	22,000	49	108	160	193	224
22,000	23,000	55	122	180	216	252
23,000	24,000	63	140	206	249	288
24,000	25,000	71	158	233	280	326
25,000	26,000	79	176	259	313	362
26,000	27,000	88	193	287	344	399
27,000	28,000	96	211	313	377	435
28,000	29,000	104	229	340	408	473
29,000	30,000	112	247	366	441	509
30,000	31,000	120	265	393	472	546
31,000	32,000	128	283	420	504	583
32,000	33,000	137	301	446	536	620
33,000	34,000	145	319	472	568	657
34,000	35,000	153	337	499	600	693
35,000	36,000	161	355	526	631	731
36,000	37,000	169	373	552	664	767
37,000	38,000	178	391	578	696	804
38,000	39,000	186	409	605	727	841
39,000	40,000	194	427	632	759	878
40,000	41,000	202	445	658	791	915
41,000	42,000	210	463	685	823	951
42,000	43,000	218	481	712	854	989
43,000	44,000	227	498	739	886	1,026
44,000	45,000	235	516	765	919	1,062
45,000	46,000	243	534	792	951	1,098
46,000	47,000	251	552	819	982	1,136
47,000	48,000	259	570	845	1,015	1,172
48,000	49,000	268	588	871	1,047	1,209
49,000	50,000	276	606	898	1,078	1,246
50,000	51,000	284	624	925	1,110	1,282
51,000	52,000	292	642	951	1,142	1,320
52,000	53,000	300	660	978	1,174	1,356
53,000	54,000	308	678	1,004	1,206	1,394
54,000	55,000	317	695	1,032	1,237	1,430
55,000	56,000	325	713	1,058	1,270	1,467
56,000	57,000	333	732	1,084	1,301	1,504
57,000	58,000	341	750	1,110	1,334	1,540
58,000	59,000	349	768	1,137	1,365	1,578
59,000	60,000	358	785	1,164	1,397	1,615
60,000	62,000	370	812	1,204	1,445	1,670
62,000	64,000	386	848	1,257	1,509	1,743
64,000	66,000	403	884	1,310	1,573	1,817
66,000	68,000	419	920	1,363	1,637	1,890
68,000	70,000	435	956	1,417	1,700	1,964
70,000	72,000	452	991	1,470	1,764	2,038
72,000	74,000	468	1,027	1,524	1,827	2,112
74,000	76,000	484	1,063	1,577	1,891	2,186
76,000	78,000	501	1,099	1,630	1,955	2,259
78,000	80,000	517	1,135	1,683	2,019	2,333
80,000	85,000	546	1,198	1,776	2,130	2,462
85,000	90,000	587	1,287	1,909	2,291	2,645
90,000	95,000	627	1,377	2,042	2,450	2,830
95,000	100,000[2]	668	1,467	2,175	2,609	3,014

[1] For the last tax year of the lease, use the amount for the preceding year.
[2] If the fair market value of the car is more than $100,000, see Revenue Procedure 97-20 (1997-11 IRB 10).

Chapter 11

HOME OFFICE EXPENSE STRATEGIES FOR THE 21ST CENTURY

The home office expense deduction is one of the most misinterpreted and misunderstood areas of the tax law affecting small business owners today. Only a modest few know the actual eligibility requirements for the deduction. Fewer know the long-range implications of claiming a deduction for your home office. Thanks to recent tax reform, however, this often controversial deduction will prove beneficial to some taxpayers.

PASS THE PRIMARY TEST

It is now confirmed that to claim a deduction for home office expense, you must show that the area in your home was used *exclusively* and on a *regular basis* as:

♦ The principal place of your business; or

♦ The place you deal with your clients, patients, or customers in the normal course of business.

IRS agents are quick to take issue with the *exclusive use* test. Some auditors visit a taxpayer's home and discover evidence that the office was also used as something else. For example, certain articles in the room — a sewing machine, a day bed, or children's toys — might be used to support the position that the office is actually a guestroom or a child's play room.

✎ PLANNING TIP

If you do use a portion of your residence for business, remove all nonbusiness-related items. Although not essential, you might consider physically separating these office quarters, possibly with partitions.

The key is to demonstrate that the space was used exclusively on a **regular basis**; that means you have to show *continuing* use in your particular work — not just occasional or incidental use.

THE FOCAL POINT TEST

A few years ago, the U.S. Supreme Court ruled on another crucial requirement of home office expense taxpayers. In addition to the primary test, taxpayers must pass a focal point test. For a certain class of taxpayers, particularly those who have a place of business elsewhere, the test makes approval of the deduction more difficult.

The test suggests that your true place of business is at the point where goods and services are being rendered or delivered. Greater emphasis is given to the place that you see customers or patients, rather than to the place where you tend to relatively less important details, like billing or report writing.

The key determinant is not the amount of time spent at the place of business, rather it is the focal point, or the place where the important part of the business transaction occurred. This is the key to an allowable deduction.

TAX LAW UPDATE

The IRS has recently allowed some slack from the harsh new rules. It is now becoming evident that the issue is not so clear-cut. Many practitioners have been too hasty in assuming that unless you could clearly pass the focal point test, you may just as well forget the deduction. The reality is that there is actually a two-prong test that needs to be applied to determine qualification.

In addition to the focal point test, the IRS still plans to look at the actual amount of time that you spend at each location performing duties — duties that are of relative importance to your work

Accordingly, if your work arrangements cause you to spend a considerable amount of time inside your home office, you may still qualify for the deduction even though the focal point — the primary function of your business operation — is at an outside location. Illustration 11.1 cites a clear example of this two-prong test.

Illustration 11.1

◆ Diane is a self-employed costume jewelry retailer. She places orders from wholesalers and sells the jewelry at craft shows, on consignment, and through mail orders.

◆ Diane spends about 25 hours per week at home placing orders, shipping, ordering, and keeping her books. She also spends 15 hours per week at craft shows and other marketing locations.

◆ In this example, the IRS states that Diane is entitled to claim the home office deduction. Clearly, the majority of her time is spent at home carrying on a function relatively important to her business.

The message is clear. Many taxpayers have not tried to deduct their home office because of the Supreme Court's well-publicized position on the focal point test. The bottom line is that **the focal point test is not necessarily the only test**, particularly when it is unclear where the principal place of business is located. Tax experts still consider this a controversial area. Remember, after December 31, 1998 there will be some slack for those who need to use their home for administrative purposes and no other office space is available.

EXCLUSIVE BUSINESS USE RULE PUT TO THE TEST

If you have ever gone through the exercise of calculating your home office expense, you may have been dismayed by the surprisingly small deduction as a result of your efforts. Those who clearly qualify for the home office deduction often limit themselves to the bare minimum to avoid the wrath of the IRS. Many feel that claiming more than 10 to 15% of the home is just asking for trouble.

Once again, the issue was brought before the tax court. From the court's ruling it appears that no set norms for calculating the allocation of business use of your home exist, although you can attract an audit with an allocation that is too large. As explained in Illustration 11.1, the tax court had no problem allowing a major portion of a married couple's ranch-style house, which was dedicated exclusively to business use.

Illustration 11.2

♦ Ron and Rose operate a home-based business printing legal documents in Columbus, Ohio. In their home office they keep various pieces of equipment, including machines needed to duplicate the documents, as well as, computer systems for word processing and for reading materials.

♦ The couple originally tried to deduct 94% of the home (nearly the entire house) for the years 1985 through 1987.

♦ An IRS audit revealed 64% of the home should be allowed as a deduction.

♦ After a follow up with the tax court, it was decided that 78% of the total usable space was used exclusively for business and, thus, could be deducted.

Two observations in this decision should capture your attention as a small business owner. First, observe the importance of the calculation of floor space used for business. Second, look at the real meaning of the term *exclusive business use*.

CALCULATING THE FLOOR SPACE USED FOR BUSINESS

In Ron and Rose's case, the tax court set a precedent when it allowed an additional deduction for space in their house that the IRS ordinarily would consider as nonfunctional or having minimum usability. Here, the attic, which was used to store shipping and packing materials, was allowed — in spite of its sloping roof and awkward design.

DETERMINING EXCLUSIVE BUSINESS USE

The tax court also made another interesting concession when it allowed, as part of the home office allocation, the expenses attributable to the couple's garage. Although the garage housed two large printing presses and a paper cutter, the court observed that some nominal personal property items were also stored there. This usually gives the IRS enough ammunition to disallow the use of any room or area of one's home.

Breaking with the traditional definition of *exclusive business use*, the tax court found that the IRS was oversensitive in its argument. The court felt that the lawnmower stored in the couple's garage was a matter too trivial to warrant disallowance of the deduction.

The lesson here is to be aware of the space you utilize for your home business operations. Look around your home office areas. Are there any personal items you should remove? Keep a keen eye for ways to increase the tax deductibility of your operation.

THE PRINCIPAL PLACE OF BUSINESS TEST

To meet this important test, you need to review the activity being carried on at all your business locations — and the relative importance of your work at each location. First, the location at which you might meet with customers and patients or provide specific services or deliver goods is usually considered your principal place of business. If this is difficult to analyze, you will want to review the amount of time spent at each location to help you determine the "relative importance."

Occasional use of a home office area will not qualify. You must be able to prove that the area in your home is used regularly and exclusively to meet with your clients and customers. Also, under the old law, you may run into a problem if you are using part of your home merely to do administrative or paperwork.

❒ *Special Note: After December 31, 1998, a home office will satisfy the principal place of business test if it is used to carry on management or administrative activities and it can be shown that there is no other fixed location to carry on such activities.*

TWO LONG-TERM TAX TRAPS: MAJOR RELIEF UNDER THE NEW LAW

One of the most unwelcome surprises that has long faced taxpayers is the unexpected tax bill that sometimes accompanies the sale of their personal residences. Upon the day of sale, the last thing **you** need is a capital gains tax on what may be the most important investment of your life.

To avoid a long-term tax trap, often taxpayers have forgone the home office deduction because they were fearful of paying a price later. They did not want to lose either one of the special tax breaks under the old law, which are:

♦ The once-in-a-lifetime exclusion, which permitted taxpayers to avoid tax on up to $125,000 in profits on the sale of a residence; and

♦ The deferral provision in the law, which allowed taxpayers to defer profits on the sale of a residence in situations where a new home was purchased within a prescribed time period.

It is understandable why so many small business owners have long been wary about running any risk of losing either of these valuable tax benefits by converting a portion of their home to a business office. After the 1997 Tax Reform Act, however, a revolutionary change has taken place that changes the whole approach to determining tax liability when you sell your personal residence.

☐ *Special Note: After May 6, 1997, taxpayers can exclude up to $250,000 of the gain that would be generated on the sale of a personal residence. (Married couples can exclude up to $500,000.) In general, all a taxpayer needs to do (to take advantage of the exclusion) is to own and use the property as a "principal residence" for at least two of the five years before the sale.*

This new law provision has already opened up some wonderful planning opportunities for anyone who one day plans to sell his or her home. And, the ability to be relieved of tax liability on as much as $250,000 (or $500,000) in profits appears to be extended to those who have converted a portion of their residence to a business office.

The only apparent cost of selling a home that has a business office within it is that the taxpayer will have to pay a tax on the depreciation claimed after May 6, 1997. This seems to be a modest price to pay in view of the major tax-saving benefits.

Illustration 11.3

◆ Reggie had a home office for which he claimed depreciation deductions of $10,000 before May 6, 1997 and $3,000 after that date. The house was sold on June 1, 1998 generating a gain of $200,000.

◆ Reggie can exclude $197,000 of the gain from taxes. He is only liable to report $3,000 of the gain on his 1998 tax return (the depreciation after the new transition date).

CHAPTER SUMMARY

Clearly, the increase in the number of home-based businesses over the last five years shows that this trend is here to stay. Individuals using their home offices either part-time or full-time must be wary of the tax implications. As pointed out in this chapter, the current latest tax law focuses on the principal place of business test. If you intend on claiming a deduction for your home office, can you meet the requirements of this test? Also, have you considered the long-term tax consequences — specifically the ramifications of the eventual sale of your home? In this regard, you need to be aware of the revolutionary 1997 tax law change that provides unprecedented tax relief. One thing is for certain, as more taxpayers claim this controversial deduction, there will be more IRS auditors looking for misuse or abuse. Your best plan is to remain informed of the latest tax law legislation. Chapter 15 provides resources that will help you stay abreast of these changes.

Chapter 12

SMART RETIREMENT PLANNING AND TAX DEFERRALS

Any technique that allows a legal deferment of income tax liability will always be attractive to taxpayers. With income tax rates on the rise, business owners are particularly interested in securing every possible tax-deferral measure.

EMPLOYER RETIREMENT PLANS

Heading the list of legal tax-deferral schemes are the employer plans that provide retirement benefits for employees. At their best, these plans offer the luxury of an upfront tax deduction by the employer, while no taxable income need be reported by the affected employee. As income is generated from the invested funds in the plan, continued tax deferral allows for further, compounding tax advantages.

The real tax savings of a qualified retirement plan in action is shown in the following illustration.

Illustration 12.1

♦ Quill Corporation, owned by Dexter, Ellen, and Frances, approaches the end of its business year with a projected $15,000 profit.

♦ The original plan was to pay Dexter, Ellen, and Frances, also the corporation's only employees, $5,000 each for the extra time and effort spent with the business that year.

♦ Since they were all in the 31% tax bracket, they arranged for the three $5,000 payments to go into a qualified retirement plan instead.

♦ Quill Corporation is allowed a $15,000 upfront deduction.

♦ Dexter, Ellen, and Frances are each spared from paying $1,550 on their share of bonuses, or $5,000 multiplied by 31%.

♦ In addition, the $15,000 invested by the plan will be allowed to compound, fully tax deferred, during future years.

Interestingly, many small business owner-operators don't bother taking advantage of an employer-sponsored retirement plan because they are simply intimidated by its complexity. Further, many are not certain as to the **amount** of possible tax deferral that can be attained under today's complex rules. You may ask, "How much deferral makes sense at this time?"

A single chapter cannot begin to provide all the answers for this highly specialized and complex topic. However, you will at least be left informed as to the general choices of tax-favored plans that are now available under the current law. In addition, you should have a better idea as to which would meet your particular needs for tax saving retirement benefits.

The tax-favored retirement plan options for the small business owner are:

♦ The Individual Retirement Arrangement (IRA);

♦ Company qualified plans, also known as profit-sharing or pension plans;

♦ The Keogh, or self-employed plan;

♦ The Simplified Employee Pension Plan (SEP);

♦ The 401(k), or deferred salary plan; and

♦ The SIMPLE Plan.

Before you follow the traditional approach of deciphering each of the tax-favored retirement plans in their given order, first ask yourself two specific questions.

1. Which plan is the simplest and least cumbersome to operate in securing my retirement planning objectives?

2. Which will allow the most tax write-off without requiring an unnecessarily high cost of administration?

First, take a look at the plan alternatives in view of these underlying questions.

The IRA

Without question, the IRA is clearly the simplest and least expensive plan to set up and operate. Because of its simplicity and low costs, many small business owners choose the IRA because they don't want to be bothered with anything more complex. The problem, as you are probably well aware, is that the amount that can be socked away as a deductible contribution is quite limited. The maximum you can contribute is up to $2,000 of your earnings, provided you have wage, salary, or self-employment income.

TAX LAW UPDATE

Starting in 1997, a new tax law provision allows a taxpayer's nonworking or low-earning spouse an additional $2,000 deduction. This makes for a combined deduction of as much as $4,000 as long as their combined compensation is that much. If you or your spouse are an active participant in another employer retirement plan, that deduction is reduced as follows:

Taxable Years Beginning in:	Phase-out Range for Joint Returns	Phase-out Range for Single Taxpayers
1998	$50,000–$60,000	$30,000–$40,000
1999	$51,000–$61,000	$31,000–$41,000
2000	$52,000–$62,000	$32,000–$42,000
2001	$53,000–$63,000	$33,000–$43,000
2002	$54,000–$64,000	$34,000–$44,000
2003	$60,000–$70,000	$40,000–$50,000
2004	$65,000–$75,000	$45,000–$55,000
2005	$70,000–$80,000	$50,000–$60,000
2006	$75,000–$85,000	$50,000–$60,000
2007 and thereafter	$80,000–$100,000	$50,000–$60,000

⬭ *Special Note: A nondeductible contribution can be made to the plan if the deduction is not permitted because of the **income phase-out rule**. Thus, if you have a higher income level and still want to take advantage of the tax-free compounding of an IRA investment, you may do so as long as you, or your spouse, are not active participants in another employer retirement plan.*

Illustration 12.2

♦ Ralph, a married man, owns a small construction company with three employees.

♦ The company generated a rather meager profit during the current year. His wife participates in a qualified retirement plan.

♦ With a modest AGI of $24,000, Ralph found himself in the lowest 15% tax bracket for the year.

♦ Although short on cash, he begins an IRA for himself at no cost. To this account he contributes the maximum $2,000.

♦ Ralph saves only $300 in taxes that year, or $2,000 multiplied by 15%. However, he gets to participate in an investment program that will accumulate tax-free dollars compounded annually for future years.

You may wonder if Ralph made a smart move. You may ask, "Is the upfront tax deduction and tax deferral that Ralph gets worth it in the long run?" The answer depends on how you might respond to two individualized observations about this particular small business owner's circumstances.

1. The 15% tax deduction and $300 tax savings won't amount to much, in relative terms, if Ralph's business continues to grow with increasing tax brackets in future years. For example, he will not have won the game if he reaches retirement age and starts to withdraw his IRA money, only to pay taxes at 39.6% rates.

2. Although $2,000 doesn't sound like much money, it could be critically important to a struggling new business owner like Ralph. He might get much better leverage with any excess dollars being invested in the business, rather than in an IRA that can't be touched until retirement.

As shown, the hype over the advantages of **any** tax-deferred retirement plan must be viewed with extreme care. Whether you're looking at a simple IRA or a more substantive tax-favored retirement plan, the smart small business owner should look at the entire picture. Be sensitive to your current tax bracket and your probable bracket at retirement. In addition, you must consider the risks of having your funds tied up until you are 59½-years-old.

☐ ***Special Note:*** *For all tax-favored retirement plans, the participant is not permitted to take distributions from the retirement account until age 59½, without incurring a penalty except in unique circumstances.*

Q. Where can your IRA contributions be invested?

A. The assets of an IRA account must be invested in a trustee, or custodial account with a bank, savings and loan association, credit union, brokerage firm, or other qualified person operating as trustee or custodian. However, you can stay in charge and self direct the investment plan as long as you put your money into vehicles like certificates of deposit, stocks, bonds, mutual funds, annuity contracts, and a few other specified areas. (To establish an IRA account refer to *Form 5305* located in Appendix D.)

From the above data and illustration, you can see that the IRA alternative is quite limited with regard to its tax-saving capability. Although it is simple and inexpensive to administer, some find its low contribution limits make the IRA hardly worthwhile from a tax-saving standpoint.

THE ROTH IRA

When Congress passed the Taxpayer Relief Act of 1997, it created an entirely new dimension in the art of retirement planning. Although the decision to establish a Roth IRA is not one for business owners specifically, its widespread popularity makes it important for the purpose of tax saving. Further, whether or not a small business owner is eligible to participate in a Roth IRA is not restricted or otherwise limited because he or she has elected to participate in one of the various tax-deferral retirement schemes described in this chapter. In short, it is available to all taxpayers who have earned income as long as certain general income limitations are met (see below).

Although contributions to a Roth IRA are nondeductible, the real value is that a participant can put away money each year and watch it grow tax free until it comes time to pull out distributions. The key benefit, however, is that the distributions can be taken out tax free after five years as long as that individual has reached age 59½.

Clearly, the ability to receive tax-free distributions to supplement your retirement income stream makes for an attractive retirement planning alternative — one that needs to be explored by all taxpayers.

Q. How much can I contribute to a Roth IRA?

A. You can contribute up to $2,000 annually, provided you have earned that much in compensation. In general, however, there are limitations for higher earners. These limitations will apply if you are single and your adjusted gross income is expected to exceed $95,000. If you are married, the threshold is $150,000.

THE ROTH IRA ROLLOVER QUESTION

Perhaps the most-asked question about the popular Roth IRA is whether or not an individual should roll over his or her traditional IRA into a Roth plan in order to secure a tax-free income stream. This can be an extremely important question for those who are looking to enhance their planned cash flow at retirement with an attractive tax-free income stream.

In very general terms, all that you need to do is to roll over the IRA funds into the Roth plan within 60 days after receipt and to pay the tax on the distribution at that time. If you happen to be under age 59½, you will not be subject to the usual 10% penalty tax that is usually applied.

Finally, the other significant advantage of the rollover process is that the taxpayer is entitled to spread out the normal tax liability that may exist over a four-year period — beginning with the year that the distribution takes place. This special option is available only until January 1, 1999.

◻ *Special Note: The qualified rollover cannot be made if your adjusted gross income is over $100,000 or if you are married and filing a separate return.*

If you have a traditional IRA, carefully consider the possibility of rolling over your tax-deferred investment into a Roth plan. Although there may be something of a price to pay in terms of an initial tax cost, the long-range benefits may outweigh that cost in the long run. Also, if you have made nondeductible contributions to your traditional IRA, you will not be taxed on those particular contributions.

COMPANY QUALIFIED PLANS: PROFIT-SHARING AND PENSION PLANS

If you have an ownership interest in a small business corporation and you are concerned about the increasing tax bill on your profits, chances are you need to look closely at a *company qualified plan*. *Company qualified retirement plans* often provide substantial tax write-offs upfront. In addition, there are long-range benefits as your investment dollars compound and grow unfettered by current taxes. Before you participate, have an experienced pension consultant explain all the related costs and obligations that are part of the program. Also, remain aware that there are strict anti-discrimination rules, so that excessive retirement benefits cannot be allocated to owners and key employees in an unfair manner.

Consider Ralph (Illustration 12.2) who, after a point in time, witnesses some reasonable growth and development in the closely held corporation that he operates. Assume that with his steadily increasing salary he is now well beyond the IRA stage.

Illustration 12.3

◆ Ralph's corporation, during the last month of a particular fiscal year, projects a $20,000 profit. Ralph, in the 31% tax bracket that year, sees no economic merit to adding another $20,000 to his salary via his *W-2*.

◆ He decides to set up a *company qualified retirement plan*. Although his other two employees will be entitled to a small portion, $15,000 goes to Ralph's retirement account based on the plan.

◆ The corporation can deduct the $20,000 contribution leaving no corporate tax liability. Ralph pays no tax on the contribution. Further, he has $15,000 tax free working for him until retirement.

How are small business owners like Ralph supposed to know what kind of company qualified retirement plan is best for their purposes?

If you are a small corporate owner like Ralph, you need to look at all your retirement planning options before you start making profits and paying excessive taxes on such. Before you start spending money on professional advisers and "pension experts," familiarize yourself with some of the general planning alternatives so you know which questions to ask.

In Ralph's case, before he socked away a hefty $15,000 (Illustration 12.3), he first had to contemplate some pervasive, long-range issues before he decided what kind of company qualified plan would be best for him. He had to consider that whichever plan he chose, there would be strict anti-discrimination rules to follow.

This meant he would have to evaluate the amount that would also have to be put in the plan for his other two employees each year. Even though he would probably continue to attain the "lion's share" of the benefits, an evaluation of the overall out-of-pocket costs must be made before deciding the best route.

If you decide that a qualified plan, with employees included, is a worthwhile endeavor, then ask yourself the following two questions:

- Would I be better off with a plan that requires the company to contribute a certain percentage of employee's salaries every year or should I gear it to the profits of the company?

- What is the maximum tax free amount that can be legally "socked away" in the plan?

With these questions in mind, you will better appreciate the pros and cons of the two general plan alternatives available with a company qualified plan. Your general choices are between the *profit-sharing plan* and the *pension plan*.

THE PROFIT-SHARING PLAN

The comforting advantage of the *profit-sharing plan* is that, for the most part, it provides you as the employer with a totally discretionary contribution formula. In other words, if you don't want to be obligated to make contributions each year, set up a *profit-sharing plan* that essentially states: **no profit, no contributions to the plan.**

◻ **Special Note:** *Although an employer is not required to contribute any particular percentage of profits, the profit-sharing plan must have a written formula for allocating the profits consistently among the participants. It is also important to remember that, in general terms, the most you can contribute is 15% of the employee's compensation. Also, the maximum amount of compensation that can be considered for the computation is set by an IRS formula, which cannot exceed $30,000 per employee in any one year.*

Consider the circumstances of Tanya (Illustration 12.4), the owner of a small consulting corporation with three people on the payroll, including herself. Tanya anticipates some healthy profits over the next few years but she has some long-range concerns about the company's continuing profitability. She decides that the best and most conservative retirement plan to choose from under the circumstances is a *profit-sharing plan*. For peace of mind, Tanya takes the position that, **"no profit, no obligation to make retirement contributions"** is the best policy.

Illustration 12.4

♦ Tanya anticipates a $20,000 corporate profit for the current year; she does not favor paying taxes on such.

♦ Tanya sets up a *profit-sharing plan* that calls for a contribution of 10% of each employee's salary for the year, including her own.

♦ Although she could contribute as much as 15%, for the current year, the 10% contribution to the retirement plan is just enough to bring the corporate profits down to zero.

♦ Instead of paying corporate taxes on $20,000 that year, Tanya pays nothing.

♦ Tanya attains the conservative goal of her plan. A reasonable retirement plan is in place, and she is not saddled with future obligations when no profit or cash is available.

☞ KEY OBSERVATION

As an employer, you may have one other option available with *profit-sharing plans*. You may elect to make a plan contribution in a given year, even though the corporation **does not** make a profit. This is a good idea if it makes sense to tie up cash dollars to get some long-range, tax-deferred benefits for the earnings on your investment.

THE PENSION PLAN

We have seen where the *profit-sharing plan* gives the small corporate owner an opportunity to increase the amount of deductible plan contributions by as much as 15% of employee compensation paid during the year. The *pension plan* adds another dimension and helps you increase those contributions even more. First, be aware that the pension plan can be set up either as:

♦ A *defined contribution* type of pension plan; or

♦ A *defined benefit* plan.

THE *DEFINED CONTRIBUTION* PLAN: A JOINT EFFORT

With the *defined contribution* type of plan, an employer makes an agreement promising to make a specific contribution into a retirement plan on behalf of the qualified employees. The contribution is usually an expressed percentage of the employee's compensation and **is not based on profits**. Thus, you need to be careful when you set these percentage requirements because you may be required to make retirement contributions in amounts that may be difficult to come up with during times of faltering cash flow.

What is the maximum contribution? For *defined contribution* plans, the maximum amount that can be contributed to an employee's account is 25% of the employee's compensation — up to a maximum of $30,000.

In addition, the maximum amount of that employee's compensation that can be used in the calculation is set by the IRS. The most recent (1998) maximum amount is $160,000.

Illustration 12.5

♦ Jeff is an employee and the sole owner of Crinkle Corporation. He has one other employee, Fred.

♦ Anticipating a $31,000 profit in the current year, Jeff sets up a *defined contribution* pension plan. He elects to use the maximum contribution percentage of 25%.

♦ With Jeff drawing a salary of $100,000 and Fred drawing $24,000, the corporation gets the maximum tax advantage.

♦ The allowed contribution for Jeff is $25,000, or $100,000 multiplied by 25%. For Fred it's $6,000, or $24,000 multiplied by 25%. So with a total contribution of $31,000, Jeff has managed to eliminate any corporate tax liability for the year.

☞ KEY OBSERVATION

Unless he changes the plan, Jeff needs to remain aware that the corporation will continue to be obligated to make the same contributions, or 25% of the employee's compensation, regardless of the availability of cash.

THE *DEFINED BENEFIT* PLAN: THE ULTIMATE IN TAX-FAVORED RETIREMENT BENEFITS

Unlike other qualified retirement plans whereby contributions are usually based on a flat percentage of employees' salaries, the *defined benefit* arrangement allows for some major exceptions to the deduction limits. The key is this special plan permits deductions for the required amount to fund the retirement plan so that it meets your planning objective. Your objective, of course, is to secure a targeted amount of retirement benefits that you need to be comfortable when you reach the "magic" age of 59½-years-old, or a later retirement age if you so choose.

Q. Why has the *defined benefit* plan become such a popular windfall as a tax saving measure?

A. By applying a rather complex formula based on actuarial assumptions, older owner-employees are able to design a plan that permits a disproportionately generous retirement contribution on their own behalf. Sometimes these deductible contributions can even exceed their salary in a given year. In designing the plan with its targeted objectives, the anticipated retirement benefits cannot exceed an indexed dollar amount each year.

Illustration 12.6

♦ Marla owns 100% of Presley Corporation, which is anticipated to generate about $60,000 in income for the current year. During the year, she earns $45,000 in salary while her other three employees earn $20,000 each.

♦ Marla, the only employee close to retirement, sets up a *defined benefit* plan for the current year. This type of plan calls for a substantial contribution on her behalf to meet this targeted retirement objective.

♦ With help from a pension consultant, it is theoretically possible that a $60,000 deductible contribution can be made to the defined benefit plan with $50,000 (an amount more than her salary) going to Marla's account, and the balance going to the employees.

♦ The deduction would, of course, eliminate any tax liability.

THE KEOGH PLAN: WHEN YOU ARE SELF-EMPLOYED AND NOT OPERATING AS A CORPORATION

An individual starting out in business should be aware that the tax-saving benefits of *qualified retirement plans* are available to self-employed individuals as well as employees of corporations. Further, the qualification rules for self-employed plans are, in many regards, no different than that of corporate plans.

If you set up a self-employed retirement plan, make a written communication of the plan arrangement to your employees — just like other qualified employee retirement plans. As with regular *qualified retirement plans,* you can make a choice to use either:

♦ A *profit-sharing Keogh* plan which, as stated earlier, means that you are **not required** to make a contribution unless you make a profit.

♦ A *pension plan*, based on either a fixed percentage of the employees' salaries or a *defined benefit* plan.

☞ KEY OBSERVATION

Self-employed plans must be established for the benefit of the employees or their beneficiaries. In this regard, the self-employed person is treated as both employer and employee.

WHO IS ELIGIBLE

If you are self-employed and have no other employees, you can still qualify for the tax-saving benefits of the plan. A self-employed individual, in general terms, is an individual who has earned income during any taxable year. In this regard, earned income refers to earnings with respect to a business in which **personal services** are a material factor.

Self-employed individuals could include lawyers, accountants, doctors, architects, and all types of consultants. It could also include those who operate a business such as real estate, home repair, a bakery, a gift shop, or independent sales.

Q. How much of a deductible contribution can be made to a self-employed Keogh retirement plan?

A. As indicated above, it depends on whether you use profit-sharing or the regular type pension plan.

If you select the profit-sharing Keogh variety, the maximum amount you could contribute for yourself is approximately 13% of your own net earnings. The greatest amount that you could contribute on behalf of your employees is a flat 15%. If you decide to do a regular pension plan, you have another choice.

♦ You could select a *defined contribution* plan. This would permit you to make a deductible contribution for yourself up to a maximum amount of 20%. For other employees, the limit goes to 25%; or

♦ As with qualified corporate plans, you can elect the *defined benefit* arrangement. This more complicated version may permit a substantially greater allocation of the contribution to go toward the owner's benefit.

☞ KEY OBSERVATION

Although the *defined benefit* plan is usually designed to allow a larger contribution benefit for the owner-participant, its advantages are not as significant as with corporate defined benefit arrangements. Generally, when such plans are run through self-employed Keogh plans, the most that can be contributed for the owner is limited to the self-employed individual's net income for the year. You will recall that with corporate plans, the contributions can in some cases go well beyond the owner-participant's compensation.

THE SIMPLIFIED EMPLOYEE PENSION PLAN (SEP)

Although company qualified retirement plans continue to be widely used as a major tax saver and retirement vehicle, there has been a noticeable downfall in their cost effectiveness. The ever-increasing complexity and restrictions on these plans are causing many small business owners to question the value of the amount that they are allowed to treat as a tax deferral. For some, the answer points to the old reliable alternative known as the Simplified Employee Pension Plan (SEP).

A SEP plan set up by small business owners allows contributions to the regular IRA accounts of their employees. The key, however, is that the amount contributed can go well beyond the usual restrictive IRA limitations.

What it Takes to be Eligible

One nice feature about the SEP retirement plan is that it may be entirely discretionary each year. If you, the small business owner, don't have the funds in any one year, you simply don't have to make any contributions to the plan. When you **do** make a contribution, you must cover everybody who:

- Is over 21-years-old;

- Earns more than $400 during the year (based on a 1998 figure); and

- Has worked for you at **any** time during at least three of the past five years.

The SEP retirement plan is thought of as a simple, convenient arrangement that can be used by almost any small business — provided there is no discrimination in favor of the owner-employees and those that are highly compensated. Thus, a corporation, a partnership, or a sole-proprietorship can qualify.

Q. How much can be contributed and deducted to a SEP plan?

A. The answer depends on whether you have 1) an *ordinary* SEP plan, or 2) a *salary reduction arrangement*.

The differences between the two types of plans are:

♦ The maximum contribution for an ordinary SEP is the lesser of 15% of each of the employee's compensation or $30,000. (The maximum that can be contributed on behalf of a sole proprietor is about 13% of that proprietor's net income.)

♦ If you have a *salary reduction plan*, the maximum contribution is significantly reduced. The limit is $9,500 for 1997 and will be adjusted for inflation.

Realistically look at the two alternatives. Put yourself in the shoes of the small business owner who doesn't have much cash available to fund retirement plans. You already may be starting to look with interest at the SEP concept in general. As pointed out, it is not only incredibly easy to set up, it also costs practically nothing in the process.

🗍 *Special Note: Under current law, new salary reduction SEPs for plans started after December 31, 1996 are not allowable. Old plans are still okay under the same rules as before.*

If you plan to implement an *ordinary* SEP plan, remember that you are getting into a wholly employer-funded arrangement. If you have the available cash and wish to contribute something to a retirement plan for yourself and your employees across the board, then this plan is for you.

Illustration 12.7 – Ordinary SEP Plan

♦ Marco, the owner of Zenith Corporation, anticipates a $17,000 profit for the current year.

♦ Marco draws $60,000 in salary while his one employee, Marie, draws $50,000.

♦ Mindful of the extra cash reserves on hand, Zenith sets up an ordinary SEP IRA account. The *maximum* is contributed to a SEP IRA account that Marco opens for himself and for Marie.

♦ Zenith gets a deductible contribution of $16,500, with a flat 15% discretionary payment. $9,000 goes to Marco's account, or $60,000 multiplied by 15%; and $7,500 to Marie's account, or $50,000 multiplied by 15%.

Illustration 12.8 – Salary Reduction Plan

♦ Here the same facts apply, except that Zenith Corporation doesn't have any significant available cash.

♦ Marco makes an arrangement with Marie who agrees to take a $7,000 cut in salary.

♦ The $7,000 will be used to fund Marie's contribution to her SEP IRA account.

♦ He also elects to contribute the maximum toward his own SEP IRA account. $17,000 has been excluded from the employees' incomes — $10,000 for Marco (the maximum) and $7,000 for Marie.

♦ Since the *salary reduction plan* places a limit on the SEP IRA deduction, Zenith may be required to pay a modest corporate tax on the remaining profit.

☐ *Special Note: The maximum SEP IRA contribution allowed under a salary reduction plan for 1998 will be $10,000.*

☞ KEY OBSERVATION

There are three other eligibility requirements that you must consider if you want to take advantage of a SEP salary reduction arrangement.

♦ Only small companies with no more than 25 employees may offer such plans;

♦ At least 50% of the eligible employees must agree with the salary reduction; and

♦ The amount deferred for the highly compensated employees cannot be more than 125% of the average contribution of the other employees. (To establish a SEP IRA, refer to sample *Form 5305-SEP* in Appendix D.)

THE 401(K) PLAN

The 401(k) plan is nothing more than another form of a salary reduction arrangement. If, as a small business owner, you do not have the cash available to contribute into one of the aforementioned retirement plans, you may consider the 401(k) plan.

This plan is another way to say that employees have an extra option to forego a certain amount of income on an their *W-2*s and have it put into a retirement plan instead. Put another way, it allows the employer to treat those salary reduction amounts as if they were in fact made by the employer instead.

The 401(k) plan is generally tied to a profit-sharing plan or a stock bonus plan that must be in existence. And, as with other qualified plans, the employer contributes an amount for the employees' benefit to a special trust account. The income, of course, is allowed to accumulate tax free until it is withdrawn by the employee.

FIVE SPECIAL REQUIREMENTS TO QUALIFY FOR A 401(K) PLAN

1. The employee-participant must be given the option of having the employer give the employee cash or make the contribution to the plan.

2. The plan must prohibit certain early distributions to the employee.

3. The employee-participants must have certain vested rights to the value of their account at all times.

4. The plan cannot require, as a condition of participation in the plan, that an employee complete more than one year of service with the employer.

5. It cannot make conditions to get benefits under the 401(k) plan that are based on the employee's elective contributions.

THE SIMPLE IRA

Portions of the following article entitled "Finally, A Retirement Plan Small Businesses Can Afford" by Jim Vonachen are reprinted with permission from McGraw Hill Companies, Inc.

"In the midst of tax season it's good to know there's something in the IRS code that's cause for celebration. It's the new, congressionally mandated SIMPLE-IRA plans. This fresh twist on the individual retirement account lets more small business owners save for their own — and their employees' — retirement while greatly increasing regulatory burdens that may have discouraged them in the past.

"Congress, of course, is gaga over acronyms, and it dubbed the Savings Incentive Matching Plan for Employees (SIMPLE) to signify the streamlined paperwork requirements for small businesses setting up these plans.

"While the SIMPLE regulations are easier and cheaper to digest than the previous rules, they are, alas, a product of Congress and the IRS, which means they're not that simple. To make the best use of them, it's helpful to trace their family tree.

"By now you've probably discovered the first rule of small business retirement planning: it's hard to do. That's mainly because of expense but also because of the IRS rules that govern so-called qualified plans like 401(k)s. (The term "qualified" simply means a plan conforms to specified limits on the amount business owners can contribute in comparison to their lowest paid employee.)

"Qualified plans, however, are by far the most lucrative way to save funds for retirement. The employer gets a tax deduction for money going into the plan, and both employees and employer-owners get to watch their contributions grow tax free.

"Aside from finding money to fund a qualified plan, small businesses have had to cope with:

♦ The cost of starting a plan, normally $1,000 to $2,000. Ongoing administrative changes can easily run more than $75 per employee, per year, since small employers typically hire an outside service to keep track of the plan.

♦ The additional cost and complexity of meeting the IRS's discrimination rules that determine if top management's saving options are unfairly generous compared to other employees'. The IRS-required start-up documentation often totals 50 to 75 pages.

♦ The cost of educating employees about the savings plans as well as the cost of completing annual IRS and labor department reports. Penalties are levied on companies that file improperly.

"Of course, larger employers can more easily absorb the costs and risks of these qualified plans. For them, annual administrative expenses can run as low as $25 per participant, which is three to four times less than the typical cost to small companies.

"The bottom line: For small-business owners to run a qualified plan they not only have to spend thousands of start-up dollars but they also must invest substantial time and money in recordkeeping, employee education, and government compliance. And this doesn't even include the actual cash contributions to employees' plans. In all, qualified plans demand a level of commitment few small businesses are capable of meeting.

"In the past, an alternative to qualified plans was the Simplified Employee Pension Plan (SEP) and a more recent variation — the SEP coupled with a Salary Reduction feature (SAR-SEP). With the SEP, an employer contributes up to 15% of a participant's total annual compensation to an individual retirement account. Using the SAR-SEP, the employees make contributions of their own pre-tax dollars.

"Although both of these plans were typically an improvement over the qualified plans, they both had significant drawbacks for many small employers. The SEP was entirely employee funded, and since the rules liberally defined who was an eligible employee (generally, those who made over $400 per year), the expense to small business was traditionally too high to maintain.

"The SAR-SEP was often referred to as the Poor Man's 401(k) for business owners, because using it, the owners could avoid the IRS "qualifying" costs. They did, however, have to meet some strict criteria before the SEP-SAR could start. Half of the eligible employees had to participate for the plan to take effect. And the government allowed only 25 eligible participants for each company.

Also, owners and highly compensated employees were allowed to set aside only 125% of the average salary deferral of their employees. Thus, if the employees saved an average of 4%, the owner could only put 5% into a personal plan. If the employees didn't contribute anything, the owner couldn't either.

Despite its complexities, the SAR-SEP was still much less complex than the 401(k). But as part of new tax laws, SAR-SEPs were discontinued as of December 31, 1996. Congress intends for the SIMPLE to replace the SAR-SEP, although existing SAR-SEPs can continue under the prior rules.

"Given this background — the complicated compliance rules and the fact that SEP and SAR-SEP plans were not attracting the participants Congress had hoped for — the lawmakers authorized the SIMPLE-IRA, a new form of the individual retirement account.

"Do not confuse the SIMPLE-IRA with the SIMPLE-401(k). Although they are similar in many respects, the SIMPLE-401(k) is not nearly as advantageous to the employer as the SIMPLE-IRA. Since the SIMPLE-401(k) must meet many of the same requirements as a traditional "qualified" 401(k), the cost is substantially higher to business owners.

"The first rule of the SIMPLE-IRA is to forget all of the rules for qualified and SEP plans. Qualified plans and SEPs are designed for the primary benefit and protection of employees. SIMPLE-IRA plans are designed for their benefit too, but offer employers much more discretion. Congress shifted the emphasis because it found small businesses were wary of the other plans' red tape. That virtually paralyzed their retirement offerings. Now, the qualified plans' discrimination tests are gone

The SIMPLE-IRA allows for employees (as well as the business owner) to place up to $6,000 of salary into an IRA account. Employees contribute pre-tax dollars, which lower their taxable income, and thus their income tax, just as would happen with a 401(k). Of course, once the funds are deposited into an IRA account, they are governed by most standing IRA rules. However, the early withdrawal penalty under SIMPLE-IRAs is 25% instead of the normal 10%. The 25% penalty does not apply in the case of death, disability, or withdrawals made after the age of 59½.

"Employers can save money for their own retirement plan regardless of whether employees do so or not. The maximum total amount per year is $12,000 — $6,000 of salary deferral plus a 3% match on a salary of $200,000 or more.

Technical Requirements for the Simple IRA

"Employees must be given 60 days each year to decide whether or not to participate in the plan. And to be an eligible sponsor of a SIMPLE-IRA, an employer must have had 100 or fewer employees receiving compensation of $5,000 or more each the preceding tax year. Once an employer has established a valid SIMPLE plan, he or she may generally be able to continue on the program for two more years even if the number of employees exceeds 100.

"There is no long-term fixed commitment on the behalf of an employer. Once started, the law only requires that the plan run for the entire calendar year, although it can be terminated the year after. Further, a plan document is required — either the six-page IRS *Form 5305, SIMPLE,* or a commercial provider's prototype document. This once-a-year filing is the only necessary IRS form.

"The SIMPLE-IRA must be offered to all employees who have received at least $5,000 of compensation in at least two prior years and those who expect to receive at least $5,000 of compensation in the current year. Note, these are minimum requirements. An employer can choose to lower cutoffs as well. As an employer, you can choose to exclude union employees, certain airline pilots, and nonresident aliens who receive non-U.S. source income from the plan and you cannot maintain any other active qualified plan or SEP plan while the SIMPLE-IRA is in existence. Keep in mind, employee salary deferrals are subject to Social Security and federal unemployment taxes.

"Once an employee has decided to participate in the SIMPLE-IRA, he or she can end participation at any time; though once an employee is dropped out of the plan, that individual cannot re-enter until the start of the next year. Also, an employer has the option of allowing participants to modify their salary deferrals during the course of the year. Thus, the employer could present the employee participants with the option of either terminating all participation in the plan or requiring employees to maintain a designated level of contributions.

"This flexibility only increases the plan's attractiveness to a small-business owner. Its main attraction, of course, is savings in administrative costs. Since start-up fees are minimal and employees' own contributions fund most of the savings, an employer can offer a means of retirement savings without going broke. Part of the plan, however, does require employers to contribute a small percentage to the employees' savings. The contribution can be either in the form of am employer match or an across-the-board contribution.

"The SIMPLE-IRA can be a very effective retirement vehicle for your small business. The pervasive marketing of plans by financial service companies — which will set up plans for you — makes them sound like the solution for every small business. That may not always be the case, but they do provide significant benefits to employers who want to reduce the cost of retirement programs while at the same time funding their own retirement.

CHAPTER SUMMARY

It can be argued that the most effective way to secure relief from your oppressive income tax liability is to contribute to a tax deductible retirement plan. In addition to the immediate tax savings, the contributor secures:

◆ The long-term benefit of having his or her investment compound and grow (tax free) all the way to retirement; and

◆ A program to set the stage for a continuing and systematic savings plan which he for she would ordinarily not adhere to.

Fortunately, for the small business owner, there are a number of options that may be considered to gain the best advantage. The options range from the most basic IRA to the most complex pension or profit sharing arrangement. Every small business owner should take a look at each of these options before deciding which makes the best sense in terms of the lowest cost to set up, the least amount of effort to operate, and the maximum tax savings.

Chapter 13

ESTATE PLANNING TIPS FOR THE SMALL BUSINESS OWNER

Perhaps the most overlooked area of tax planning by small business owners involves their own personal estate. Too often, entrepreneurs are eager to learn about the latest in income tax shelters and deferrals, but do nothing to protect themselves from the ultimate tax liability — the federal estate tax.

One reason for the lack of concern over potential estate tax problems is that small business owners often fail to acknowledge that their operating entity has a going concern value. In many cases, that prospective value may trigger a federal estate tax liability that they could have never possibly imagined.

Once the value of your estate passes a certain mark (currently $625,000), it's time to do some serious estate planning. This means your overall estate — life insurance included. The tax rate on those assets starts at 37% and can increase as high as 55%.

You heard it right — the federal estate tax rate (for some estates) can be downright catastrophic. For larger estates, the government actually can step in and take more than half of everything you own.

☞ **KEY OBSERVATION**

Most businesses have some fair market value attached to them as an operating entity. Even the simple sole proprietorship has some elements of intangible worth, including goodwill, copyrights, and patents. Although these items are not visible, they nevertheless have value and must be counted along with other assets shown on the company's books, such as inventory, equipment, and supplies. Remember, the overriding purpose is to determine the full market value of the business as a whole.

Whether you have a sole proprietorship or are involved in a partnership or corporation, know that your interest in the business is an asset for estate purposes. Should you die without a well-devised plan, a good portion of your assets will go to the government for taxes, rather than to your loved ones.

Remember, under ordinary circumstances, the IRS insists that estate taxes be paid upfront and in cash. There are no exceptions, unless certain circumstances exist. You may not claim that your estate includes business property and investments that cannot readily be converted into cash. Ordinarily, you must pay by cash no matter what kind of property you own.

HOW YOUR BUSINESS IS VALUED FOR ESTATE TAX PURPOSES

No set techniques for valuing going business concerns exist — whether the evaluation is needed to help you get a loan at the bank, or is to be used for estate planning purposes. Even if an expert does an appraisal, you, as owner-operator, have a better sense of what your business is really worth. You will want to provide the appraiser with all current offers, inventory lists, accounts receivable and payable, and any information on intangibles, such as goodwill.

The considerations for determining fair market value of a business are similar to those for determining the value of any individual business asset. The criteria used in a professional evaluation for the purchase of a business include the following observations.

♦ The prime reason for buying the business is to make money.

♦ The decision to purchase should only be made after you consider alternative places to invest your money.

♦ You need to look closely at the return on the investment and the risk factors involved.

Clearly, the job of appraising a closely held business is best handled by a financially well-versed professional, who also has first-hand experience in business matters. His/her attestation of value will be needed to support the valuation for your estate tax purposes.

Regardless of who does your business valuation, you must follow generally accepted procedures and guidelines if you expect the IRS to agree with the "bottom line."

A professional valuation will be driven by one or more of the following three factors:

1. **Assets.** With this guideline, the primary focus is on the value of the assets within the business.

2. **The income stream.** The value is based on the income stream that is generated in the ordinary course of business.

3. **Comparable sales.** Prime consideration is given to the sales of the same or similar types of businesses.

☞ KEY OBSERVATION

If you are looking to evaluate your business for estate planning purposes, remember that there is no one single method or approach. IRS and professional appraisers alike will accept any one valuation method, or a combination of the three methods. Often, the experts will strongly disagree. For example, some courts have applied an inordinate amount of weight to the income stream factor, while others have looked more closely at the other approaches.

Remember, when an independent valuation is made for your business, don't be shy about questioning the experts when that valuation appears to contradict your objectives. Your input as owner-operator may very well be key ingredients to the valuation.

Once you have gained a good sense of the value of your business operation, you could reasonably ascertain your overall net worth. With this, you will know your potential estate tax exposure.

A LOOK AT THE FEDERAL ESTATE AND GIFT TAX RULES

Each individual is entitled to a lifetime tax credit — a credit that allows one to give away, tax free, a certain amount of assets to family or loved ones. Put another way, the credit works by allowing a prescribed equivalent amount of assets to be transferred to others without paying any federal estate taxes.

And now, Congress finally has raised the familiar $600,000 exemption equivalent — an amount that seemed to have been carved in stone with no thought given to inflation and other real life factors. For years, estate planners had to keep a watchful eye on that $600,000 threshold amount while realizing that any accumulation of assets over that amount might trigger a heavy price to be paid by their family and loved ones. Now, thanks to the 1997 Taxpayer Relief Act, this lifetime exclusion has finally been raised — closer to reality — in the following phase-in formula.

For estates of persons dying, and gifts made, during:	The applicable exemption amount is:
1998	$625,000
1999	$650,000
2000 and 2001	$675,000
2002 and 2003	$700,000
2004	$850,000
2005	$950,000
2006 and thereafter	$1,000,000

All taxpayers are allowed to make further gift transfers of $10,000 to any donee each year without any accounting whatsoever. That means that you can give away $10,000 without using any portion of your lifetime phased-in allowance. If the donor happens to be married, a split gift provision in the rules can raise the annual exclusion to $20,000 per donee.

☞ KEY OBSERVATION

There is no limit on the number of those $10,000, or $20,000 tax-free transfers that can be made.

✎ PLANNING TIP

A married person, who makes the maximum tax-free transfer to a total of ten children and grandchildren, can give away $200,000 each year, or $20,000 multiplied by 10. Thus, none of the *lifetime* allowance is wasted and no taxes are due, if gifts up to this amount are given away each year.

$10,000 ANNUAL EXCLUSION IS ADJUSTED FOR INFLATION

Most people are aware that the old rule that allows one to transfer $10,000 free from lifetime gifts has been around forever. The $10,000 annual exclusion has long been a valuable planning tool for those who have been interested in gifting property to family members, thereby eliminating such transfers from estate/transfer taxes.

In spite of the value of this annual exclusion, many have begun to think that Congress didn't even know that inflation exists. This is because there has never been an interest in increasing the allowance to stay up with the times. After 1998, the $10,000 annual exclusion for gifts will be adjusted for inflation.

NEW ESTATE TAX RELIEF FOR SMALL BUSINESS OWNERS AFTER 1997

At long last, owners of many small family businesses are allowed relief from the oppressive estate tax after their death. In addition to the new increasing lifetime exemption Congress now permits a special tax break for qualified small business owners. For the most part, any interest in any form of business qualifies if it is in the United States and more than 50% of one's estate consists of the family-owned business. (There are different ownership requirements if there are more families that have an interest.)

How much can be excluded from taxability in one's estate? The amount excludable is based on a sliding scale. The allowance is, for most part, the lesser of: 1) the value of the business, or 2) the difference between $1.3 million and the applicable lifetime exclusion for that particular year. (Remember, the lifetime increases each year up to 2006.)

Illustration 13.1

♦ Mark Mayberry dies in 1998 when the lifetime exclusion from estate taxes is $625,000. His estate includes a qualified family business worth.

♦ The amount that can be excluded from Mark's estate is $675,000 ($1.3 million less $625,000).

♦ If the business were only worth $400,000, then the exclusion would be limited to $400,000 (the lesser amount).

⬚ *Special Note: After 1998, a new tax law provision will permit further tax-saving benefits by revising the formula for the* *exclusion for small businesses. After 1998, a full $675,000 exclusion may be allowed for certain businesses in future years regardless of the date of death.*

Illustration 13.2

♦ Toby, an unmarried man, is the owner of a small gift shop. (Note: His business is not qualified under the new law since its value is less than 50% of his estate.)

♦ He reviews his assets to determine if he needs to do any estate planning. The first draft of his net worth is

Cash and investments	$ 50,000
IRA's and annuities	100,000
Personal residence and misc. assets	300,000
Beach cottage	100,000
Net worth (no liabilities)	$550,000

♦ He is advised that the gift shop would also have a distinct value even in the event of his death. In light of this, Toby has it appraised for estate planning purposes.

♦ The valuation of the business is a startling $200,000, bringing his overall net worth to $750,000.

♦ After checking the 1998 estate tax rates, Toby learns that his potential estate tax liability could be as high as $46,250, or $248,300 minus the lifetime credit of $202,050.

♦ Toby is now prepared to take some aggressive estate planning measures that involve some gift transfers to his son, Ted.

To gain a better perspective of the relative impact of the tax as your estate increases in value, consider Toby's growing estate implications in the following illustration.

Illustration 13.3

♦ Toby decided to protect his son Ted's long-range needs, knowing he would not always be alive to help him manage the business affairs.

♦ He was advised to buy a balanced life insurance policy that would pay $250,000 to Ted in the event of his death.

♦ Toby learns that this action would raise his potential estate tax burden.

♦ Because insurance proceeds are normally included in your gross estate, Toby's estate is technically now worth $1 million. His potential estate tax on this amount is $143,750 and his new estate tax bracket is 41%.

☐ *Special Note: The potential tax liability increases in proportion to the size of your estate. Taxable estate or gift transfers can go as high as 55% when the transfers exceed $3 million. (Refer to sample of Form 706 Federal Estate Tax Return and corresponding estate tax rates located in Appendix C.)*

TWO ESTATE PLANNING OPTIONS FOR SMALL BUSINESS OWNERS

To get a feel of some of the major estate planning options available to the small business owner, know the alternatives that are available in cases like Toby's.

THE INSURANCE PLANNING ALTERNATIVE

Because of the added insurance policy, Toby (Illustration 13.3) increased his potential estate tax bill by another $97,500. He didn't realize that life insurance is taxable in the estate. To prevent this, he could arrange for his son Ted to purchase and maintain control of the insurance policy on his life. Further, a trust can be used to buy the policy. As long as Toby is not the direct owner of the policy, the policy proceeds are not taxed in his estate.

⬚ *Special Note: Although there are some minor risks involved under the current law, Toby could still get the insurance out of his estate by transferring ownership of the old policy to Ted at a later date. He could eliminate all risks by having Ted, or a trust, purchase a new policy instead.*

LIFETIME GIFT TRANSFERS BY SMALL BUSINESS OWNERS

Although there are several other estate planning options available to taxpayers, none are as effective as a sensible gift transfer plan. For Toby and other small business owners, a systematic gift plan involving the transfers of interests in the business to family each year can be most effective. Specifically, the gift transfers can serve several purposes.

♦ They provide a mechanism for including younger family members in the business operation.

♦ They lower income taxes by the process of income splitting.

♦ They remove a substantial portion of asset values from the small business owner's estate right now.

THE APPRECIATION FACTOR AND GIFT GIVING

The main reason that discerning estate planners make annual gift transfers is that they don't want a year to pass without availing themselves of the $10,000 tax-free allowance and $20,000 for married donees — to be adjusted for inflation after 1998.

Another advantage is found in the realization that whatever is currently given has the potential for significant appreciation in the future. The astute planner calculates factors like inflation and earning potential in determining the real tax savings.

If you give away $10,000 **in cash** today, you will literally extract no more than $10,000 from your overall estate. You might argue, however, that you have also extracted the interest that you might have made on those funds had they stayed in a bank account over the years.

Keep in mind, if you make a gift of an asset with **strong growth potential** you are actually doing some creative planning. Consider the tax shelter if you transfer, to your son or daughter, assets like:

♦ An interest in high growth business real estate, or

♦ A portion of a small business operation that is destined to increase in value over the years.

☞ KEY OBSERVATION

There are always potential risks when you give **anything** of value, and it no longer remains under your management and control. Theoretically, individuals like Toby (Illustrations 13.2 and 13.3) could continue to make gift transfers of up to $10,000 every year, and eventually eliminate their entire potential estate tax liability. However, there are considerations that are more important than implementing a clever estate planning program.

First, questions of control of the business need to be asked, as greater portions of the business are relinquished to a younger, less experienced, family member. Second, be aware of legal exposure that may develop as these younger family members are allowed to own a significant portion of **your** hard-earned business.

Clearly, these are important issues that must be addressed by competent legal counsel before you give away too much of your business in your zeal to save estate taxes.

Be aware of the negative aspects of excessive gift giving to your children and other family members. Be aware that enormous estate tax consequences could take a toll on your hard-earned assets if no action is taken at all.

When you start looking at a 37% or even a 55% federal tax bite, consider some aggressive estate planning action. There are several legitimate, yet complex alternatives that you could discuss with your advisers. However, one of the most sensible starting points is to devise a well-thought-out gift plan — one that involves the transfer of interests in business property. (Refer to sample *Form 709 Federal Gift Tax Return* in Appendix C.)

TAKE POSITIVE ACTION FOR FEDERAL ESTATE PLANNING PURPOSES

There are many taxes to be saved by income splitting with other family members who are in lower tax brackets. You can transfer assets out of your name through gift, loan, or sale. If those assets are the types that produce income, the instant result is lower income taxes for everyone. See the following chapter for more on family planning income tax strategies.

When outright gifts of business property are made to younger family members, major tax savings result. This involves the federal estate tax liability which, in some cases, could be as much as half the value of your entire estate.

Illustration 13.4

♦ Bud is a 67-year-old widower who owns a small hardware store recently valued at $200,000. (Note: Bud's business is not a qualified business under the new law.) He operates as a sole proprietorship.

♦ The value of his overall estate exceeds $600,000. In December, he plans to transfer part interest in the business to his son, Joe.

♦ Unfortunately, interests in sole proprietorships are not readily transferable.

♦ Although Bud wants to bring Joe into the business before the end of the year, he must consider other measures.

Q. What steps could Bud take to facilitate the transfer of a portion of the business to his son, Joe?

A. Bud could possibly reorganize his business into a family corporation, or even a partnership. With these kinds of entities, he would have the tools to effectively transfer business interests to other parties.

⬭ *Special Note: There is a tax-free provision in the tax law that permits sole proprietors to transfer their business assets to a newly formed corporation. In general terms, this provision is permitted when the same owner is at least an 80% shareholder of the newly formed corporation.*

INCORPORATING: A SIMPLE AND EFFECTIVE SOLUTION

If your small business is operating as a family corporation, you can begin a systematic gift transfer program. By giving shares of stock to family members over a period of time, you can methodically shift large portions of the business to shelter it from the IRS. With a corporate entity, you need not worry about re-titling the underlying business assets every time a transfer occurs. Except for an attorney-drafted corporate resolution, all you need to do is sign over the shares and record the same in the stock transfer record. This applies to both the ordinary C corporation and S corporation status.

Remember, with the flexibility of a corporation you can arrange a systematic plan to vary the number of transferred shares so that little, if any, gift transfer taxes are paid.

Illustration 13.5

♦ Margaret is married and is the sole owner of a corporation that operates a small business. Its value has measurably increased over the years.

♦ In line with her estate planning goal, Margaret begins transferring shares to her three sons. Her goal is to relinquish the entire business to her sons and avoid estate and gift taxes.

♦ During the first year, and each year thereafter, Margaret transfers enough shares to each son to equal the annual exclusion of $20,000 for married persons.

♦ Over a few years, at $60,000 per year, the entire business can be transferred to the sons — completely tax free!

✎ PLANNING TIP

The transfer of a small number of shares to new family shareholders can sometimes save income taxes by income splitting. Future dividends from the corporation can be directed to the lower brackets of the new shareholders. If you will operate your business as an S corporation, you can save income taxes by dividing some of the profits with the younger shareholders as if they were partners. Remember, S corporations are taxed in the same manner as partnerships.

Each time you elect to make a gift transfer of stock in a small business corporation, first know the full fair market value of the overall corporation. To know the true value of the shares given away, you must have an appraisal.

Keep in mind, the IRS is interested in knowing if the shares that you give away are actually worth what you claim. If it is later determined that those shares were worth more at the time of the gift, you might owe unanticipated gift taxes. Further, you might waste a portion of your *lifetime* exclusion of $625,000 up to $1,000,000. Therefore, it is important that you have a competent professional prepare a valuation of the business each time a gift transfer is made.

✎ PLANNING TIP

When you value a minority interest in a small corporation, you may be allowed to discount the value of those shares for gift tax purposes. Minority shareholders do not have any real control over corporate management. Further, their shares cannot be readily sold to outside parties. Remember to inquire about this discount, which can easily enhance your estate planning efforts. That discounted value may easily permit you to give away significantly more shares tax free.

A TOUGH DECISION: GIVING UP CONTROL OF THE BUSINESS

By far, the toughest decision that the small business owner has to face when relinquishing shares of stock is the loss of control. For this reason, many corporate operators **never** give more than 49% of the voting stock of the corporation.

Anxiety about turning over control is also heightened when the prospective donees are younger and less experienced family members. You may think that your young son or daughter is capable of managing the transferred income from the operation, but not the business operation itself. With this kind of thinking, many business owners make an effort to transfer corporate stock while retaining the voting rights.

Whether you have a regular C or an S corporation, voting rights allow control. There are several ways to retain your voting rights. All are subject to IRS scrutiny, which may claim that a true ownership in the business has not truly been given to your son or daughter. In spite of your efforts, the entire corporation may be taxed in your estate.

Q. How can voting rights be retained while I transfer stock to my young son or daughter?

A. There are several ways this can be done, however all are subject to the risk that the IRS will later try to claim that a true ownership in the business has not been given to your son or daughter. In these cases, the entire corporation may be taxed in your estate in spite of your efforts.

Probably the safest way to transfer stock and retain voting rights is to transfer the shares to a trust for the benefit of your son or daughter and reserve the right to vote the shares under the trust agreement.

◌ *Special Note: An experienced attorney is essential to help ensure that a qualified "arms-length" trust agreement is in place.*

USE A PARTNERSHIP TO PASS BUSINESS INTERESTS TO FAMILY MEMBERS

Although the corporation is the most flexible vehicle for transferring business interests to other individuals, some business owners prefer other methods. For example, you may not want the extra paperwork or the extra fees that accompany the administration of corporate activities.

On the other hand, many experts feel that the use of a partnership to transfer business interests can be even more costly and a more cumbersome approach. Instead of signing over a few shares of stock each year with a corporation, you might incur a variety of extra costs and administrative steps. These include revising partnership agreements and the allocations of income among the respective partners. In spite of its potential downsides, the partnership is still regarded by many to be a viable alternative for family tax planning.

☞ KEY OBSERVATION

If you decide to take the partnership route, be aware of several hazards when transferring business interests to family members. Specifically, those family members will not be viewed as the legitimate owners of the partnership interests, if the donor retains any power over the transferred interests.

Illustration 13.6

♦ For tax planning purposes, Frank makes some systematic gift transfers of partnership interests to his son, Sherman, and his daughter, Diane.

♦ Frank is warned to avoid the following:

♦ A partnership agreement that places full management powers in Frank with no limitations or restrictions.

♦ Power given to control the distributions of partnership income to remain with Frank.

♦ Full control given over certain assets essential to the partnership business is Frank's.

♦ Restriction on Sherman or Diane from selling or liquidating their interests in the partnership.

♦ Any one of these circumstances can cause the donees to be viewed by the IRS as bogus partners in the business. If that assertion is upheld, then the donor's gift giving plan will have been for naught.

♦ Frank's income splitting plan will be foiled, and the entire business will be taxed in his estate at 100% of the fair market value.

You should inquire about the increasingly popular "family limited partnership," which can provide a greater degree of flexibility for your gift transfer plan

SMALLER ESTATES

As a small business owner, you may find it highly unlikely that your overall estate will ever reach the $625,000 to $1,000,000 marks. Is it still a good idea, then, to start transferring portions of the business to your children under a methodical gift plan. Without a federal estate tax liability with which to contend, there is not much tax incentive to start making gift transfers. However, there are some less important issues that you should know, including:

♦ Probate requirements;

♦ Inheritance and state assessments that may be required by the state in which you reside; and

♦ Income tax saving potential

As a small business owner, you may not foresee your overall estate ever reaching the $625,000 to $1,000,000 marks. You may ask yourself, "Is it still a good idea to start transferring portions of my business to my children under a methodical gift plan?"

Most states have an interest in the estates of those who die while residing in their jurisdiction. The amount of tax on estate property, however, is minimal — at least when compared to the federal estate tax schedule. In many states, for example, there is an inheritance tax, which is as low as 1%.

Because of the comparatively low tax cost, many feel that the only real concern is probate administration. In simple terms, any assets that are owned by a decedent must go through a formal administration process. In addition to some prescribed fees, the process usually requires the estate assets be inaccessible for an unspecified period of time. During this period, the state takes steps to ensure that creditors and legal heirs are given proper consideration.

The threat of probate administration causes many small business owners to take aggressive steps to spare their loved ones from what they feel is an insidious, bureaucratic intrusion. On the other hand, some experts feel that there is too much over-reaction in this regard. In fact, tax experts find that aggressive action can sometimes do more harm than good.

Although debate in this area continues, you may want to consider the following example to help you decide if you should give away business interests when **federal** estate tax is not an issue.

Illustration 13.7

♦ Melvin, a 63-year-old, had a successful landscaping business, which recently was appraised at $250,000.

♦ His only other assets consisted of some stocks, bonds, and a few personal belongings. He figured his entire net worth could not exceed $350,000 and no federal estate tax would be due.

♦ Although he was not yet ready to retire, Melvin wanted to take some aggressive estate planning steps and started relinquishing ownership of the business to his son, Mike.

♦ Melvin was concerned about the probate administration of his estate. In fact, he became very concerned after hearing rumors about government intervention through probate and inheritance taxes.

♦ Melvin proceeded to relinquish ownership of the entire business to Mike within a one-year period. Melvin then took on the role as a consultant to the corporation.

♦ Melvin eliminated all potential estate tax problems.

Remember, his federal estate was well below $625,000 to $1,000,000 and not subject to federal tax. More important, Melvin gained assurance that when he dies, his son would not have to deal with outrageous probate costs and inheritance taxes. In his mind, Melvin had beaten the system. Take a closer look at Melvin's so-called rewards.

◆ He gained nothing under the federal rules since neither he nor his estate would have had to deal with federal gift or estate taxes anyway.

◆ Melvin's idea of state intervention and subjection to death taxes was distorted. Depending on his state, the inheritance tax would probably be $3,500 (assuming a 1% tax rate). In addition, there might be another $3,500 in attorney and accountant fees for handling probate matters. His only reward is that he probably saved his estate about $7,000 in out-of-pocket costs by giving away the business in a *lifetime* transfer.

In reality, the alleged hazard that his estate would have undergone is, in fact, a relatively simple process. In most cases, the estate's representatives are free to ensure that business is carried on as usual.

The biggest and most obvious risk to Melvin is having an inexperienced family member in control of the business operation. Melvin has won nothing if Mike loses the entire business. You must ask yourself, "Is that kind of risk worth saving only a few thousand dollars and some administrative duties?"

Often, small business owners hasten to relinquish control over assets to save what some consider to be an insignificant tax obligation. This adds to the psychological trauma associated with the possibility of death taxes and probate that sometimes moves individuals to create more risks than rewards.

☞ KEY OBSERVATION

The decision to transfer any kind of business assets to your children is not something that you should view lightly. Regardless of the size of the estate, always consult a capable attorney about the potential risks and exposure to the family's assets, when those assets are placed outside of your control. Find out what could happen to those assets if the donee(s) run into problems of their own, such as lawsuits, divorce, or bankruptcy. Remember, once the assets are legally relinquished, the process is irreversible.

MARRIED COUPLES ENJOY THE *BY-PASS TRUST*

Remember, the general rule is that **all** estates are subject to the federal estate tax when the estate value exceeds $625,000 to $1,000,000. However, the tax does not apply when the estate assets are directly passed to a surviving spouse. This special tax relief provision is known as the unlimited marital deduction.

With married couples, the estate tax problem only becomes a concern when the surviving spouse eventually dies. With no spouse remaining to pass assets, there is no marital deduction; hence, the regular tax will apply.

To avoid this tax crunch, seek advice about a *by-pass trust*. If you are married, ask how this special trust provision might enable you to shelter up to an additional $625,000 to $1,000,000 in your estate planning program.

Illustration 13.8

♦ Richard owned a business worth $625,000 and his wife Marcia had various investments that were also worth $625,000. Their total net worth is $1.25 million.

♦ After Richard dies, the business is placed in a trust with income to be paid to Marcia for the remainder of her life. Upon her death, the income from the trust will continue for their children.

♦ Marcia dies in 1998, leaving the only asset in her name valued at $625,000. The other $625,000 value attached to the business passes her estate tax free, since it was not an asset for which she had direct control.

♦ Through a common *by-pass trust*, neither Richard nor Marcia paid any tax. Neither estate exceeded the lifetime allowance of $625,000. Thus, the entire $1.25 million in assets is free from estate taxes.

CHARITABLE TRUSTS: A BENEFIT TO BOTH PARTIES

Through a variety of charitable trusts, business owners can get a significant tax break by helping their favorite charity. The key is to follow a plan that allows an immediate tax deduction for certain business property or investments placed in trust. The income from the property is paid to you for life and then the proceeds are simply transferred over to the charity.

Illustration 13.9

♦ Rosa, a 69-year-old, places $50,000 worth of stock into an annuity trust. The trust will pay her 6% for life, or $3,000 per year.

♦ After her death, the balance in the account goes to Community Hospital.

♦ The original cost of the stock is $10,000.

♦ Rosa gets an immediate, upfront tax deduction for the stock, plus she is spared from reporting the capital gains on the increase in value.

♦ Since the ultimate beneficiary is a charitable entity, there is no estate tax with which to reckon.

There are numerous possibilities for gaining immediate tax advantages when working with business and investment properties that ultimately might be directed to go to qualified charities. In fact, your own family-operated business might qualify for this effective tax-saving maneuver.

Because of the costs and administrative problems associated with this highly technical area, associate with a charitable institution that can provide financial expertise on this procedure. Of course, use your own professional advisers to review any documents or contracts.

CHAPTER SUMMARY

It is all too common for the small entrepreneur to pay meticulous attention to various tax-saving options for business owners while overlooking what may be the most unwelcome tax bite of all — the final estate tax. The estate tax could be a major concern for many and (with a tax rate reaching as high as 55%) it could prove to be downright catastrophic if too much net worth is accumulated.

Some are surprised to learn that the going concern value of one's business operation needs to be included in the gross taxable estate — notwithstanding the value of the actual assets owned by the company. This business valuation too often sets the stage for an unwelcome tax bite upon the owner's death. Now, thanks to new tax reform, smaller operators will be given a substantial break which will enable more of their hard-earned assets to go to their loved ones instead of to unnecessary estate taxes. This break comes in the form of an increased lifetime exemption for all taxpayers and a special break for the owners of relatively small business operations.

In addition to the tax-saving benefits in the revised tax law, most business owners can gain even more estate tax relief with estate planning maneuvers that include:

♦   Tax sheltered life insurance plans; or

♦   The establishment of certain kinds of business entities that facilitate the transfer of interests in the business to certain family members or loved ones.

Make sure you read the following chapter to learn more about transferring assets to your family members.

Chapter 14

UNDERSTAND FAMILY PLANNING TAX STRATEGIES

In addition to the potential estate planning advantages when you shift income and assets to other family members, there are a number of income tax savings advantages as well.

Tax savings are clearly available to small business owners who shift business ownership and business income from their higher tax bracket, to the lower brackets of other family members. In previous years, taxpayers didn't use this tax-saving tactic for three reasons.

1. There weren't enough tax savings to make it worth the effort. The difference between the parents' and the children's tax rates is usually too small to generate an overall significant tax savings.

2. Too many feared loss of control when turning over the ownership of assets to younger, less experienced family members.

3. Many feared the IRS's repercussions for maneuvering with such an aggressive tax-shelter procedure.

Each one of these is a legitimate issue. However, the facts are often distorted and can sometimes be considered downright myths.

CAN YOU SAVE ENOUGH TAXES BY SPLITTING INCOME?

Whether you operate as a corporation, a partnership, an LLC, or a sole proprietorship, the final measure of savings will directly depend on your current **individual** tax rate. (To better understand your individual rate, refer back to Chapter 1.)

All business owners, at one time or another, have to account for business profits on their personal tax returns. If enough disparity exists between the income and tax bracket of one family member and that of another, there could be an opportunity to save significant tax dollars. The only way to be certain of this is to check your tax brackets and run a computation. **Remember, the strategy does not work between husband and wife.**

Illustration 14.1

♦ Small business owner, Eileen has been relegated to the 28% tax bracket by the current tax law.

♦ She determines that her 19-year-old son, Mike, is currently in the 15% bracket now and will remain there for a number of years.

♦ Legally, she manages to allocate $10,000 of business profits for the year to Mike instead of herself for that year.

♦ Eileen generates a tax savings of $1,300. Because of her strategic planning, the family will owe $1,500 on this part of the profit instead of $2,800.

☞ KEY OBSERVATION

Other taxpayers may now face a 39.6% tax bite under the new law. For these taxpayers, the need to evaluate the tax savings through family income splitting is of critical importance.

If Eileen (Illustration 14.1) had reached that top bracket, her overall savings would have been $2,460 on the $10,000 distribution. In other words, she would have a $1,500 tax instead of $3,960.

Clearly, there is a potential to gain measurable savings in income taxes by shifting income from owner-operators to other family members. To gain these savings there are two ways that the income is legitimately shifted.

First, pay the family member(s) a salary or fee for services. Keep records of each individual's work, withhold the appropriate taxes, and issue a *W-2*.

Second, share some of the profits. Make a gift transfer of a part of the business to the family member(s) so that they can share in the profits of the operation. The easiest way to accomplish this is to operate as a corporation. A corporation readily facilitates the transfer of ownership of shares back and forth between family members. Another alternative is to use a partnership in which partnership units of ownership may be transferred to other family members.

THE FICA TAX

Throughout the years, the added burden of Social Security tax was not a major factor in evaluating the benefits of income splitting. Today, with the increase of the FICA tax rates, a completely different strategy may be required.

Under the current rate, wages paid to an individual require a 7.65% tax to be paid by that individual. In addition, the employer needs to match that payment bringing the overall cost to a whopping 15.3%. For the most part, the FICA tax bite applies to $68,400 in earnings. A small fraction of additional tax continues for Medicare beyond the $68,400 limit.

With an additional 15.3% tax, reevaluate the income splitting alternative. Consider Eileen from Illustration 14.1 who is now looking to distribute $10,000 to her 19-year-old son, Mike, to generate healthy tax savings. If she were to make a **salary** payment to Mike, requiring FICA taxes, then the planned savings are drastically reduced.

Whether Eileen operates as a sole proprietorship, a corporation, or a partnership has a major significance on the end result. Study each of the following scenarios and find out which will generate your desired tax savings.

SPLITTING INCOME AS A SOLE PROPRIETORSHIP

If you operate your small business as a sole proprietorship, the easiest way that you could distribute income to your teenagers is to simply put them to work. If your teenager works for you for a few hours after school and on weekends on a regular basis, you can:

♦ Deduct the costs of the teenager's salary. To do this, keep adequate time records and be prepared to show that the reasonable amount of paid salary was an *ordinary and necessary* cost of doing business.

♦ Get a special bonus. This is available because a son or daughter, employed by a parent's unincorporated business, is exempt from Social Security until age 18. When you pay a minor child out of your sole proprietorship, the exemption will apply.

Illustration 14.2

♦ Eileen, operating her business as a sole proprietorship, is in the 28% tax bracket, while her son Mike pays 15%.

♦ The $10,000 paid to Mike is in the form of salary payments.

♦ Because of the special rule for sole proprietorships dealing with salaries paid to a son or daughter under age 18, Mike's wages are exempt from FICA tax.

♦ Thus, the $1,300 tax savings on the salary payment is not offset by the burden of an added FICA tax.

Q. Does this mean that the only way I could beat the FICA tax dilemma by using my minor aged children is to pay them through a sole proprietorship?

A. Interestingly, the special exemption also applies to partnerships that pay children under age 18 when both partners happen to be the parents of those children. For ordinary C or S status corporations, however, the full 15.3% Social Security tax will apply.

THE KIDDIE TAX

Income splitting is a cost effective and perfectly legitimate planning tool for saving income taxes if you play by the rules. However, one rule you must follow involves what is known as the kiddie tax. The kiddie tax primarily applies to investment income over $1,400 earned by minor aged children. The key is that such income is taxed at the parent's top tax rate rather than the child's. Clearly, this special tax was created by Congress to discourage income splitting between parents and their minor children.

How does the well-known kiddie tax fit into this discussion on family tax planning strategies and income splitting? You probably don't want to go through the time and effort of shifting income to a lower income family member and pay at the same high rate. The following observations will help you plan around the penalty provisions of the kiddie tax.

♦ The penalizing provisions of the kiddie tax only apply to minor children who are under age 14. You might consider splitting income with older children or else wait until a certain child reaches the prescribed age.

♦ Since the special tax only applies to investment income, be careful that you don't distribute too much income in the form of interest, dividends, rents, and profits on sales of property. Remember, once the child receives $1,400 in income from these sources, the tough kiddie tax rules apply.

♦ Wages paid to your minor children are not subject to the kiddie tax and could be ignored in an effort to split income.

✎ PLANNING TIP

You can enjoy significant tax savings by splitting income with other family members, particularly with your own children. Further, there is practically no risk involved when the income splitting comes is the result of salary payments that are properly documented.

On the other hand, when you seek to split income by transferring ownership in your business, you'll face an important organizational change, requiring that you carefully play by the rules.

♦ First, you are giving up a legal interest in your business entity; thus, you should ask your attorney to check the legal issues surrounding this action.

♦ Second, you are changing the ground rules for tax reporting purposes. The IRS is notified that you are sharing the profits of your business entity with your son, daughter, or another close family member. Your strategic action will create a generous tax savings, and there is nothing the IRS can do if you have the appropriate legal documentation.

☞ KEY OBSERVATION

> The S corporation, like the partnership, is a convenient device for sharing the ordinary profits of the business with other family members. In many cases, it's as simple as signing over a few shares of stock to those individuals.

Also, S corporations and partnerships ordinarily do not pay taxes on generated income. Instead, an information report is filed at the end of the year to identify the individual partners or shareholders who share in the profits. With this information, the IRS is notified of the income amount that is taxable by each of the new owner-participants.

A CHECKLIST OF STRATEGIC FAMILY PLANNING TIPS

✓ **Try to make your gift transfers tax free.**

If you give your son or daughter a small interest in your business — say some stock or a partnership unit — try to get an independent estimate of the value of the business. This will help you prove the value of the portion given away. Your child won't have to report this value as income, but you may be required to file a gift tax return if the amount is over $10,000 in any one year. Keep in mind, that filing a gift tax return doesn't necessarily mean that you will have to pay any gift taxes. In many cases, such filing is nothing more than a mere formality.

✓ **Be careful about giving your children a partnership interest if they are still minors.**

Children of minor age are not recognized as partners unless they are competent enough to manage their own property. If not, the control over the partnership unit must be given to a fiduciary or custodian for the benefit of the minor. The safest approach is to set up a trust to hold the partnership interest for that child.

⬭ *Special Note: When you pass control of a portion of the business to a trust, you must show that you, as a general partner, are not trying to exert ownership rights over the transferred share. The IRS may check the terms of the trust to ensure that this isn't the case.*

✓ **The kind of partnership that you have can make a difference in splitting income.**

Shifting income with partnership interests usually is not a problem when capital is not a material income-producing factor in the business. However, if yours is a service oriented business, such as real estate, insurance, or accounting, then a gift of a partnership interest is inappropriate. The only way the partnership can split the profits with another family member is by that individual actually performing services for the partnership. Be careful about transferring stock in your S corporation to your minor children. If you wish to transfer stock in your S corporation to your minor aged child you face problems, unless you have that stock put into a special trust for the benefit of the child. A sub-chapter S trust can be used for this purpose. Keep in mind, failure to use a qualified trust can cause your S status to be revoked.

✓ **Make sure that the income splitting of your S corporation has a sound basis.**

The IRS likes to check the method of splitting up profits by S corporations when family members are involved. For these purposes, the term family includes spouses, parents, grandparents, children, and trusts for the benefit of such persons. For example, if one relative of an S corporation shareholder performs substantial services without receiving reasonable pay or interest for capital contributions, a disproportionate share of income will pass through to other shareholders. This will create a significant tax savings, because the income will be split up with lower bracket shareholders; the IRS may question this. Most likely, the IRS will re-calculate the income to be distributed to each of the shareholders. Then proper credit is given for the compensation and interest that initially **should have been** paid to the higher bracket shareholders.

CHAPTER SUMMARY

If you are the owner of a small business operation and you have a family member who has a smaller income (and a lower tax bracket) you may want to evaluate the possibility of transferring a small portion of the business to him or her. The purpose: to split some of the net income earned and to lower the overall tax bill by having it taxed at a lower rate. Before you take a step, however, you need to calculate the tax savings by: 1)comparing your marginal tax brackets; 2)checking the impact of the FICA tax; and, 3) determining if the so-called *kiddie tax* for minors could thwart your tax-saving efforts.

If you determine that you could save taxes by transferring a portion of your business to a family member, you need to determine what kind of business entity would provide the best vehicle for this purpose. That transfer should be accompanied by the least amount of cost and/or gift taxes.

Chapter 15

KEEP CURRENT ON THE LATEST TAX-SAVING TRENDS AND IDEAS

During the past several years, Congress has enacted a myriad of IRS code provisions that have been specifically designed to provide additional tax breaks for the small business owner. Many of these provisions are quite revolutionary in that they manifest a reform mentality of a Congress that is not afraid to change certain tax law concepts that have been with us forever.

Many of these new loopholes and enhancements have already been discussed throughout other chapters in this book, however there are other issues that need recognition. It is impossible to define each and every tax-saving benefit in the law. However, an attempt has been made to identify those that are new along with those that appear to spark a continuing interest among a large segment of small business operators in recent years.

EXPENSING OPTIONS: A WELCOME RELIEF FOR MANY

Even the most unsophisticated business owners are keenly aware of the seemingly restrictive rules on depreciation. In short, they lay out money for certain business assets (that have a presumed life expectancy) and the government tells them how much, and when, they will get their coveted tax deduction.

Because of a special tax code section (written for the small business owner) there is instant relief when certain business equipment is purchased. The popular "Section 179" deduction has long been around to grant this special deduction. And now, its benefits have been enhanced even further.

Eligible personal property used in a trade or business can generally be expensed in the very first year that it is purchased. The maximum amount that can be expensed under this tax-friendly code section is outlined below.

Amount	Year
$18,000	1997
$18,500	1998
$19,000	1999
$20,000	2000
$24,000	2001 or 2002
$25,000	2003 and thereafter

☐ *Special Note: The special deduction will be reduced if the taxpayer places in service business equipment in excess of $200,000. Also, the deduction cannot be more than the taxable income from the trade or business.*

CAPITAL GAINS TIPS

For most, the only remaining advantage of selling investment property is that the amount of the actual capital gains tax cannot exceed 20%. For many investors, however, that is still a high price to pay especially when they might be required to pay a state tax as well. It may seem unfair to exact such a price on small business owners who have not only risked their capital, but tied it up for lengthy periods as well.

Illustration 15.1

♦ Mabel, a retired widow, owns a piece of rental property, which she purchased 20 years ago to help supplement her retirement needs.

♦ Although her tax basis is only $100,000, she now plans to sell the property for $300,000, a gain of $200,000.

♦ She is advised that her $200,000 gain is subject to the 20% capital gains tax and a state tax as well.

♦ Mabel realizes that she stands to lose nearly one-fourth of that gain to taxes, or $50,000.

♦ Now that she has $50,000 (with no adjustment made for depreciation) less to place in fixed yield investments, Mabel is hard pressed to meet her retirement income goal.

To solve her problem, Mabel could consider arranging an *installment sale* that would allow her extra leeway by deferring the tax and paying the capital gains tax in smaller amounts as the note payment is received. This *installment sale* approach would keep her money working at full value.

Instead of taking cash in full payment for her property, Mabel agrees to take a down payment and a note requiring monthly payments with 8% interest. During the first year, Mabel receives $21,000 toward her principal. In this scenario, she is only required to report $14,000 even though she had a $200,000 profit, or $21,000 multiplied by two-thirds of her profit percentage, or $200,000 divided by $300,000 equals 66%. If Mabel is against paying any upfront capital gains tax at all, she might consider a *tax-free exchange*.

ANOTHER SENSIBLE SOLUTION – *TAX-FREE EXCHANGES*

Frustrated investors are looking more closely at the *tax-free exchange* alternative as they argue that any capital gains tax at all on their long-term investments is both oppressive and unnecessary.

HOW THE TAX-FREE EXCHANGE ALTERNATIVE WORKS

Generally, you are not required to report a taxable gain when business or investment property is exchanged for *like kind* business or investment property.

The term *like kind* refers to the nature or character of the property — not to its grade or quality. To get a better sense of how you can qualify for this definition, take a look at one of the most common types of **investment** property used with this planning loophole — real estate. When one kind of investment real estate is traded for another, the capital gains tax is fully deferred.

With this broad definition, note the wide variety of real estate exchanges that could qualify for this special treatment. Some examples of tax-free exchanges are:

♦ A rental house traded for an apartment building;

♦ Land traded for a building;

♦ Farm land for city lots; and

♦ Certain leasehold interests exchanged for outright ownership in realty.

Illustration 15.2

♦ Instead of selling her rental house outright, Mabel (Illustration 15.1) decides to trade the property for a real estate investment that generates a higher cash flow.

♦ Remember, she needs that extra income stream for her retirement budget.

♦ After locating an attractive small commercial building, she arranges for the potential buyer of the rental house to place a contract on the building and then make a trade with her.

♦ Mabel meets the prescribed deadlines for the property transfers and successfully acquires a new investment property without paying any taxes. The $50,000 in taxes is fully deferred.

☛ KEY OBSERVATION

If cash is received in a *tax-free exchange*, you may have to report some capital gain to the extent of the cash received.

Although the capital gains tax may seem confiscatory to many, there are those who will find a relative tax savings in the maximum 20% capital gains rate prescribed in the current law.

Q. What should higher income earners look for in investments when trying to take advantage of the relatively lower capital gains rate of 20%?

A. One planning idea favors making investments that are geared toward appreciation, rather than those that generate high rents, dividends, and interest. The latter types of income are taxed at the ordinary rates. On the other hand, a long-term investment in real estate, growth securities, or certain small business corporations can qualify you to take advantage of the lower capital gains rate limited to 20%. Surely this is a better option than paying 31%, 36%, or 39.6%.

INCENTIVE STOCK OPTIONS – ANOTHER ATTRACTIVE STRATEGY FOR SECURING THE CAPITAL GAIN ADVANTAGE

Incentive Stock Options (ISOs) are popular devices used by corporations to provide shareholders with special rights to acquire stock. When qualified options are exercised, the employee has no tax liability. If the stock acquired with the option is held for a certain period of time, a major portion of any gain realized will get favorable capital gain treatment. Because of the capital gain advantage under the new tax rates, it is easy to see why the ISOs are becoming increasingly attractive to higher income taxpayers.

MEDICAL EXPENSE: SPECIAL BREAK FOR SOLE PROPRIETORS

Everyone is aware how tough it is for any individual to get a tax deduction for any kind of medical expenses. Because of the tough threshold requirement, you need to spend a small fortune in medical expenses to be eligible for any benefit whatsoever. Small business owners had found a way around this problem by forming a regular corporation.

In Chapter 3, it was shown that the ordinary corporation could provide a convenient way to beat the threshold requirement and get a full deduction. All that is needed is a corporate medical benefit plan for employees. Forming a corporation had become a popular solution, particularly because of the devastating increase in medical insurance premiums.

Now, as a result of the latest tax law updates, some might not have to go through the cost and effort of forming a corporation to get a write-off for those sky-rocketing health insurance premiums (see Chapter 3). Many self-employed individuals are now getting a realistic break for the amount paid for medical insurance for the entire family without incorporating.

Starting in 1998, a revised program allows a self-employed individual to deduct 45% of the amount paid for the insurance. Then, this percentage is slated to rise in incremental stages all the way up to 100% in 2007. Yes, by 2007 you won't need to form a corporation just to get the full fringe benefit of that important tax write-off for medical insurance premiums.

PASSIVE LOSS RELIEF FOR REAL ESTATE PROFESSIONALS

Those small business owner-operators and investors who have been involved in real estate are well aware of the restrictive passive loss rules that have been around since 1986. Under these tough rules, anybody that incurs a loss in a business that was deemed to be a *passive activity* is not allowed to write off the loss of that business against other income. However, there is an exception allowing up to $25,000 in rental losses when your income is below $150,000.

The *passive activities* that are subject to the restriction on tax write-offs generally include any business in which the owner-operator does not materially participate. Unfortunately, for many real estate investors, rental activities are treated as *passive activity* regardless of the amount of material participation.

Illustration 15.3

♦ · Janet earns $300,000 per year as a planning consultant.

♦ She also owns several rental properties.

♦ Last year the properties generated a $40,000 loss.

♦ The rental loss is not deductible from her consulting income because it is passive.

After 1993, special relief from the passive loss rules is extended to taxpayers who devote more than half their time to the real estate business. Because of the new law, taxpayers can now get a tax write-off for businesses involving real estate activities if:

♦ The taxpayer can show that more than half of the personal services performed are real estate activities; and

♦ The taxpayer performs more than 750 hours of service during the year carrying on a real estate trade or business.

AMORTIZATION OF GOODWILL

This recently revised provision in the law is a welcome tax break to many **new** business owners. For many years, controversy existed between the IRS and taxpayers over the tax implications of goodwill in a newly acquired business. The IRS's position has been clear and unrelenting. Goodwill simply was not allowed as a deduction, because the tax law does not allow a deduction for an intangible asset that doesn't have a fixed useful life in a trade or business.

Nearly every individual who purchased a business that is currently in operation has a goodwill issue for which to be concerned. Whether or not the purchase price was properly allocated on the books of new business owners has been the subject of debate by the IRS for many years.

Illustration 15.4

♦ Calvert purchased a printing business for $100,000. Although the seller had been in operation for 35 years and was greatly supported by the community, he agreed that the contract would only show $1,000 as the price to be paid for the goodwill.

♦ The rest of the contract identified $60,000 as the price for the equipment and $39,000 for inventory and supplies — all of which would soon be deducted by Calvert in his new operation.

♦ The IRS determined that $30,000 was the appropriate value of the goodwill and not $1,000.

♦ After re-allocating the purchase price, the value of the $30,000 in goodwill needed to be carried on the books indefinitely, never to be written off as a business expense.

Under the current rules, goodwill is now deductible if it is acquired after August 10, 1993. It can now be amortized over 15 years on a straight-line basis.

Assume that Calvert (Illustration 15.4) had bought the business in January 1994. He would be entitled to write off $2,000 in goodwill amortization for 1994 and for each of the next 14 years, or $30,000 divided over the course of the 15 years.

AMORTIZATION OF OTHER INTANGIBLE ASSETS

Other intangible assets have also been the source of much controversy and guesswork over the years. Unlike goodwill, many of these assets at least had some sort of finite life and could be amortized accordingly. The problem, however, was determining the appropriate life span and separating them from the goodwill that might have been engendered in the transaction.

Once again, the new act takes away the guesswork. It provides that most intangible assets acquired after August 10, 1993 can be amortized on a straight-line basis over a uniform 15-year period. The new law also repeals the inconsistent amortization periods of certain intangibles, and it allows amortization when it wasn't even permitted in the past. The following assets are permitted to be amortized under the new uniform procedure over a uniform 15-year period.

♦ Workforce in place;

♦ Information bases, including business books and records, operating systems, and technical and training manuals;

♦ "Know-how," including secret formulae, designs, patterns, sound recordings, video tapes, and similar items;

♦ Customer lists, patient, and client files;

♦ Supplier-based intangibles;

♦ Franchises, trademarks, and trade names; and

♦ Covenants not to compete and similar agreements.

Likewise, the new act specifically prohibits the special uniform amortization deduction for several named intangibles. These include the following:

♦ Accounts receivable and interests in patents and copyrights;

♦ Numerous other intangibles not acquired in a business acquisition; and

♦ Interests in land or other business entities.

A FICA Tax Credit Allowance to Restaurants and Bars

Under the general rule, all income earned by employees from tips is handled as if it were paid by the employer for Social Security purposes, also known as FICA. Therefore, the employer is required to pay the FICA tax at the rate of 7.65%. Because of this, the employer is entitled to a deduction.

Special Note: As with any deduction in business, the dollar value of the deduction to the employers is only as much as the tax bracket they are in. For example, if as an employer you are in the lowest 15% bracket, you could only expect to get back 15% (in taxes saved) for every dollar you put out on behalf of the employees for the required FICA payment.

Instead of a mere deduction, a dollar-for-dollar tax credit is now allowed. The credit goes to all employers who provide food or beverages to customers at the employer's place of business. The

PROVE YOUR HOBBY LOSSES – PASS THE PRESUMPTION TEST

Do you have a side business where you race or train horses? Do you collect and sell coins or stamps? Do you engage in work as an artist or entertainer? It is always interesting to note that when you make money at enterprises such as these, the IRS will tax this income under the usual reporting rules. Further, if you begin to lose money, the IRS may prohibit you from writing off your losses.

As long as there is a profit from your operation, you are able to deduct all the *ordinary and necessary* expenses of running your business. However, if expenses exceed your income, and an IRS agent succeeds in characterizing your activity as a hobby, you can deduct expenses only up to the amount of your gross income.

WHAT YOU CAN DO

There are two ways to defeat the IRS's allegation that you are merely operating a hobby and not a legitimate business.

First, you must pass the *presumption test*. If you can show a profit in three out of the past five consecutive years, then you are safe.

The presumption is that you have a legitimate business operation and your losses will probably be allowed. Incidentally, if you breed, race, train, or show horses, you only have to show a profit in two out of seven consecutive years.

Second, if you can't pass the *presumption test*, the burden of proof is greater and you must show that you have:

♦ Spent considerable time and effort trying to make a profit;

♦ Kept a detailed set of books and records;

♦ Sought and relied on expert advice;

♦ Expected the assets to appreciate in value; and

♦ Proved that losses are common in the early or start-up phase of your type of business.

Remember, do not despair if you are unable to pass the *presumption test*. Failure to do so will not automatically cause your losses to be disallowed under the law. All it does is shift the burden back to you to prove that you are entitled to the claim.

☞ KEY OBSERVATION

Many taxpayers have successfully challenged the allegation that they were engaged in hobby activities, even when they had lost money for several years in a row.

KNOW THE FACTS WHEN WORKING WITH INDEPENDENT CONTRACTORS

Most small business consultants agree that the IRS has been steadily increasing its focus on small businesses that carry their workers as independent contractors on a continuing basis. The new IRS policy is to identify those that have been misclassified. Their overall goal is to set up a tax liability for the unpaid withholding tax and penalties.

If you have never had to administer a regular payroll, you cannot appreciate the extent of the cost and the responsibility for meeting the withholding rules for regular employees. It begins the moment you are placed in the fiduciary role that requires you to withhold and pay the substantial tax costs set by strict federal and state guidelines. These costs include:

♦ Matching FICA taxes that have been withheld;

♦ Federal and state unemployment taxes;

♦ Health insurance and certain fringe benefits that are normally provided to employees; and

♦ Pension and profit sharing requirements.

Your first step is to ascertain any existing exposure for unpaid withholding tax. You may want to review your contractual relationship with your independent workers. You will want to make certain that your documents are in order and the requirements for independent contractor status are being met. Equipped with computerized cross-matching technology, the IRS has recently begun to team up with the state agencies to inspect the subcontract records of small business owner-operators. If a determination is made that an employer-employee relationship exists, the resulting tax liability can be retroactively assessed. For some, the results could be devastating.

States like California, Illinois, Georgia, New York, Michigan, and Texas are actively pursuing this current team effort. To safeguard the independent contractor status of your various workers, you must get acquainted with the state and federal rules to assure compliance. If you don't already have a properly thought-out independent contractor's agreement in your files, have one drafted immediately.

For federal purposes, the following example will help you provide the framework for the contract. Additionally, it will alert you to the kind of questions that an examining officer is likely to raise during the course of an audit.

Illustration 15.5

♦ Bryan is a commercial building contractor who sub-contracts with Joe, a painter who works on a number of projects with the owners of several office buildings. The IRS auditor asks the following questions:

♦ "As a contractor, do you give instructions to the painter about when, where, and how the job is to be done?" If Bryan does instruct the painter, this is one strike against him.

♦ "Does the painter work for others?" This is a big plus for Bryan if the painter has other clients.

♦ "Does the painter run certain risks of loss in the projects?" For example, if Joe has to buy his own materials and pay assistants, the chances are good that he will succeed in proving his independent contractor status.

♦ "Does he set his own hours and days of work?"

♦ "Does he publicly advertise as an independent painting contractor?" It's a major plus if Joe has his own business cards, stationery, business license, or if he advertises in directories or trade journals.

♦ "Does the commercial contractor reserve the right to fire the painter?" Generally, independent contractors cannot be fired as long as they are producing results in accordance with the terms of the contract.

♦ "Is the painter paid 'by the job?'" Payment made by straight commission or 'by the job' is indicative that an independent contractor relationship exists.

♦ "Does he pay for his own insurance?"

Clearly, not one of the above criteria can settle the issue of independent contractor status on its own. If viewed together, however, the merit of the overall responses will definitely set the tone for the resulting decision.

Q. Can occasional payments for so-called "casual labor" be treated as independent contractor status in a business?

A. As with any other worker, you need to evaluate the prescribed tests for independent contractor status. Casual employees, unfortunately, are usually subject to enough control to require classification as employees. There is an exemption from withholding, however, when these "occasional workers" are paid less than $50 and work less than 24 days in a quarter.

Independent contractors cover a wide spectrum of business activities as evidenced by the following sampling.

- ◆ Accountants;

- ◆ Health and accident insurance salespeople who are free to solicit business on their own;

- ◆ Barbers renting chairs in shops;

- ◆ Church organists;

- ◆ Commercial fishermen who provide their own equipment and sell to the public;

- ◆ Consultants;

- ◆ House-to-house canvassers who are not under the direction and control of a crew manager;

- ◆ Models who operate on a freelance basis;

- ◆ Sales agents of a manufacturing company who have an exclusive right to sell in certain territories;

- ◆ Sales personnel in real estate who have unlimited discretion in their activities and whose work is not supervised;

- ◆ Tennis professionals who sell their service on the premises of a club. (Although the club controls the desired results, it does not control how it is to be done.); and

- ◆ Writers who furnish a weekly column to a newspaper and have complete control over its content.

Under certain circumstances, though, individuals that perform these same services may also be classified as employees.

TAX-DEFERRED ANNUITIES AND OTHER SCHEMES TO DEFER TAX LIABILITY

Ever since the government eliminated real tax shelters in 1986, many small business owners have been busy trying to find other tax-friendly places to put some of their extra cash profits. If they put their money in CDs for example, they have found that not only are they victimized by low interest rates, but the IRS wants a portion of the earnings as well — perhaps as much as 39.6%.

Say, for example, you put $10,000 into a short-term CD paying 4.5%. If your effective tax rate, federal and state, is 33%, your true earning on your investment is only 3%. If inflation exceeds 3%, then obviously you're losing money instead of making it.

With this backdrop, it is easy to see why tax-deferred annuities have become so popular; particularly since their tax-sheltering benefits to remain unscathed. Before you sign up for an investment, know the exact terms of the investment.

The following segment is borrowed from a well-known Prentice-Hall Publishing Company publication entitled *Executive's Tax Report*. "Tax Deferred Annuities: Getting Beyond the Hype," by Thomas J. Stemmy is reproduced with permission, and has been modified to fit the needs of the small business owner in the current environment.

"HOW DOES IT [the Tax Deferred Annuity] WORK? You simply hand over a cash payment (as little as $5,000) to an insurer. You then can choose whether you want a fixed interest rate or a variable rate — similar to choosing a mortgage. The fixed interest rate can be locked in for varying periods from one to ten years. The variable rate fluctuates with the prices of the stock and bond markets. There are several ways to take the money out when you need it. You can make a lump sum withdrawal, or you can get monthly income for life or for a predetermined number of years.

"The tax advantages: Tax-deferral is the biggest selling point for an annuity. The tax law says that you don't have to pay taxes on the interest you are earning until you actually withdraw the money (unlike the situation at your local bank where you pay tax on the interest as it accumulates). That can be a big money-saver, especially if your tax rate declines between the time you earn the interest and the time you have to pay on it.

"Annuity salespeople like to point out that when you invest in an annuity, not only are you earning interest on your principal and interest on your interest, you're also earning interest on dollars you would have normally paid away in taxes. Below is a comparison of what a $10,000 investment will yield using a tax-deferred annuity (TDA) and without tax-deferral. In both cases a 28% tax rate is assumed.

$10,000 at	10 years with a TDA	10 years no TDA	20 years with a TDA	20 years no TDA
8%	$18,340	$17,510	$36,360	$30,650
10%	21,470	20,040	51,240	40,170

"There is considerable money to be saved through tax-deferral — especially over longer periods and at higher interest rates. However, don't overlook the fact that this is not tax elimination, just putting off the inevitable. Of course, the idea is that by the time you have to pay tax, you will have retired and your income will have dropped to the point where the tax bite is minimized.

"Is it safe? How safe is money that you entrust to an insurer? After all, the newspapers are full of reports of reputable insurers going bust. The answer is that while annuities are a relatively safe investment, your money is only as safe as the company you choose. You should not be shy in asking the insurer its rating. Find out how the insurer fared under the scrutiny of Standard & Poor's, A.M. Best, Moody's, Duff and Phelp's, and the real tough grader, Weiss Research. Also, keep an eye on continuing performance.

"Earning potential: While interest paid is comparable to bank rates, it is not unusual for insurers to advertise high starting yields (say 9%), then drop to 6% or 7% after the honeymoon (the initial guarantee period) is over.

"Access to your money: Some insurers impose fees as high as 15% if you pull money out in the early years. Most will allow you to take out 10% of your account value without penalty. Generally speaking, though, your money is always available for an emergency. In addition, the money is readily available to your heirs upon your death — without the delay of probate proceedings. The same cannot be said for a CD at your local bank. However, keep in mind that the IRS generally imposes a 10% penalty tax on any withdrawals you make from the annuity before you reach age 59½.

"Planning Key: The best candidates for fixed annuities are conservative investors over 50 years old who are prepared to tie up their funds for 10 years before drawing on them for retirement."

OTHER TAX-FRIENDLY INVESTMENT OPTIONS

Voluntary tax-deferral programs, such as tax-deferred annuities, may not be for every small business owner who is looking for a place to invest some of the profits. Accordingly, you may be wondering what other tax-sheltered options are available as an alternative to CDs or other securities that produce a fixed yield. Discuss the following three options with your investment adviser.

MUNICIPAL BONDS

Except in rare cases, municipal bonds still retain their tax-free feature with the federal government. Advice should be sought, however, on factors such as:

♦ Quality or inherent risk of each bond;

♦ The length of time that you must hold the bond until maturity; and

♦ The attached commissions and fees.

CORPORATE STOCK

If your business entity is an ordinary corporation, you have a special tax advantage for investments. If you choose to take some of your cash reserves and buy stock in other corporations, in most cases you are permitted to exclude from income 70% of the dividends received. This feature becomes particularly attractive when you make the right kind of investment. Ask your broker to recommend the highest yielding and safest stock positions that he can find for your account. (See Chapter 3 for this tax-free feature.)

OTHER LONG-TERM INVESTMENT OPTIONS

You can save by focusing your investment dollars on capital appreciation rather than current yield. For one thing, the tax may be lower at capital gains rates. For another, you don't have to pay taxes until the asset is sold — a tax-deferral feature always worthy of merit.

Other equally subtle, tax-saving possibilities exist to put some of your cash reserves to work. Another increasingly popular alternative is tied to the tax-deferral features of certain life insurance products. One such product has to do with *split-dollar* life insurance. Ask your insurance consultant how you, as an employer, could recoup your insurance investment, tax free, from the increasing cash surrender value of an insurance policy.

OFFER IN COMPROMISE – DEBT RELIEF FOR MANY TAXPAYERS

The government allows some leeway for all those taxpayers who are overwhelmed by their tax obligations to the IRS. Before you begin negotiating with a revenue officer, consider submitting an offer in compromise. For an investigative officer to consider an offer in compromise the following criteria must be met.

♦ First, the offer in compromise is to be considered a useful collection tool and a practical alternative to a prolonged installment agreement.

♦ Second, the offer plan should conform to the goal of achieving collection at the earliest time possible and at the least possible cost to the government.

♦ Third, the ultimate goal is a compromise in the best interest of the government *and* the taxpayer.

Many of you burdened with tax debt will find **the key** in the second bulleted item. Here, you will learn that a relatively small amount of cash is your answer — as long as that amount meets a prescribed minimum. (Refer to Illustration 15.6.) To further simplify this process, the IRS has made the offer in compromise user-friendlier with easy-to-complete forms and a less bureaucratic approach.

REDUCED BUREAUCRACY

The delegation of authority to accept offers is now streamlined and the IRS will go out of its way to assist. The IRS states:

"In cases where an offer in compromise appears to be a viable solution to a tax delinquency, the service employee assigned to the case will discuss the compromise alternative with the taxpayer and, when necessary, assist in preparing the required forms. The taxpayer will be responsible for initiating the first specific proposal for compromise."

EASIER FORMS AND FEWER CONTINGENCIES

For many years, taxpayers, particularly, business owners, had been plagued with long and complicated "information forms" that needed to be prepared before an offer could even be considered. Now, three forms have been designed to make the job simpler and shorter.

♦ *Form 656 – Offer in Compromise*

♦ *Form 433 – A, Collection Information Statement for Individuals*

♦ *Form 433 – B, Collection Information Statement for Businesses.* (For a look at samples of these forms, refer to Appendix A.)

Under the most current procedures, a collateral agreement will not be required with every offer as was the case in the past. These side agreements are now being de-emphasized. Thus, taxpayers are not subjected to as many restrictions and contingencies in connection with future activities.

Clearly, the offer in compromise is now becoming a significant planning tool for those small business owners who are financially hard-pressed and whose purpose is to get a fresh start. There are two significant prerequisites.

First, for the IRS to waive a large tax bill, you need to have a current, specified amount of cash. That amount must be no less than the amount of equity that you have in everything that you own.

Second, for the deal to work, the IRS also must be satisfied that the amount being offered is not less than the amount that could be generated by the taxpayer's income now and later. In essence, the IRS is ensuring that the amount of upfront money is worth as much now as it will be in future years.

Illustration 15.6

♦ Kim, the sole proprietor of a small cleaning service business, owes the IRS $200,000 in back taxes after filing three years of delinquent returns.

♦ The only asset that she owns is her personal residence with a fair market value of $175,000; her mortgage debt is $150,000.

♦ Since it can be ascertained that the net equity of all her assets is $25,000, she will need to come up with at least this amount of cash to make the compromise work.

♦ The value of her present and future income is calculated by taking her monthly income and subtracting her necessary living expenses and multiplying the result by 60 months. Kim's total monthly income was $4,000 and her total expenses were $3,800 — the value of her present and future income was $12,000 ($200 multiplied by 60).

♦ In preparing the prescribed offer in compromise forms, Kim sat down to calculate the minimum amount that she would have to submit to satisfy her $200,000 obligation to the IRS.

♦ She made the following computation

♦ A) Her equity in her assets $25,000

♦ B) The value of her present and future income $12,000

♦ Total $37,000

♦ With this information, she set out to borrow $37,000 from a family member and she promptly wrote out a check to the IRS, which was then submitted with the offer in compromise.

☞ KEY OBSERVATION

The IRS will closely look at any illegal or questionable maneuvering of assets. This includes the sale of assets to friends and relatives for less than full fair market value or the transfer of assets beyond the reach of the government, like to foreign countries. (Refer to Appendix A for a sample of the offer in compromise and its related forms.)

LOOK FOR MORE INTERPRETATIONS OF THE TAX LAWS

As more taxpayers challenge the new tax laws, you can be assured of different interpretations that will potentially favor your small business. Keep your eyes and ears open for more tax court rulings that may allow a tax savings for your operation. Several organizations throughout the country have publications to help you stay abreast of the latest IRS rulings. To learn more about such publications, contact any one of the following offices.

HELPFUL TAX RESOURCES

Daily Tax Report

The Bureau of National Affairs, Inc. (BNA)
9435 Key West Avenue
Rockville, MD 20850
(800) 372-1033
http://www.bna.com (Web site)

The Tax Adviser

The American Institute of CPAs (AICPA)
1211 Avenue of the Americas
New York, NY 10036-8775
(212) 575-6200
http://www.aicpa.org (Web site)

Weekly Alert

Research Institute of America (RIA)
95th Avenue
New York, NY 10011
(800) 431-9025
http://www.riatax.com (Web site)

APPENDIX A

Form 656 – Offer in Compromise

Form 433-A – Collection Information Statement for Individuals

Form 433-B – Collection Information Statement for Business

Form 656 – Offer in Compromise

Department of Treasury
Internal Revenue Service

Form 656 (Rev. 1-97)
Catalog Number 16728N

Form 656

Offer in Compromise

■ What you should know before submitting an offer in compromise

■ Worksheets to calculate an acceptable offer amount using
Form 433-A and/or 433-B and Publication 1854*

■ How to correctly complete Form 656, Offer in Compromise

■ Two copies of Form 656

*Required forms can be obtained by calling 1-800-829-1040

Offer in Compromise *(continued)*

What You Should Know Before Preparing an Offer in Compromise

Legal Limitations on Compromise	IRS *may* legally compromise a tax liability owed based only on: ■ **Collectibility**—doubt that IRS can collect the full amount owed and/or ■ **Liability**—doubt as to whether you owe the amount	IRS *cannot* legally accept a compromise based solely on hardship.
Are You an Offer Candidate?	*Do not* submit an offer if: ■ The entire amount you owe can be collected through liquidation of your assets or through a monthly install-ment plan. ■ IRS can collect more from your assets and/or future income than you are offering.	IRS *will not* decide that "something is better than nothing" and accept the offer because you currently have no assets or income.
Additional Agreements	The IRS may require additional agreements which would require you to:	■ Pay a percentage of future earnings ■ Give up certain present or potential tax benefits
Suspending Collection	Submitting an offer does not automatically suspend collection activity. ■ If there is an indication that you filed the offer to delay collection of the tax or if delay of collection would inter-fere with the Service's ability to collect the tax, then IRS will continue collection efforts.	■ If you have an installment agreement prior to submit-ting the offer, you must continue making those payments while the offer is being considered.
Substitute Form 656	Offer in Compromise Form 656 is the official Offer in Compromise agreement. If you are using a substitute Form 656 that is a computer generated or photocopied substitute Form 656 be aware that:	■ By signing the substitute Form 656 you affirm: 1. That this form is a verbatim duplicate of the official Form 656. 2. That you agree to be bound by all terms and condi-tions set forth in the official Form 656.
Can We Process Your Form 656?	IRS will return your offer to you and ask for clarification if you do not fill in every line item on the form. Refer to "How To Correctly Complete Form 656", page 6 that explains how to fill out the form. IRS cannot process your offer if it contains any of these problems: ■ Substitute Form 656 is not a verbatim duplicate of the official Form 656 ■ Pre-printed terms of the offer form are altered ■ Taxpayer is not identified ■ Taxpayer Identification Number is not included	■ An amount is not offered and/or payment terms are not stated ■ Appropriate signatures are not present ■ Forms 433-A and/or 433-B, if required, are missing or are incomplete ■ IRS determines that the amount you offered is less than the equity and available income indicated on the attached Form 433-A and/or 433-B

z

Offer in Compromise *(continued)*

Worksheet to Calculate an Acceptable Offer Amount Using Forms 433-A or 433-B

Read the terms and definitions below before preparing Forms 433-A or 433-B. You must use the National Standard expense amounts found in Publication 1854 to prepare Form 433-A.

Terms and Definitions

Current Market Value—The amount you could reasonably expect to be paid for the asset if you sold it. Do not guess at the value of an asset. Find out the value from realtors, used car dealers, publications, furniture dealers, or other experts on specific types of assets. If you get a written estimate, please include a copy with your financial statement.

Present and Future Income—Generally the amount collectible is your income minus necessary living expenses. We usually consider what we can collect over 5 years.

Necessary Expenses—*(Not for business entities)* Expenses needed to provide for you and your family's health and welfare and the production of income. All expenses must be reasonable in amount. IRS expense amounts are determined from the Bureau of Labor Statistics (BLS) Consumer Expenditure Survey. IRS also developed local standards for housing (includes utilities) from information received from the Bureau of Census.

Note: If the amount of your necessary expenses is unreasonable based on the BLS and local standards, IRS will not allow these expenses.

Expenses Not Generally Allowed—Tuition for private elementary and secondary schools, public or private college expenses, charitable contributions, voluntary retirement benefits, unsecured debts, cable television charges and any other expense that does not meet the "necessary expense" test.

Worksheet Instructions

Follow the steps in the appropriate worksheet below to compute the offer amount.

1. Use Form 433-A if you are an individual wage earner (go to worksheet 1)

2. Use Forms 433-A and 433-B if you are self-employed or if you are both self-employed and a wage earner (go to worksheet 2)

3. Use Form 433-B if the offer is for a business entity (go to worksheet 3)

Note: The offer investigator will review the form and compute an amount acceptable to compromise your liability. The amount you offered may have to be increased based on the investigator's review.

Worksheet 1: Individual Wage Earners

Step 1: Equity in Assets	Enter the dollar amount from line 30, Form 433-A		$_____
Step 2: Present and Future Income	(a) Enter the amount from line 41, Form 433-A	$_____	
	(b) Necessary Expenses (Total lines 42-51)	$_____	
	Line (a) minus line (b) =	$_____	
	Multiply by 60 months =		$_____
Step 3: Offer Amount	Add total of steps 1 and 2 above = offer amount		$_____
	Note: If the offer amount is more than your total liability, you are not an offer candidate. Contact your local IRS office to resolve your liabilities.		
Step 4: Form 656	Enter the total amount from step 3 above in item 7 of Form 656.		

Offer in Compromise *(continued)*

Worksheet 2:
Self-Employed or Self-Employed and Wage Earners

Step 1: Equity in Assets	(a) Enter the dollar amount from line 30, Form 433-A	$	
	(b) Enter the dollar amount from line 27, Form 433-B	$	
	Enter total of lines (a) and (b)		$
Step 2: Present and Future Income	Enter the amount from line 33, Form 433-B on line 34, Form 433-A. Include line 34 in total on line 41, Form 433A		
	(a) Enter the amount from line 41, Form 433-A	$	
	(b) Enter expenses (Total lines 42-51, Form 433-A)	$	
	Line (a) minus line (b) =	$	
	Multiply by 60 months =		$
Step 3: Offer Amount	Add total of steps 1 and 2 above = offer amount		$
	Note: If the offer amount is more than your total liability, you are not an offer candidate. Contact your local IRS office to resolve your liabilities.		
Step 4: Form 656	Enter the total amount from step 3 above in item 7 of Form 656.		

Worksheet 3:
Business Entities

Step 1: Equity in Assets	Enter the dollar amount from line 27, Form 433-B		$
Step 2: Present and Future Income	(a) Enter the amount from line 33, Form 433-B	$	
	(b) Enter expenses (Total lines 34-44)	$	
	Line (a) minus line (b) =	$	
	Multiply by 60 months =		$
Step 3: Offer Amount	Add total of steps 1 and 2 above = offer amount		$
	Note: If the offer amount is more than your total liability, you are not an offer candidate. Contact your local IRS office to resolve your liabilities.		
Step 4: Form 656	Enter the total amount from step 3 above in item 7 of Form 656		

Offer in Compromise *(continued)*

How to Correctly Complete Form 656

Two Forms 656 are provided. Use one form to submit your offer in compromise. The other form may be used as a worksheet and retained for your personal records.

Failure to read and follow these instructions could result in IRS returning your offer. Questions may be directed to your local IRS office.

Item 1
Enter the taxpayer's name and home or business address. You should also include a mailing address, if different.

If the tax liability is owed jointly by a husband and wife and both wish to make an offer, show both names. If you owe one amount by yourself (such as employment taxes), and other amounts jointly (such as income taxes),

but only one person is submitting an offer, list all tax liabilities on one Form 656. If you owe one amount yourself and another amount jointly, and both parties submit an offer, you must complete two Forms 656, one for the amount you owe individually and one for the joint amount.

Item 2
Enter the social security number for the person submitting the offer. For example, if both husband and wife are submitting an offer on a joint income tax liability, the

social security number of both persons should be entered. However, if only the husband is submitting the offer, only his social security number should be entered.

Item 3
If the liability being compromised is owed by a business, enter the employer identification number.

Item 4
Show the employer identification numbers for all other businesses (excluding corporate entities) which you own. Under the terms of the offer in compromise, you

are required to comply with the filing and paying requirements of the tax laws for a period of 5 years for all the businesses that you own.

Item 5
Check the blocks that identify your tax liability and enter the tax year or period of the liability. If you owe a type of tax not preprinted, list it in the "other" block, specifying the type of tax and tax year and/or period. Tax periods

related to Trust Fund Recovery assessments can be found on copies of notices and from the Notice of Federal Tax Lien.

Item 6
Check the applicable block describing the basis for your offer.

∎ If **Doubt as to Liability** you must submit a written statement describing in detail why you do not believe you owe the liability. You *must complete item 7.*

∎ If **Doubt as to Collectibility** you must submit Collection Information Statement, Form 433-A for individual and/or Form 433-B for businesses. You *must complete item 7.*

∎ If you are submitting an offer on **both Doubt as to Liability and Doubt as to Collectibility,** please be advised that IRS will first determine whether your offer is acceptable based on Doubt as to Collectibility. If your offer is acceptable based on Doubt as to Collectibility, the liability issue will not be considered.

Offer in Compromise *(continued)*

Item 7

■ Enter the total amount of your offer from the work-sheet. Do not include amounts you have already paid, IRS has already physically collected or is due to receive.

■ Enter the amount of your deposit. A deposit is not required, however IRS encourages deposits because it reflects your good faith effort to reach an acceptable compromise. However, the law requires that your deposit go into a special fund. IRS will not pay you interest whether the deposit is applied to an accepted offer, applied to your tax liability, or refunded to you. *When the IRS cashes your check it does not mean your offer is accepted.*

■ Enter how and when you will pay the remainder of your offer. We have provided some specific time periods: 10 days, 30 days, 60 days, or 90 days. You should pay the full amount of the offer as soon as possible. If we determine that you can pay in a shorter time frame, we will require earlier payment or we will reject your offer.

■ Enter other proposed payment terms if you cannot pay the offer amount within 90 days or if you intend to make more than one payment within the specific time frames above. Include the specific dates and payment amount that we will receive. For example, $1000.00 to be paid on 12-31-97. When IRS reviews your financial statement, if we determine that you can pay in a shorter time frame, we will require earlier payment or we will reject your offer.

Item 8

It is important that you thoroughly read and understand the contractual requirements listed in this section.

Item 9

All persons submitting the offer should sign and date Form 656. Where applicable, include titles of authorized corporate officers, executors, trustees, Powers of Attorney, etc.

If you are using a substitute Form 656 be aware that:

■ By signing the substitute Form 656 you affirm:

1) That this form is a verbatim duplicate of the official Form 656.

2) That you agree to be bound by all the terms and conditions set forth in the official Form 656.

■ If the substitute form is two single sided pages, the taxpayer(s) must initial and date the first page in addition to signing and dating the second page.

Where to File

File your offer in compromise in the IRS district office in your area. If you have been working with a specific IRS employee, file the offer with that employee.

Review your offer form to ensure that all line items are entered correctly.

7

Offer in Compromise *(continued)*

Department of Treasury
Internal Revenue Service
Form 656 (Rev. 1-97)
Catalog Number 16728N

Form 656

Offer in Compromise

(If you need more space, use another sheet titled "Attachment to Form 656", and sign and date it.)

Item 1
Taxpayer's Name and Home or Business Address

Name

Street Address

City   State   Zip Code

Mailing Address (if different from above)

City   State   Zip Code

Item 2
Social Security Numbers

(a) Primary

(b) Secondary

Item 3
Employer Identification Number (included in offer)

Item 4
Other Employer Identification Numbers (Not included in offer)

Item 5

To: Commissioner of Internal Revenue Service
I/we (includes all types of taxpayers) submit this offer to compromise the tax liabilities plus any interest, penalties, additions to tax, and additional amounts required by law (tax liability) for the tax type and period marked below: (Please mark an "X" for the correct description and fill-in the correct tax period(s), adding additional periods if needed.)

☐ 1040/1120 Income tax— Year(s)

☐ 941 Employer's Quarterly Federal Tax Return—Quarterly Period(s)

☐ 940 Employer's Annual Federal Unemployment (FUTA) Tax Return— Year(s)

☐ Trust Fund Recovery Penalty as a responsible person of (enter corporation name)

for failure to pay withholding and Federal Insurance Contributions Act Taxes (Social Security taxes)—Period(s)

☐ Other Federal taxes (specify type and period(s))

Item 6
I/we submit this offer for the reason(s) checked below:

☐ Doubt as to Liability— "I do not believe I owe this amount." You must include a detailed explanation of the reasons you believe you do not owe the tax.

☐ Doubt as to Collectibility— "I have insufficient assets and income to pay the full amount." You must include a complete financial statement (Form 433-A and/or Form 433-B).

Item 7
I/We offer to pay $

☐ Paid in full with this offer.
☐ Deposit of $_____ with this offer.
☐ No deposit.
Check one of the following boxes:
☐ Balance to be paid in   10.   30.   50. or   90 days from notice of acceptance of the offer. If more than one payment will be paid during the time frame checked, provide the amount of the payment and date to be paid on the line below.

☐ Other proposed payment terms. Enter the specific dates (mm/dd/yy format) and dollar amounts of the the payment terms you propose on the lines below.

In addition to the above amount, IRS will add interest from the date IRS accepts the offer until the date you completely pay the amount offered, as required by section 6621 of the Internal Revenue Code. IRS compounds interest daily, as required by section 6622 of the Internal Revenue Code.

Offer in Compromise *(continued)*

Item 8

By submitting this offer, I/we understand and agree to the following conditions:

(a) I/we voluntarily submit all payments made on this offer.

(b) IRS will apply payments made under the terms of this offer in the best interest of the government.

(c) If IRS rejects the offer or I/we withdraw the offer, IRS will return any amount paid with the offer. If I/we agree in writing, IRS will apply the amount paid with the offer to the amount owed. If I/we agree to apply the payment, the date the offer is rejected or withdrawn will be considered the date of payment. I/we understand that IRS will not pay interest on any amount I/we submit with the offer.

(d) I/we will comply with all provisions of the Internal Revenue Code relating to filing my/our returns and paying my/our required taxes for 5 years from the date IRS accepts the offer. This condition does not apply to offers based on Doubt as to Liability.

(e) I/we waive and agree to the suspension of any statutory periods of limitation (time limits provided for by law) for IRS assessment and collection of the tax liability for the tax periods identified in item (5).

(f) IRS will keep all payments and credits made, received, or applied to the amount being compromised before this offer was submitted. IRS may keep any proceeds from a levy served prior to submission of the offer, but not received at the time the offer is submitted. If I/we have an installment agreement prior to submitting the offer, I/we must continue to make the payments as agreed while this offer is pending. Installment agreement payments will not be applied against the amount offered.

(g) IRS will keep any refund, including interest, due to me/us because of overpayment of any tax or other liability, for tax periods extending through the calendar year that IRS accepts the offer. I/we may not designate a refund, to which the IRS is entitled, to be applied to estimated tax payments for the following year. This condition doesn't apply if the offer is based only on Doubt as to Liability.

(h) I/we will return to IRS any refund identified in (g) received after submission of this offer. This condition doesn't apply if the offer is based only on Doubt as to Liability.

(i) The total amount IRS can collect under this offer can not be more than the full amount of the tax liability.

(j) I/we understand that I/we remain responsible for the full amount of the tax liability, unless and until IRS accepts the offer in writing and I/we have met all the terms and conditions of the offer. I/we won't remove the original amount of the tax liability from its records until I/we have met all the terms of the offer.

(k) I/we understand that the tax I/we offer to compromise is and will remain a tax liability until I/we meet all the terms and conditions of this offer. If I/we file bankruptcy before the terms and conditions of this offer are completed, any claim the IRS files in the bankruptcy proceeding will be a tax claim.

(l) Once IRS accepts the offer in writing, I/we have no right to contest in court or otherwise, the amount of the tax liability.

(m) The offer is pending starting with the date an authorized IRS official signs this form and accepts my/our waiver of the statutory periods of limitation. The offer remains pending until an authorized IRS official accepts, rejects or acknowledges withdrawal of the offer in writing. If I/we appeal the IRS decision on the offer, IRS will continue to treat the offer as pending until the Appeals Office accepts or rejects the offer in writing. If I/we don't file a protest within 30 days of the date IRS notifies me/us of the right to protest the decision, I/we waive the right to a hearing before the Appeals Office about the offer in compromise.

(n) The waiver and suspension of any statutory periods of limitation for assessment and collection of the amount of the tax liability described in item (5), continues to apply: while the offer is pending (see (m) above), during the time I/we have not paid all of the amount offered, during the time I/we have not completed all terms and conditions of the offer, and for one additional year beyond each of the time periods identified in this paragraph.

(o) If I/we fail to meet any of the terms and conditions of the offer, the offer is in default, then IRS may: immediately file suit to collect the entire unpaid balance of the offer; immediately file suit to collect an amount equal to the original amount of the tax liability as liquidating damages, minus any payments already received under the terms of this offer; disregard the amount of the offer and apply all amounts already paid under the offer against the original amount of tax liability; or file suit or levy to collect the original amount of the tax liability, without further notice of any kind.

IRS will continue to add interest as required by section 6621 of the Internal Revenue Code, on the amount IRS determines is due after default. IRS will add interest from the date the offer is defaulted until I/we completely satisfy the amount owed.

Item 9

If I/we submit this offer on a substitute form, I/we affirm that this form is a verbatim duplicate of the official Form 656, and I/we agree to be bound by all the terms and conditions set forth in the official Form 656.

Under penalties of perjury, I declare that I have examined this offer, including accompanying schedules and statements, and to the best of my knowledge and belief, it is true, correct and complete.

(9a) Signature of taxpayer proponent

Date

(9b) Signature of taxpayer proponent

Date

For Official Use Only

I accept waiver of the statutory period of limitations for the Internal Revenue Service.

Signature of authorized Internal Revenue Service Official

Title

Date

Form 433-A – Collection Information Statement for Individuals

Form **433-A**
(Rev. September 1995)

Department of the Treasury — Internal Revenue Service

Collection Information Statement for Individuals

NOTE: Complete all blocks, except shaded areas. Write "N/A" (not applicable) in those blocks that do not apply.
Instructions for certain line items are in Publication 1854.

| 1. Taxpayer(s) name(s) and address | 2. Home phone number | 3. Marital status |
| | 4. a. Taxpayer's social security number | b. Spouse's social security number |

County_____

Section I.   Employment Information

5. Taxpayer's employer or business (name and address)	a. How long employed	b. Business phone number	c. Occupation
	d. Number of exemptions claimed on Form W-4 ___	e. Pay period ☐ Weekly ☐ Bi-weekly ☐ Monthly ___ Payday: ____ (Mon - Sun)	f. (Check appropriate box) ☐ Wage earner ☐ Sole proprietor ☐ Partner
6. Spouse's employer or business (name and address)	a. How long employed	b. Business phone number	c. Occupation
	d. Number of exemptions claimed on Form W-4 ___	e. Pay period ☐ Weekly ☐ Bi-weekly ☐ Monthly ___ Payday: ____ (Mon - Sun)	f. (Check appropriate box) ☐ Wage earner ☐ Sole proprietor ☐ Partner

Section II.   Personal Information

| 7. Name, address and telephone number of next of kin or other reference | 8. Other names or aliases | 9. Previous address(es) |

10. Age and relationship of dependents living in your household (exclude yourself and spouse)

| 11. Date of Birth | a. Taxpayer | b. Spouse | 12. Latest filed income tax return (tax year) | a. Number of exemptions claimed | b. Adjusted Gross Income |

Section III.   General Financial Information

13. Bank accounts (include savings & loans, credit unions, IRA and retirement plans, certificates of deposit, etc.) Enter bank loans in item 28

Name of Institution	Address	Type of Account	Account No.	Balance
			Total (Enter in Item 21)	

Form **433-A** (Rev. 9-95)

ISA
STF FED1060F 1

Form 433-A *(continued)*

Section III - *continued* General Financial Information

14. Charge cards and lines of credit from banks, credit unions, and savings and loans. List all other charge accounts in item 28.

Type of Account or Card	Name and Address of Financial Institution	Monthly Payment	Credit Limit	Amount Owed	Credit Available
	Totals *(Enter in item 27)* ▶				

15. Safe deposit boxes rented or accessed *(List all locations, box numbers, and contents)*

16. Real Property *(Brief description and type of ownership)*	Physical Address
a.	
	County_____
b.	
	County_____
c.	
	County_____

17 Life Insurance *(Name of Company)*	Policy Number	Type	Face Amount	Available Loan Value
		Whole / Term		
		Whole / Term		
		Whole / Term		
		Total *(Enter in item 23)* ▶		

18. Securities *(stocks, bonds, mutual funds, money market funds, government securities, etc.)*

Kind	Quantity of Denomination	Current Value	Where Located	Owner of Record

19. Other information relating to your financial condition. If you check the yes box, please give dates and explain on page 4. Additional information or Comments.

a. Court proceedings	☐ Yes ☐ No	b. Bankruptcies	☐ Yes ☐ No
c. Repossessions	☐ Yes ☐ No	d. Recent sale or other transfer of assets for less than full value	☐ Yes ☐ No
e. Anticipated increase in income	☐ Yes ☐ No	f. Participant or beneficiary to trust, estate, profit sharing, etc.	☐ Yes ☐ No

Form 433-A page 2 (Rev 9-95)

STF FED1060F 2

Form 433-A *(continued)*

Section IV.   Assets and Liabilities

Description	Current Market Value	Current Amount Owed	Equity in Asset	Amount of Monthly Payment	Name and Address of Lien/Note Holder/Lender	Date Pledged	Date of Final Payment
20. Cash							
21. Bank accounts *(from Item 13)*							
22. Securities *(from Item 18)*							
23. Cash or loan value of insurance							
24. Vehicles *(model, year, license, tags)*							
a.							
b.							
c.							
25. Real property *(From Section III, Item 16)* a.							
b.							
c.							
26. Other assets							
a.							
b.							
c.							
d.							
e.							
27. Bank revolving credit *(from Item 14)*							
28. Other Liabilities *(Including bank loans, judgments, notes, and charge accounts not entered in Item 13.)* a.							
b.							
c.							
d.							
e.							
f.							
g.							
29. Federal taxes owed (prior years)							
30. Totals			$	$			

Internal Revenue Service Use Only Below This Line

Financial Verification/Analysis

Item	Date Information or Encumbrance Verified	Date Property Inspected	Estimated Forced Sale Equity
Personal Residence			
Other Real Property			
Vehicles			
Other Personal Property			
State Employment *(Husband and Wife)*			
Income Tax Return			
Wage Statements *(Husband and Wife)*			
Sources of Income/Credit *(D&B Report)*			
Expenses			
Other Assets/Liabilities			

Form **433-A**   page 3   (Rev. 9-95)
STF FED1060F 3

Form 433-A *(continued)*

Section V.   Monthly Income and Expense Analysis

Total Income			Necessary Living Expenses		
Source	Gross			Claimed	*(IRS use only)* Allowed
31. Wages/Salaries *(Taxpayer)*	$	42. National Standard Expenses[1]		$	$
32. Wages/Salaries *(Spouse)*		43. Housing and utilities[2]			
33. Interest - Dividends		44. Transportation[3]			
34. Net business income *(from Form 433-B)*		45. Health care			
35. Rental Income		46. Taxes *(income and FICA)*			
36. Pension *(Taxpayer)*		47. Court ordered payments			
37. Pension *(Spouse)*		48. Child/dependent care			
38. Child Support		49. Life insurance			
39. Alimony		50. Secured or legally-perfected debts *(specify)*			
40. Other		51. Other expenses *(specify)*			
41. Total Income	$	52. Total Expenses		$	$
		53. *(IRS use only)* Net difference *(income less necessary living expenses)*		$	$

Certification   Under penalties of perjury, I declare that to the best of my knowledge and belief this statement of assets, liabilities, and other information is true, correct, and complete.

54. Your signature	55. Spouse's signature *(if joint return was filed)*	56. Date

Notes

1. Clothing and clothing services, food, housekeeping supplies, personal care products and services, and miscellaneous.

2. Rent or mortgage payment for the taxpayer's principal residence. Add the average monthly payment for the following expenses if they are *not* included in the rent or mortgage payment: property taxes, homeowner's or renter's insurance, parking, necessary maintenance and repair, homeowner dues, condominium fees and utilities. Utilities includes gas, electricity, water, fuel oil, coal, bottled gas, trash and garbage collection, wood and other fuels, septic cleaning and telephone.

3. Lease or purchase payments, insurance, registration fees, normal maintenance, fuel, public transportation, parking and tolls.

Additional information or comments:

Internal Revenue Service Use Only Below This Line

Explain any difference between item 53 and the installment agreement payment amount:

Name of originator and IDRS assignment number	Date

Form 433-A   page 4   (Rev. 9-95)

STF FED1060F 4

Form 433-B – Collection Information Statement for Business

Form **433-B**
(Rev. June 1991)
Department of the Treasury
Internal Revenue Service

Collection Information Statement for Businesses

(If you need additional space, please attach a separate sheet.)

Note: Complete all blocks, except shaded areas. Write "N/A" (not applicable) in those blocks that do not apply.

1 Name and address of business	2 Business phone number ( )

3 (Check appropriate box)
☐ Sole proprietor ☐ Other (specify)
☐ Partnership
County .... ☐ Corporation

4 Name and title of person being interviewed	5 Employer identification number	6 Type of business

7 Information about owner, partners, officers, major shareholder, etc.

Name and Title	Effective Date	Home Address	Phone Number	Social Security Number	Total Shares or Interest

Section I   General Financial Information

8 Latest filed income tax return ▶ | Form | Tax year ended | Net income before taxes

9 Bank accounts (List all types of accounts including payroll and general, savings, certificates of deposit, etc.)

Name of Institution	Address	Type of Account	Account Number	Balance

Total (Enter in item 17) ▶

10 Bank credit available (Lines of credit, etc.)

Name of Institution	Address	Credit Limit	Amount Owed	Credit Available	Monthly Payments

Totals (Enter in items 24 or 25 as appropriate) . . . . ▶

11 Location, box number, and contents of all safe deposit boxes rented or accessed

Cat. No. 16649P   Form **433-B** (Rev. 6-91)

Form 433-B *(continued)*

Section I (continued)   **General Financial Information**

12   Real property

Brief Description and Type of Ownership	Physical Address
a	County ....
b	County ....
c	County ....
d	County ....

13   Life insurance policies owned with business as beneficiary

Name Insured	Company	Policy Number	Type	Face Amount	Available Loan Value

Total (Enter in item 19) . . . . ►

14a Additional information regarding financial condition (Court proceedings, bankruptcies filed or anticipated, transfers of assets for less than full value, changes in market conditions, etc. Include information regarding company participation in trusts, estates, profit-sharing plans, etc.)

b If you know of any person or organization that borrowed or otherwise provided funds to pay net payrolls:	**(i)** Who borrowed funds?
	(ii) Who supplied funds?

15   Accounts/notes receivable (Include current contract jobs. loans to stockholders, officers, partners, etc.)

Name	Address	Amount Due	Date Due	Status
		$		

Total (Enter in item 18) . . . . ► $

Form 433-B *(continued)*

Form 433-B (Rev. 6-91)   Page 3

Section II — Asset and Liability Analysis

(a) Description	(b) Cur. Mkt. Value	(c) Liabilities Bal. Due	(d) Equity in Asset	(e) Amt. of Mo. Pymt	(f) Name and Address of Lien/Note Holder/Obligee	(g) Date Pledged	(h) Date of Final Pymt.
16 Cash on hand							
17 Bank accounts							
18 Accounts/Notes receivable							
19 Life insurance loan value							
20 Real property *(from item 12)* a							
b							
c							
d							
21 Vehicles *(model, year, and license)* a							
b							
c							
22 Machinery and equipment *(specify)* a							
b							
c							
23 Merchandise inventory *(specify)* a							
b							
24 Other assets *(specify)* a							
b							
25 Other liabilities *(including notes and judgments)* a							
b							
c							
d							
e							
f							
g							
h							
26 Federal taxes owed							
27 Total							

Form 433-B *(continued)*

Form 433-B (Rev. 6-91)   Page **4**

Section III   Income and Expense Analysis

The following information applies to income and expenses during the period _____ to _____		Accounting method used	
Income		**Expenses**	
28 Gross receipts from sales, services, etc.	$	34 Materials purchased	$
29 Gross rental income		35 Net wages and salaries (Number of employees ....)	
30 Interest		36 Rent	
31 Dividends		37 Allowable installment payments *(IRS use only)*	
32 Other income *(specify)*		38 Supplies	
		39 Utilities/telephone	
		40 Gasoline/oil	
		41 Repairs and maintenance	
		42 Insurance	
		43 Current taxes	
		44 Other *(specify)*	
33 Total income	▶ $	45 Total expenses *(IRS use only)*	▶
		46 Net difference *(IRS use only)*	▶

Certification: Under penalties of perjury, I declare that to the best of my knowledge and belief this statement of assets, liabilities, and other information is true, correct, and complete.

47 Signature	48 Date

Internal Revenue Service Use Only Below This Line

Financial Verification/Analysis

Item	Date Information or Encumbrance Verified	Date Property Inspected	Estimated Forced Sale Equity
Sources of income/credit (D&B report)			
Expenses			
Real property			
Vehicles			
Machinery and equipment			
Merchandise			
Accounts/notes receivable			
Corporate information, if applicable			
U.C.C. senior/junior lienholder			
Other assets/liabilities			

Explain any difference between item 46 (or P&L) and the installment agreement payment amount.

Name of originator and IDRS assignment number	Date

APPENDIX B

Publication 1542 – Per Diem Rates in the United States

Publication 1542 – Per Diem Rates in the United States

Department of the Treasury
Internal Revenue Service

Publication 1542
(Rev. February 1998)
Cat. No. 12684I

Per Diem Rates

(For Travel Within the Continental United States)

Get forms and other information faster and easier by:
COMPUTER
- World Wide Web ➤ www.irs.ustreas.gov
- FTP ➤ ftp.irs.ustreas.gov
- IRIS at FedWorld ➤ (703) 321-8020
  FAX
- From your FAX machine, dial ➤ (703) 368-9694
See *How To Get More Information* in this publication.

Contents

Introduction

This publication is for employers who pay a per diem allowance to employees for business travel away from home, on or after January 1, 1998, within the continental United States (CONUS). It gives the maximum per diem rate you can use without treating part of the per diem allowance as wages for tax purposes. For a detailed discussion on the tax treatment of a per diem allowance, see chapter 16 of Publication 535, *Business Expenses*, or Revenue Procedure 97–59, 1997–52 I.R.B. 31.

High-low method. The *Localities Eligible for $180 ($40 M&IE) Per Diem Amount Under the High-Low Substantiation Method* chart on pages 2 and 3 lists the localities that are treated under that method as high cost localities for 1998 or the part of the year shown in parenthesis. All other localities within CONUS are eligible for $113 ($32 M&IE) per diem under the high-low method.

Regular federal per diem rate method. The *Maximum Federal Per Diem Rates* chart that begins on page 4 of this publication gives the regular federal per diem rate, including the separate rate for meals and incidental expenses (M&IE), for each locality.

Travel outside CONUS. The federal per diem rates for localities outside CONUS, including Alaska, Hawaii, Puerto Rico, the Northern Mariana Islands, U.S. possessions, and all foreign localities, are published monthly. You can buy the per diem supplement, *Maximum Travel Per Diem Allowances for Foreign Areas*, from the U.S. Government Printing Office. Call (202) 512–1800 (not a toll-free number) or write: U.S. Government Printing Office, P.O. Box 371954, Pittsburgh, PA 15250–7974.

Per diem rates on the internet. You can access the federal per diem rates on the internet.

- The rates for travel within CONUS are at:
  www.fss.gsa.gov
- The rates for travel outside CONUS are at:
  www.state.gov or *gopher://gopher.state.gov*

Per Diem Rates in the United States *(continued)*

Localities Eligible For $180 ($40 M&IE) Per Diem Amount Under the High-Low Substantiation Method*

Key City	County and Other Defined Location
Arizona	
Grand Canyon	All points in the Grand Canyon National Park and Kaibab National Forest within Coconino County
California	
Los Angeles	Los Angeles, Kern, Orange, and Ventura Counties; Edwards Air Force Base; Naval Weapons Center,
Napa	and Ordnance Test Station, China Lake
(April 1–October 31)	Napa
Palo Alto/San Jose	Santa Clara
Point Arena/Gualala	Mendocino
San Francisco	San Francisco
Colorado	
Aspen	Pitkin
Keystone/Silverthorne	Summit
Telluride	San Miguel
Vail	Eagle
(November 1–March 31)	
Delaware	
Lewes	Sussex
(June 1–September 14)	
District of Columbia	
Washington, DC	Washington, DC; the cities of Alexandria, Falls Church, and Fairfax, and the counties of Arlington, Loudoun, and Fairfax in Virginia; and the counties of Montgomery and Prince George's in Maryland
Florida	
Key West	Monroe
(December 15–April 30)	
Naples	Collier
(December 15–April 30)	
Illinois	
Chicago	Du Page, Cook, and Lake
Indiana	
Nashville	Brown
(June 1–October 31)	
Maine	
Bar Harbor	Hancock
(July 1–September 14)	
Maryland	For the counties of Montgomery and Prince George's, see District of Columbia.
Baltimore	Baltimore and Hartford
Ocean City	Worcester
(May 1–September 30)	
Saint Michael's	Talbot
(April 1–November 30)	
Massachusetts	
Boston	Suffolk
Cambridge/Lowell	Middlesex
Martha's Vineyard	Dukes
(June 1–October 31)	
Nantucket	Nantucket
(June 1–October 31)	
Nevada	
Incline Village	All points in the Northern Lake Tahoe area within Washoe County
(June 1–September 30)	
New Hampshire	
Hanover	Grafton and Sullivan
(June 1–October 31)	
New Jersey	
Ocean City/Cape May	Cape May
(May 15–September 30)	
Parsippany/Dover	Morris, Picatinny Arsenal
New Mexico	
Santa Fe	Santa Fe
(May 1–October 31)	
New York	
New York City	The boroughs of Bronx, Brooklyn, Manhattan, Queens, and Staten Island; Nassau and Suffolk Counties
Tarrytown/White Plains	Westchester
North Carolina	
Kill Devil/Duck/Outer Banks	Dare
(May 1–September 30)	

Page2

Per Diem Rates in the United States *(continued)*

Localities Eligible For $180 ($40 M&IE) Per Diem Amount Under the High-Low Substantiation Method *(continued)*

Key City	County and Other Defined Location
Pennsylvania	
Philadelphia	Philadelphia; city of Bala Cynwyd in Montgomery County
Rhode Island	
Newport/Block Island (May 1–October 14)	Newport and Washington
South Carolina	
Hilton Head (March 1–September 30)	Beaufort
Myrtle Beach (May 1–September 30)	Horry; Myrtle Beach Air Force Base
Utah	
Park City (December 1–March 31)	Summit
Virginia	For the cities of Alexandria, Fairfax, and Falls Church, and the counties of Arlington, Fairfax, and Loudon, see District of Columbia.
Washington	
Friday Harbor (June 1–October 31)	San Juan
Seattle	King
Wyoming	
Jackson (June 1–October 14)	Teton

*The per diem rate for all other localities within the continental United States is $113 ($32 M&IE).

Page 3

Per Diem Rates in the United States (continued)

Maximum Federal Per Diem Rates*

Per Diem Locality		Maximum Lodging Amount (a)	+	M&IE Rate (b)	=	Maximum Per Diem Rate⁴ (c)
Key City¹	County and/or Other Defined Location²,³					
CONUS. Standard rate . . . . (Applies to all locations within CONUS not specifically listed below or encompassed by the boundary definition of a listed point. However, the standard CONUS rate applies to all locations within CONUS. including those defined below. for certain relocation subsistence allowances. See parts 302-2, 302-4. and 302-5 of this subtitle.)		$50		$30		$80
ALABAMA						
Birmingham.	Jefferson	64		38		102
Gulf Shores.	Baldwin					
(May 1-September 30) . .	. . . .	104		34		138
(October 1-April 30). . .	. . . .	60		34		94
Huntsville	Madison	64		34		98
Mobile	Mobile	62		38		100
Montgomery	Montgomery	67		30		97
ARIZONA						
Casa Grande	Pinal					
(January 1-April 30)	. . . .	61		30		91
May 1-December 31)	. . . .	54		30		84
Chinle	Apache					
(April 1-October 31).	. . . .	93		30		123
(November 1-March 31) .	. . . .	60		30		90
Flagstaff.	All points in Coconino County not covered under Grand Canyon per diem area.					
(April 1-October 31). . .	. . . .	79		34		113
(November 1-March 31) .	. . . .	59		34		93
Grand Canyon	All points in the Grand Canyon National Park and Kaibab National Forest within Coconino County.	111		38		149
Kayenta	Navajo					
(April 1-October 31). .	. . . .	105		30		135
(November 1-March 31)	. . . .	68		30		98
Phoenix/Scottsdale . . .	Maricopa					
(October 1-May 14). . .	. . . .	106		38		144
(May 15-September 30) .	. . . .	72		38		110
Prescott.	Yavapai	59		34		93
Sierra Vista	Cochise	56		30		86
Tucson	Pima County; Davis-Monthan AFB.					
(November 1-May 31)	. . . .	85		34		119
(June 1-October 31) . .	. . . .	67		34		101
Yuma	Yuma	64		30		94
ARKANSAS						
Little Rock	Pulaski.	61		30		91
CALIFORNIA						
Clearlake	Lake	65		34		99
Death Valley	Inyo	93		42		135
Eureka	Humboldt	76		34		110
Fresno	Fresno	70		34		104

*Effective for travel on or after January 1. 1998
Source: Federal Travel Regulations. Maximum Federal Per Diem Rates (41 CFR Part 301-7)

Page 4

Per Diem Rates in the United States *(continued)*

Key City[1]	County and/or Other Defined Location[L 3]	Maximum Lodging Amount (a)	+	M&IE Rate (b)	=	Maximum Per Diem Rate[4] (c)
Los Angeles	Los Angeles, Kern, Orange and Ventura Counties; Edwards AFB; Naval Weapons Center and Ordnance Test Station, China Lake	109		42		151
Mammoth Lakes/Bridgeport	Mono	83		42		125
Merced	Merced	54		34		88
Modesto	Stanislaus	63		34		97
Monterey	Monterey	94		38		132
Napa	Napa					
(April 1-October 31)		116		42		158
(November 1-March 31)		103		42		145
Oakhurst/Madera	Madera	61		30		91
Oakland	Alameda, Contra Costa and Marin	111		34		145
Ontario	San Bernardino	66		38		104
Palm Springs	Riverside					
(November 1-May 31)		81		38		119
(June 1-October 31)		50		38		88
Palo Alto/San Jose	Santa Clara	116		42		158
Point Arena/Gualala	Mendicino	120		42		162
Redding	Shasta	53		34		87
Redwood City/San Mateo	San Mateo	87		38		125
Sacramento	Sacramento	81		38		119
San Diego	San Diego	93		38		131
San Francisco	San Francisco	120		42		162
San Luis Obispo	San Luis Obispo	66		38		104
Santa Barbara	Santa Barbara	98		34		132
Santa Cruz	Santa Cruz					
(June 1-September 30)		87		38		125
(October 1-May 31)		51		38		89
Santa Rosa	Sonoma	64		38		102
South Lake Tahoe	El Dorado (See also Stateline, NV.)	96		38		134
Stockton	San Joaquin	55		34		89
Tahoe City	Placer	94		38		132
Visalia	Tulare	55		38		93
West Sacramento	Yolo	88		30		118
Yosemite Nat'l Park	Mariposa					
(April 1-October 31)		87		42		129
(November 1-March 31)		59		42		101
COLORADO						
Aspen	Pitkin	145		42		187
Boulder	Boulder					
(May 1-October 31)		92		38		130
(November 1-April 30)		70		38		108
Colorado Springs	El Paso					
(April 1-October 31)		76		30		106
(November 1-March 31)		63		30		93
Cortez	Montezuma					
(May 1-September 30)		57		30		87
(October 1-April 30)		50		30		80
Denver	Denver, Adams, Arapahoe and Jefferson	92		34		126
Durango	La Plata					
(June 1-October 31)		100		34		134
(November 1-May 31)		50		34		84
Fort Collins/Loveland	Larimer	55		30		85
Glenwood Springs	Garfield	69		34		103
Grand Junction	Mesa	56		30		86
Gunnison	Gunnison					
(June 1-September 30)		62		30		92
(October 1-May 31)		50		30		80

Per Diem Rates in the United States *(continued)*

Key City[1]	County and/or Other Defined Location[L 1]	Maximum Lodging Amount (a)	+	M&IE Rate (b)	=	Maximum Per Diem Rate[4] (c)
Keystone/Silverthorne	Summit	170		42		212
Montrose	Montrose	60		30		90
Pueblo	Pueblo					
(June 1-September 30)		67		30		97
(October 1-May 31)		57		30		87
Steamboat Springs	Routt					
(December 1-March 31)		97		34		131
(April 1-November 30)		50		34		84
Telluride	San Miguel					
(November 1-March 31)		129		38		167
(April 1-October 31)		110		38		148
Trinidad	Las Animas					
(June 1-September 30)		67		30		97
(October 1-May 31)		50		30		80
Vail	Eagle					
(November 1-March 31)		226		42		268
(April 1-October 31)		99		42		141
CONNECTICUT						
Bridgeport/Danbury	Fairfield	96		38		134
Hartford	Hartford and Middlesex	91		30		121
New Haven	New Haven	87		30		117
New London/Groton	New London					
(June 1-October 31)		87		34		121
(November 1-May 31)		50		34		84
Putnam/Danielson	Windham	84		30		114
Salisbury/Lakeville	Litchfield	69		34		103
Vernon	Tolland	54		30		84
DELAWARE						
Dover	Kent					
(May 1-September 30)		60		34		94
(October 1-April 30)		54		34		88
Lewes	Sussex					
(June 1-September 14)		123		38		161
(September 15-May 31)		92		38		130
Wilmington	New Castle	93		38		131
DISTRICT OF COLUMBIA						
Washington, DC (also the cities of Alexandria, Falls Church, and Fairfax, and the counties of Arlington, Loudoun, and Fairfax in Virginia; and the counties of Montgomery and Prince George's in Maryland. See also Maryland and Virginia.)		126		42		168
FLORIDA						
Altamonte Springs	Seminole	81		34		115
Bradenton	Manatee					
(January 1-May 14)		76		30		106
(May 15-December 31)		50		30		80
Cocoa Beach	Brevard	84		34		118
Daytona Beach	Volusia					
(February 1-August 31)		90		34		124
(September 1-January 31)		54		34		88
Fort Lauderdale	Broward					
(December 15-April 30)		104		34		138
(May 1-December 14)		72		34		106
Fort Myers	Lee					
(January 1-April 30)		98		34		132
(May 1-December 31)		53		34		87
Fort Pierce	Saint Lucie					
(December 1-April 30)		61		30		91
(May 1-November 30)		50		30		80
Fort Walton Beach	Okaloosa	80		30		110

Per Diem Rates in the United States *(continued)*

Key City[1]	County and/or Other Defined Location[L 2]	Maximum Lodging Amount (a)	M&IE Rate (b)	Maximum Per Diem Rate[4] (c)
Gainesville	Alachua	64	34	98
Gulf Breeze	Santa Rosa	65	34	99
Jacksonville	Duval County; Naval Station Mayport	73	30	103
Key West	Monroe			
(December 15-April 30)		147	42	189
(May 1-December 14)		94	42	136
Kissimmee	Osceola	74	30	104
Lakeland	Polk	63	30	93
Miami	Dade			
(December 15-April 30)		89	42	131
(May 1-December 14)		71	42	113
Naples	Collier			
(December 15-April 30)		126	38	164
(May 1-December 14)		65	38	103
Orlando	Orange	77	34	111
Panama City	Bay			
(March 1-September 14)		77	30	107
(September 15-February 29)		59	30	89
Pensacola	Escambia	59	34	93
Punta Gorda	Charlotte			
(December 15-April 14)		76	34	110
(April 15-December 14)		54	34	88
Saint Augustine	Saint Johns	65	34	99
Sarasota	Sarasota			
(December 15-April 30)		89	34	123
(May 1-December 14)		52	34	86
Stuart	Martin			
(January 1-April 30)		69	34	103
(May 1-December 31)		63	34	97
Tallahassee	Leon	66	34	100
Tampa/St. Petersburg	Hillsborough and Pinellas			
(January 1-April 30)		103	38	141
(May 1-December 31)		81	38	119
Vero Beach	Indian River			
(January 15-April 30)		63	30	93
(May 1-January 14)		50	30	80
West Palm Beach	Palm Beach			
(January 1-April 30)		94	38	132
(May 1-December 31)		67	38	105
GEORGIA				
Albany	Dougherty	58	30	88
Athens	Clarke	58	34	92
Atlanta	Clayton, De Kalb, Fulton, Cobb, and Gwinnett	97	38	135
Augusta	Richmond	70	30	100
Columbus	Muscogee	63	30	93
Conyers	Rockdale	65	30	95
Macon	Bibb	86	30	116
Savannah	Chatham	71	34	105
IDAHO				
Boise	Ada	68	34	102
Coeur d'Alene	Kootenai			
(May 1-September 30)		56	34	90
(October 1-April 30)		50	34	84
Idaho Falls	Bonneville	56	34	90
Ketchum/Sun Valley	Blaine	87	38	125

Per Diem Rates in the United States *(continued)*

Per Diem Locality		Maximum Lodging Amount (a)		M&IE Rate (b)		Maximum Per Diem Rate⁴ (c)
Key City¹	County and/or Other Defined Location^L ²		+		=	
McCall	Valley	59		34		93
Stanley	Custer					
(June 1–September 30). .	. . . .	57		34		91
(October 1–May 31). . .	. . . .	50		34		84
ILLINOIS						
Aurora/Elgin.	Kane	59		30		89
Champaign/Urbana . . .	Champaign	56		34		90
Chicago	Du Page, Cook and Lake . . .	120		42		162
Joliet	Will	52		30		82
Peoria	Peoria	54		34		88
Rock Island	Rock Island	85		30		115
Rockford	Winnebago	65		38		103
Springfield	Sangamon.	55		30		85
INDIANA						
Bloomington/Crane . . .	Monroe and Martin	56		34		90
Carmel	Hamilton					
(June 1–September 30). .	. . . .	82		38		120
(October 1–May 31). . .	. . . .	73		38		111
Fort Wayne	Allen	52		30		82
Indianapolis.	Marion County; Fort Benjamin Harrison	79		38		117
Lafayette	Tippecanoe	54		34		88
Madison.	Jefferson	52		30		82
Michigan City	La Porte	57		30		87
Muncie	Delaware	52		30		82
Nashville	Brown					
(June 1–October 31) . .	. . . .	117		30		147
(November 1–May 31) . .	. . . .	65		30		95
South Bend.	St. Joseph	61		30		91
Valparaiso/Burlington Beach .	Porter	65		30		95
IOWA						
Bettendorf/Davenport . . .	Scott	60		30		90
Cedar Rapids	Linn	52		34		86
Des Moines.	Polk	68		30		98
KANSAS						
Kansas City.	Johnson and Wyandotte (See also Kansas City, MO)	88		42		130
Wichita	Sedgwick	62		34		96
KENTUCKY						
Covington	Kenton	64		34		98
Florence.	Boone	59		30		89
Lexington	Fayette	62		34		96
Louisville	Jefferson	71		38		109
LOUISIANA						
Baton Rouge	East Baton Rouge Parish.	67		34		101
Bossier City.	Bossier Parish	60		30		90
Gonzales	Ascension Parish.	57		30		87
Lake Charles	Calcasieu Parish	83		30		113
New Orleans	Parishes of Jefferson, Orleans, Plaquemines, and St. Bernard	88		42		130
Opelousas	St. Landry.	62		30		92
Shreveport	Caddo Parish.	60		34		94
St. Francisville	West Feliciana	88		30		118

Page 8

Per Diem Rates in the United States *(continued)*

Per Diem Locality		Maximum Lodging Amount (a)	M&IE Rate (b)	Maximum Per Diem Rate[1] (c)
Key City[1]	County and/or Other Defined Location[2,3]		+	=
MAINE				
Bangor	Penobscot			
(July 1–October 31)		59	30	89
(November 1–June 30)		50	30	80
Bar Harbor	Hancock			
(July 1–September 14)		138	34	172
(September 15–June 30)		63	34	97
Bath	Sagadahoc			
(June 1–September 30)		61	30	91
(October 1–May 31)		52	30	82
Calais	Washington			
(July 1–September 30)		59	30	89
(October 1–June 30)		50	30	80
Kennebunk/Sanford	York			
(May 1–September 30)		91	34	125
(October 1–April 30)		59	34	93
Kittery	Portsmouth Naval Shipyard (See also Portsmouth, NH.)			
(June 1–October 31)		81	34	115
(November 1–May 31)		57	34	91
Portland	Cumberland			
(July 1–October 31)		86	38	124
(November 1–June 30)		63	38	101
Rockport	Knox			
(June 15–October 31)		102	34	136
(November 1–June 14)		58	34	92
Wiscasset	Lincoln			
(July 1–September 14)		100	30	130
(September 15–June 30)		64	30	94
MARYLAND				
(For the counties of Montgomery and Prince George s. see District of Columbia.)				
Annapolis	Anne Arundel	96	38	134
Baltimore	Baltimore and Harford.	110	38	148
Columbia	Howard	92	42	134
Frederick	Frederick	56	38	94
Grasonville	Queen Annes	59	34	93
Hagerstown	Washington	54	30	84
Lexington Park/St.Inigoes/ Leonardtown.	Saint Mary s	59	34	93
Lusby	Calvert	59	34	93
Ocean City	Worcester			
(May 1–September 30)		145	42	187
(October 1–April 30).		50	42	92
Salisbury	Wicomico	58	34	92
St. Michaels	Talbot			
(April 1–November 30)		130	38	168
(December 1–March 31)		103	38	141
MASSACHUSETTS				
Andover	Essex	78	38	116
Boston	Suffolk	116	42	158
Cambridge/Lowell	Middlesex			
(April 1–November 30)		127	34	161
(December 1–March 31)		116	34	150
Greenfield/South Deerfield	Franklin	55	30	85
Hyannis	Barnstable			
(July 1–September 30)		104	38	142
(October 1–June 30)		55	38	93
Martha's Vineyard	Dukes			
(June 1–October 31)		159	42	201
(November 1–May 31)		92	42	134
Nantucket	Nantucket			
(June 1–October 31)		149	42	191
(November 1–May 31)		92	42	134
Northampton	Hampshire	68	30	98

Per Diem Rates in the United States *(continued)*

Per Diem Locality		Maximum Lodging Amount (a)	+	M&IE Rate (b)	=	Maximum Per Diem Rate (c)
Key City[1]	County and/or Other Defined Location[L,1]					
Pittsfield	Berkshire	52		34		86
Plymouth	Plymouth					
(June 15–October 31) . .	. . . .	92		30		122
(November 1–June 14) . .	. . . .	70		30		100
Quincy	Norfolk	77		34		111
Springfield	Hampden	67		30		97
Taunton/New Bedford . .	Bristol	64		30		94
Worcester	Worcester	61		30		91
MICHIGAN						
Ann Arbor	Washtenaw	75		30		105
Charlevoix	Charlevoix					
(June 1–September 30) . .	. . . .	70		30		100
(October 1–May 31) . . .	. . . .	50		30		80
Detroit	Wayne	89		38		127
East Lansing/Lansing . .	Ingham	72		30		102
Flint	Genesee	57		30		87
Frankfort	Benzie	76		30		106
Gaylord	Otsego	59		34		93
Grand Rapids	Kent	62		34		96
Holland	Ottawa	64		30		94
Kalamazoo	Kalamazoo	54		30		84
Leland	Leelanau					
(May 1–September 30) . .	. . . .	100		30		130
(October 1–April 30) . . .	. . . .	53		30		83
Mackinac Island	Mackinac					
(June 1–September 30) . .	. . . .	94		38		132
(October 1–May 31) . . .	. . . .	61		38		99
Manistee	Manistee					
(June 1–September 30) . .	. . . .	63		30		93
(October 1–May 31) . . .	. . . .	50		30		80
Midland	Midland	58		30		88
Mount Pleasant	Isabella	56		30		86
Muskegon	Muskegon	61		30		91
Ontonagon	Ontonagon	55		30		85
Petoskey	Emmet					
(June 1–October 31) . .	. . . .	56		34		90
(November 1–May 31) . .	. . . .	50		34		84
Pontiac/Troy	Oakland	93		38		131
Sault Ste. Marie	Chippewa					
(June 1–October 31) . .	. . . .	77		34		111
(November 1–May 31) . .	. . . .	60		34		94
South Haven	Van Buren					
(May 1–September 30) . .	. . . .	85		30		115
(October 1–April 30) . . .	. . . .	54		30		84
Traverse City	Grand Traverse					
(May 1–September 30) . .	. . . .	97		34		131
(October 1–April 30) . . .	. . . .	58		34		92
Warren	Macomb	61		30		91

Per Diem Rates in the United States *(continued)*

Per Diem Locality		Maximum Lodging Amount (a)	*	M&IE Rate (b)	■	Maximum Per Diem Rate (c)
Key City[1]	County and/or Other Defined Location[2, 3]					
MINNESOTA						
Duluth	St. Louis					
(June 1-September 30)		66		38		104
(October 1-May 31)		57		38		95
Minneapolis/St. Paul	Anoka, Hennepin, and Ramsey Counties; Fort Snelling Military Reservation and Navy Astronautics Group (Detachment BRAVO), Rosemount.	91		38		129
Rochester	Olmstead	68		30		98
MISSISSIPPI						
Biloxi/Gulfport/Pascagoula/Bay St. Louis	Harrison, Jackson, and Hancock	79		34		113
Jackson	Hinds	65		34		99
Ridgeland	Madison	55		34		89
Robinsonville	Tunica	51		30		81
Vicksburg	Warren	56		30		86
MISSOURI						
Branson	Taney	68		30		98
(May 1-October 31)		54		30		84
(November 1-April 30)		54		30		84
Cape Girardeau	Cape Girardeau	55		30		85
Hannibal	Marion	52		30		82
Jefferson City	Cole	88		42		130
Kansas City	Clay, Jackson, and Platte (See also Kansas City, KS.)					
Lake Ozark	Miller	55		34		89
Osage Beach	Camden	55		34		89
Springfield	Greene	53		34		87
St. Louis	St. Charles and St. Louis	75		42		117
MONTANA						
Great Falls	Cascade	52		30		82
Polson/Kalispell	Lake	54		30		84
West Yellowstone Park	Gallatin,	52		30		82
NEBRASKA						
Lincoln	Lancaster	51		30		81
Omaha	Douglas	67		34		101
NEVADA						
Elko	All points in Elko County excluding Wendover	57		30		87
Incline Village**	All points in the Northern Lake Tahoe Area within Washoe County	119		38		157
(June 1-September 30)		76		38		114
(October 1-May 31)		80		38		118
Las Vegas	Clark County; Nellis AFB.					
Reno	All points in Washoe County not covered under Incline Village per diem locality	57		34		91
Stateline	Douglas (See also South Lake Tahoe, CA).	96		38		134
Winnemucca	Humboldt	51		30		81

**Denotes independent cities

Per Diem Rates in the United States (continued)

Key City[1]	County and/or Other Defined Location[1,1]	Maximum Lodging Amount (a)	M&IE Rate (b)	Maximum Per Diem Rate[1] (c)
NEW HAMPSHIRE				
Concord.	Merrimack			
(June 1-October 31)		68	30	98
(November 1-May 31)		50	30	80
Conway.	Carroll			
(June 1-October 31)		81	34	115
(November 1-May 31)		54	34	88
Durham.	Strafford			
(May 1-October 31)		71	30	101
(November 1-April 30)		63	30	93
Hanover.	Grafton and Sullivan			
(June 1-October 31)		113	38	151
(November 1-May 31)		86	38	124
Laconia.	Belknap	70	30	100
Manchester.	Hillsborough	73	30	103
Portsmouth/Newington	Rockingham County; Pease AFB (See also Kittery, ME.)			
(June 1-October 31)		81	34	115
(November 1-May 31)		57	34	91
NEW JERSEY				
Atlantic City.	Atlantic	84	38	122
Belle Mead.	Somerset	69	34	103
Cherry Hill/Camden/Moorestown	Camden	74	38	112
Flemington.	Hunterdon.	80	34	114
Freehold/Eatontown	Monmouth County; Fort Monmouth.	89	34	123
Millville.	Cumberland	54	34	88
Newark.	Bergen, Essex, Hudson, Passaic, and Union.	94	42	136
Ocean City/Cape May	Cape May			
(May 15-September 30)		165	30	195
(October 1-May 14).		95	30	125
Parsippany/Dover	Morris County; Picatinny Arsenal	118	38	156
Piscataway/Edison.	Middlesex.	105	38	143
Princeton/Trenton.	Mercer.	87	38	125
Tom's River.	Ocean			
(June 1-September 30).		69	34	103
(October 1-May 31).		63	34	97
NEW MEXICO				
Albuquerque	Bernalillo	70	34	104
Cloudcroft.	Otero	87	30	117
Farmington.	San Juan.	53	34	87
Gallup.	McKinley.	58	30	88
Los Alamos.	Los Alamos	81	34	115
Santa Fe.	Santa Fe			
(May 1-October 31).		122	42	164
(November 1-April 30).		83	42	125
Taos.	Taos	66	34	100
NEW YORK				
Albany.	Albany.	68	38	106
Batavia.	Genesee			
(May 1-September 30).		67	34	101
(October 1-April 30).		50	34	84
Binghamton.	Broome	54	34	88

Per Diem Rates in the United States *(continued)*

Per Diem Locality		Maximum Lodging Amount (a)	+	M&IE Rate (b)	=	Maximum Per Diem Rate (c)
Key City[1]	County and/or Other Defined Location[1, 2]					
Buffalo	Erie	78		38		116
Corning	Steuben	59		30		89
Elmira	Chemung	53		30		83
Glens Falls	Warren					
(June 1-October 31)		74		38		112
(November 1-May 31)		63		38		101
Ithaca	Tompkins	56		30		86
Kingston	Ulster	52		34		86
Lake Placid	Essex					
(June 1-November 14)		75		34		109
(November 15-May 31)		59		34		93
New York City	The boroughs of the Bronx, Brooklyn, Manhattan, Queens and Staten Island; Nassau and Suffolk Counties	198		42		240
Niagara Falls	Niagara					
(May 15-October 31)		65		34		99
(November 1-May 14)		50		34		84
Nyack/Palisades	Rockland	53		34		87
Owego	Tioga	63		30		93
Plattsburgh	Clinton	58		34		92
Poughkeepsie	Dutchess	74		30		104
Rochester	Monroe	65		42		107
Saratoga Springs	Saratoga					
(May 1-October 31)		104		38		142
(November 1-April 30)		56		38		94
Schenectady	Schenectady	52		34		86
Syracuse	Onondaga	71		34		105
Tarrytown/White Plains	Westchester	114		42		156
Utica	Oneida	66		34		100
Waterloo/Romulus	Seneca	69		30		99
Watertown	Jefferson	59		30		89
Watkins Glen	Schuyler	60		30		90
West Point	Orange	57		30		87
NORTH CAROLINA						
Asheville	Buncombe	52		34		86
Charlotte	Mecklenburg	71		38		109
Fayetteville	Cumberland	82		30		112
Greensboro/High Point	Guilford	67		34		101
Kill Devil/Duck/Outer Banks	Dare					
(May 1-September 30)		118		34		152
(October 1-April 30)		50		34		84
Morehead City	Carteret					
(April 1-August 31)		64		30		94
(September 1-March 31)		50		30		80
New Bern/Havelock	Craven	84		30		114
Research Park/Raleigh/Durham/ Chapel Hill	Wake, Durham and Orange	96		38		134
Wilmington	New Hanover					
(March 1-September 30)		65		30		95
(October 1-February 29)		55		30		85
Winston-Salem	Forsyth	80		34		114
NORTH DAKOTA						
The standard CONUS rate of $80 ($50 for lodging and $30 for M&IE) applies to all per diem localities in the state of North Dakota.						
OHIO						
Akron	Summit	72		34		106
Cambridge	Guernsey					
(June 1-October 31)		61		30		91
(November 1-May 31)		50		30		80
Canton	Stark	58		30		88
Cincinnati/Evendale	Hamilton and Warren	76		34		110
Cleveland	Cuyahoga	83		38		121
Columbus	Franklin	81		34		115

Per Diem Rates in the United States (continued)

Key City[1]	Per Diem Locality County and/or Other Defined Location[2,3]	Maximum Lodging Amount (a)	+	M&IE Rate (b)	=	Maximum Per Diem Rate[4] (c)
Dayton/Fairborn	Montgomery and Greene; Wright-Patterson AFB	74		30		104
Elyria	Lorain					
(May 1-September 30)		89		30		119
(October 1-April 30)		54		30		84
Fairfield/Hamilton	Butler	58		30		88
Geneva	Ashtabula	75		30		105
Jackson	Jackson and Pike	54		30		84
Lancaster	Fairfield	53		30		83
Norwalk/Bellevue	Huron					
(May 1-September 30)		73		30		103
(October 1-April 30)		50		30		80
Port Clinton/Oakharbor	Ottawa					
(June 1-September 30)		89		30		119
(October 1-May 31)		50		30		80
Sandusky	Erie					
(May 1-September 30)		109		30		139
(October 1-April 30)		50		30		80
Springfield	Clark	56		34		90
Toledo	Lucas	57		34		91
OKLAHOMA						
Norman	Cleveland	59		30		89
Oklahoma City	Oklahoma	65		30		95
Tulsa/Bartlesville	Osage, Tulsa, and Washington	54		30		84
OREGON						
Ashland/Medford	Jackson					
(June 1-October 31)		83		38		121
(November 1-May 31)		50		38		88
Beaverton	Washington	68		38		106
Bend	Deschutes	70		30		100
Clackamas/Milwaukie	Clackamas	65		30		95
Coos Bay	Coos	60		30		90
Florence/Eugene	Lane					
(July 1-September 30)		72		34		106
(October 1-June 30)		52		34		86
Gold Beach	Curry					
(May 15-October 31)		69		30		99
(November 1-May 14)		50		30		80
Klamath Falls	Klamath	69		38		107
Lincoln City/Newport	Lincoln					
(June 1-October 31)		85		38		123
(November 1-May 31)		58		38		96
Portland	Multnomah	89		38		127
Salem	Marion	56		30		86
Seaside	Clatsop	59		30		89
PENNSYLVANIA						
Allentown	Lehigh	66		34		100
Beaver Falls	Beaver	54		30		84
Chester/Radnor	Delaware	99		42		141
Gettysburg	Adams					
(May 1-October 31)		72		34		106
(November 1-April 30)		53		34		87
King of Prussia/Ft. Washington	Montgomery County, except Bala Cynwyd (See also Philadelphia, PA)	84		38		122
Lancaster	Lancaster	63		34		97
Mechanicsburg	Cumberland	65		30		95
Mercer	Mercer	52		30		82
Philadelphia	Philadelphia County; city of Bala Cynwyd in Montgomery County	113		38		151

Page 14

Per Diem Rates in the United States *(continued)*

Per Diem Locality		Maximum Lodging Amount (a)	+	M&IE Rate (b)	=	Maximum Per Diem Rate (c)
Key City[1]	County and/or Other Defined Location[1][1]					
Pittsburgh	Allegheny	90		38		128
Reading	Berks	57		30		87
Scranton	Lackawanna	61		34		95
Valley Forge/Malvern	Chester	95		38		133
Warminster	Bucks County; Naval Air Development Center	54		34		88
RHODE ISLAND						
East Greenwich	Kent County; Naval Construction Battalion Center. Davisville.	59		34		93
Newport/Block Island	Newport and Washington					
(May 1-October 14).		111		42		153
(October 15-April 30)		81		42		123
Providence	Providence	83		42		125
SOUTH CAROLINA						
Aiken	Aiken	70		30		100
Charleston	Charleston and Berkeley	100		34		134
Columbia	Richland	55		30		85
Greenville	Greenville	74		38		112
Hilton Head	Beaufort					
(March 1-September 30)		128		34		162
(October 1-February 29)		69		34		103
Myrtle Beach	Horry County; Myrtle Beach AFB					
(May 1-September 30)		141		34		175
(October 1-April 30).		60		34		94
Spartanburg	Spartanburg	54		30		84
SOUTH DAKOTA						
Custer	Custer					
(June 1-September 30).		64		30		94
(October 1-May 31).		50		30		80
Hot Springs.	Fall River					
(May 1-September 30)		70		30		100
(October 1-April 30).		50		30		80
Rapid City	Pennington					
(June 1-August 31)		84		30		114
(September 1-May 31)		50		30		80
Sioux Falls	Minnehaha	56		30		86
Sturgis	Mead					
(June 15-August 31)		86		30		116
(September 1-June 14).		50		30		80
TENNESSEE						
Chattanooga	Hamilton	62		30		92
Gatlinburg	Sevier					
(May 1-November 30).		85		34		119
(December 1-April 30)		61		34		95
Knoxville	Knox County; city of Oak Ridge	59		34		93
Memphis	Shelby	79		30		109
Murfreesboro	Rutherford	52		30		82
Nashville	Davidson	91		38		129
Townsend	Blount					
(May 1-October 31).		77		30		107
(November 1-April 30)		50		30		80
TEXAS						
Abilene	Taylor	55		30		85
Amarillo	Potter	59		30		89
Austin	Travis	85		34		119

Per Diem Rates in the United States *(continued)*

Key City[1]	Per Diem Locality County and/or Other Defined Location[2, 3]	Maximum Lodging Amount (a)	+	M&IE Rate (b)	=	Maximum Per Diem Rate[4] (c)
College Station/Bryan	Brazos	61		30		91
Corpus Christi/Ingelside	Nueces and San Patricio	62		30		92
Dallas/Fort Worth	Dallas and Tarrant	94		42		136
Eagle Pass	Maverick	57		30		87
El Paso	El Paso	56		34		90
Fort Davis	Jeff Davis	62		30		92
Galveston	Galveston	68		42		110
Granbury	Hood	53		30		83
Houston	Harris County; L.B. Johnson Space Center and Ellington AFB	79		38		117
Killeen/Temple	Bell	59		30		89
Lajitas	Brewster					
(September 1–May 31)		64		30		94
(June 1–August 31)		51		30		81
Lubbock	Lubbock	60		34		94
McAllen	Hidalgo	69		30		99
Midland/Odessa	Ector and Midland	52		30		82
Plano	Collin	58		34		92
San Antonio	Bexar	91		34		125
Tyler	Smith	60		30		90
Victoria	Victoria	54		30		84
Waco	McLennan	64		30		94
UTAH						
Bullfrog	Garfield	85		34		119
Cedar City	Iron					
(June 1–September 30)		67		30		97
(October 1–May 31)		50		30		80
Moab	Grand	77		30		107
Park City	Summit					
(December 1–March 31)		145		42		187
(April 1–November 30)		92		42		134
Provo	Utah	60		34		94
Salt Lake City/Ogden	Salt Lake, Weber, and Davis Counties; Dugway Proving Ground and Tooele Army Depot	83		38		121
VERMONT						
Burlington/St. Albans	Chittenden and Franklin	68		34		102
Manchester	Bennington	75		34		109
Middlebury	Addison	83		34		117
Montpelier	Washington	86		30		116
Rutland	Rutland					
(December 15–March 31)		62		30		92
(April 1–December 14)		52		30		82
White River Junction	Windsor					
(June 1–October 31)		113		30		143
(November 1–May 31)		86		30		116

Per Diem Rates in the United States *(continued)*

Per Diem Locality		Maximum Lodging Amount (a)	+	M&IE Rate (b)	=	Maximum Per Diem Rate* (c)
Key City[1]	County and/or Other Defined Location[1, 2]					
VIRGINIA						
(For the cities of Alexandria, Fairfax, and Falls Church, and the counties of Arlington, Fairfax, and Loudoun, see District of Columbia.)						
Blacksburg	Montgomery	52		30		82
Charlottesville**		55		42		97
Harrisonburg**		54		30		84
Lexington**		52		30		82
Lynchburg**		65		34		99
Richmond	Chesterfield and Henrico Counties; also Defense Supply Center	77		38		115
Roanoke**	Roanoke	51		34		85
Virginia Beach**	Virginia Beach (also Norfolk, Portsmouth, and Chesapeake)**					
(May 1-September 30)		107		38		145
(October 1-April 30)		64		38		102
Wallops Island	Accomack					
(June 1-October 14)		61		30		91
(October 15-May 31)		50		30		80
Williamsburg**	Williamsburg (also Hampton, Newport News, York County, Naval Weapons Station, Yorktown)**					
(April 1-October 31)		99		34		133
(November 1-March 31)		59		34		93
Wintergreen	Nelson	101		42		143
WASHINGTON						
Anacortes/Mt. Vernon/Whidbey Island	Skagit and Island	54		34		88
Bellingham	Whatcom	54		34		88
Bremerton	Kitsap	66		30		96
Friday Harbor	San Juan					
(June 1-October 31)		129		38		167
(November 1-May 31)		74		38		112
Lynnwood/Everett	Snohomish	77		34		111
Ocean Shores	Grays Harbor					
(April 1-September 30)		73		34		107
(October 1-March 31)		50		34		84
Olympia/Tumwater	Thurston	64		30		94
Port Angeles	Clallam					
(May 15-September 30)		71		34		105
(October 1-May 14)		50		34		84
Port Townsend	Jefferson					
(April 15-October 31)		63		30		93
(November 1-April 14)		53		30		83
Seattle	King	116		38		154
Spokane	Spokane	74		38		112
Tacoma	Pierce	83		30		113
Vancouver	Clark	62		34		96
WEST VIRGINIA						
Berkeley Springs	Morgan	89		30		119
Charleston	Kanawha	52		30		82
Harper's Ferry	Jefferson	66		30		96
Martinsburg	Berkeley	62		30		92
Morgantown	Monongalia	71		30		101
Parkersburg	Wood	57		30		87
Wheeling	Ohio	59		34		93

**Denotes independent cities

Per Diem Rates in the United States (continued)

Key City[1]	County and/or Other Defined Location[L 2]	Maximum Lodging Amount (a)	+	M&IE Rate (b)	=	Maximum Per Diem Rate[4] (c)
WISCONSIN						
Appleton	Outagamie	57		30		87
Brookfield	Waukesha	74		38		112
Eau Claire	Eau Claire	54		34		88
Green Bay	Brown	61		30		91
La Crosse	La Crosse	52		34		86
Lake Geneva	Walworth					
(May 1-October 31)		69		34		103
(November 1-April 30)		51		34		85
Madison	Dane	72		34		106
Milwaukee	Milwaukee	77		34		111
Oshkosh	Winnebago	57		34		91
Plymouth/Sheboygan	Sheboygan	52		30		82
Racine/Kenosha	Racine and Kenosha					
(June 1-September 30)		57		34		91
(October 1-May 31)		50		34		84
Rhinelander/Minocqua	Oneida	57		30		87
Sturgeon Bay	Door					
(June 1-September 14)		77		30		107
(September 15-May 31)		50		30		80
Wisconsin Dells	Columbia					
(June 1-September 14)		77		38		115
(September 15-May 31)		57		38		95
WYOMING						
Cody	Park					
(May 1-September 30)		86		30		116
(October 1-April 30)		50		30		80
Jackson	Teton					
(June 1-October 14)		105		42		147
(October 15-May 31)		76		42		118
Thermopolis	Hot Springs	54		30		84

[1] Unless otherwise specified, the per diem locality is defined as "all locations within, or entirely surrounded by, the corporate limits of the key city, including independent entities located within those boundaries."

[2] Per diem localities with county definitions shall include "all locations within, or entirely surrounded by, the corporate limits of the key city as well as the boundaries of the listed counties, including independent entities located within the boundaries of the key city and the listed counties."

[3] When a military installation or Government-related facility (whether or not specifically named) is located partially within more than one city or county boundary, the applicable per diem rate for the entire installation or facility is the higher of the two rates which apply to the cities and/or counties, even though part(s) of such activities may be located outside the defined per diem locality.

[4] Federal agencies may submit a request to GSA for review of the costs covered by per diem in a particular city or area where the standard CONUS rate applies when travel to that location is repetitive or on a continuing basis and travelers' experiences indicate that the prescribed rate is inadequate. Other per diem localities listed in this appendix will be reviewed on an annual basis by GSA to determine whether rates are adequate. Requests for per diem rate adjustments shall be submitted by the agency headquarters office to the General Services Administration, Office of Governmentwide Policy, Attn: Travel and Transportation Management Policy Division (MTT), Washington, D.C. 20405. Agencies should designate an individual responsible for reviewing, coordinating, and submitting to GSA any requests from bureaus or subagencies. Requests for rate adjustments shall include a city designation, a description of the surrounding location involved (county or other defined area), and a recommended rate supported by a statement explaining the circumstances that cause the existing rate to be inadequate. The request also must contain an estimate of the annual number of trips to the location, the average duration of such trips, and the primary purpose of travel to the location. Agencies should submit their requests to GSA no later than May 1 in order for a city to be included in the annual review.

Per Diem Rates in the United States *(continued)*

HowToGetMoreInformation

Youcangethelpfromthe IRSinseveralways.

Freepublicationsandforms. Toorderfreepublica-
tions and forms, call 1–800–TAX–FORM
(1–800–829–3676). You can also write to the IRS
Forms Distribution Center nearest you. Check your income tax package for the address. Your local library
orpostofficealsomayhavetheitemsyouneed.

For a list of free tax publications, order Publication
910, *Guide to Free Tax Services.* It also contains an
index of tax topics and related publications and describes other free tax information services available
from IRS, including tax education and assistance programs.

If you have access to a personal computer and
modem, you also can get many forms and publications
electronically. See *Quick and Easy Access to Tax Help
and Forms* inyourincometaxpackagefordetails.

Tax questions. You can call the IRS with your tax
questions. Check your income tax package or telephone book for the local number, or you can call
1–800–829–1040.

TTY/TDDequipment. Ifyouhaveaccessto TTY/TDD
equipment, you can call 1–800–829–4059 to ask tax
questionsortoorderformsandpublications. See your
incometaxpackageforthehoursofoperation.

Evaluating the quality of our telephone services.
To ensure that IRS representatives give accurate,
courteous, and professional answers, we evaluate the
quality of our "800 number" telephone services in several ways.

• A second IRS representative sometimes monitors
  live telephone calls. That person only evaluates the
  IRS assistor and does not keep a record of any
  taxpayer's name or tax identification number.

• We sometimes record telephone calls to evaluate
  IRS assistors objectively. We hold these recordings
  no longer than one week and use them only to
  measure the quality of assistance.

• We value our customers' opinions. Throughout this
  year, we will be surveying our customers for their
  opinionsonourservice.

APPENDIX C

Form 706 – United States Estate Tax Return

Form 709 – United States Gift Tax Return

Form 706 — Estate Tax Return

Form **706** (Rev. April 1997) Department of the Treasury Internal Revenue Service	United States Estate (and Generation-Skipping Transfer) Tax Return Estate of a citizen or resident of the United States (see separate instructions). To be filed for decedents dying after October 8, 1990. For Paperwork Reduction Act Notice, see page 1 of the separate instructions.	OMB No. 1545-0015

Part 1 — Decedent and Executor

1a Decedent's first name and middle initial (and maiden name, if any)	1b Decedent's last name	2 Decedent's social security no.

3a Legal residence (domicile) at time of death (county, state, and ZIP code, or foreign country)	3b Year domicile established	4 Date of birth	5 Date of death

6a Name of executor (see page 2 of the instructions)	6b Executor's address (number and street including apartment or suite no. or rural route; city, town, or post office; state; and ZIP code)

| 6c Executor's social security number (see page 2 of the instructions) | |

7a Name and location of court where will was probated or estate administered	7b Case number

8 If decedent died testate, check here ▶ ☐ and attach a certified copy of the will. | 9 If Form 4768 is attached, check here ▶ ☐

10 If Schedule R-1 is attached, check here ▶ ☐

Part 2 — Tax Computation

1	Total gross estate (from Part 5, Recapitulation, page 3, item 10)	1
2	Total allowable deductions (from Part 5, Recapitulation, page 3, item 20)	2
3	Taxable estate (subtract line 2 from line 1)	3
4	Adjusted taxable gifts (total taxable gifts (within the meaning of section 2503) made by the decedent after December 31, 1976, other than gifts that are includible in decedent's gross estate (section 2001(b)))	4
5	Add lines 3 and 4	5
6	Tentative tax on the amount on line 5 from Table A on page 10 of the instructions	6
7a	If line 5 exceeds $10,000,000, enter the lesser of line 5 or $21,040,000. If line 5 is $10,000,000 or less, skip lines 7a and 7b and enter -0- on line 7c. **7a**	
b	Subtract $10,000,000 from line 7a **7b**	
c	Enter 5% (.05) of line 7b	7c
8	Total tentative tax (add lines 6 and 7c)	8
9	Total gift tax payable with respect to gifts made by the decedent after December 31, 1976. Include gift taxes by the decedent's spouse for such spouse's share of split gifts (section 2513) only if the decedent was the donor of these gifts and they are includible in the decedent's gross estate (see instructions)	9
10	Gross estate tax (subtract line 9 from line 8)	10
11	Maximum unified credit against estate tax **11** 192,800 00	
12	Adjustment to unified credit. (This adjustment may not exceed $6,000. See page 7 of the instructions.) **12**	
13	Allowable unified credit (subtract line 12 from line 11)	13
14	Subtract line 13 from line 10 (but do not enter less than zero)	14
15	Credit for state death taxes. Do not enter more than line 14. Figure the credit by using the amount on line 3 less $60,000. See Table B in the instructions and **attach credit evidence** (see instructions)	15
16	Subtract line 15 from line 14	16
17	Credit for Federal gift taxes on pre-1977 gifts (section 2012) (attach computation) **17**	
18	Credit for foreign death taxes (from Schedule(s) P). (Attach Form(s) 706-CE.) **18**	
19	Credit for tax on prior transfers (from Schedule Q) **19**	
20	Total (add lines 17, 18, and 19)	20
21	Net estate tax (subtract line 20 from line 16)	21
22	Generation-skipping transfer taxes (from Schedule R, Part 2, line 10)	22
23	Section 4980A increased estate tax (from Schedule S, Part I, line 17) (see page 20 of the instructions)	23
24	Total transfer taxes (add lines 21, 22, and 23)	24
25	Prior payments. Explain in an attached statement **25**	
26	United States Treasury bonds redeemed in payment of estate tax **26**	
27	Total (add lines 25 and 26)	27
28	Balance due (or overpayment) (subtract line 27 from line 24)	28

Under penalties of perjury I declare that I have examined this return, including accompanying schedules and statements, and to the best of my knowledge and belief it is true, correct, and complete. Declaration of preparer other than the executor is based on all information of which preparer has any knowledge.

Signature(s) of executor(s) _____ Date _____

Signature of preparer other than executor _____ Address (and ZIP code) _____ Date _____

Cat. No. 20548R

Form 706 *(continued)*

Form 706 (Rev. 4-97)

Estate of:

Part 3.—Elections by the Executor

Please check the "Yes" or "No" box for each question. (See instructions beginning on page 3.)	Yes	No

1   Do you elect alternate valuation?

2   Do you elect special use valuation?
If "Yes," you must complete and attach Schedule A-1.

3   Do you elect to pay the taxes in installments as described in section 6166?
If "Yes," you must attach the additional information described on page 5 of the instructions.

4   Do you elect to postpone the part of the taxes attributable to a reversionary or remainder interest as described in section 6163?

Part 4.—General Information *(Note: Please attach the necessary supplemental documents. You must attach the death certificate.)*
(See instructions beginning on page 6.)

Authorization to receive confidential tax information under Regulations section 601.504(b)(2)(i), to act as the estate's representative before the Internal Revenue Service, and to make written or oral presentations on behalf of the estate if return prepared by an attorney, accountant, or enrolled agent for the executor:

Name of representative (print or type)	State	Address (number, street, and room or suite no., city, state, and ZIP code)

I declare that I am the ☐ attorney/ ☐ certified public accountant/ ☐ enrolled agent (you must check the applicable box) for the executor and prepared this return for the executor. I am not under suspension or disbarment from practice before the Internal Revenue Service and am qualified to practice in the state shown above.

Signature		CAF number	Date	Telephone number

1   Death certificate number and issuing authority (attach a copy of the death certificate to this return).

2   Decedent's business or occupation. If retired, check here ▶ ☐ and state decedent's former business or occupation.

3   Marital status of the decedent at time of death:
☐ Married
☐ Widow or widower—Name, SSN, and date of death of deceased spouse ▶ ....
....
☐ Single
☐ Legally separated
☐ Divorced—Date divorce decree became final ▶

4a Surviving spouse's name	4b Social security number	4c Amount received (see page 6 of the instructions)

5   Individuals (other than the surviving spouse), trusts, or other estates who receive benefits from the estate (do not include charitable beneficiaries shown in Schedule O) (see instructions). For Privacy Act Notice (applicable to individual beneficiaries only), see the Instructions for Form 1040.

Name of individual, trust, or estate receiving $5,000 or more	Identifying number	Relationship to decedent	Amount (see instructions)

All unascertainable beneficiaries and those who receive less than $5,000 ▶

Total

(continued on next page)   **Page 2**

Form 706 (continued)

Form 706 (Rev. 4-97)

Part 4.—General Information (continued)

Please check the "Yes" or "No" box for each question.

		Yes	No
6	Does the gross estate contain any section 2044 property (qualified terminable interest property (QTIP) from a prior gift or estate) (see page 6 of the instructions)?		
7a	Have Federal gift tax returns ever been filed? . . . . If "Yes," please attach copies of the returns, if available, and furnish the following information:		
7b	Period(s) covered	7c	Internal Revenue office(s) where filed		

If you answer "Yes" to any of questions 8–16, you must attach additional information as described in the instructions.

		Yes	No
8a	Was there any insurance on the decedent's life that is not included on the return as part of the gross estate?		
b	Did the decedent own any insurance on the life of another that is not included in the gross estate?		
9	Did the decedent at the time of death own any property as a joint tenant with right of survivorship in which **(a)** one or more of the other joint tenants was someone other than the decedent's spouse, and **(b)** less than the full value of the property is included on the return as part of the gross estate? If "Yes," you must complete and attach Schedule E		
10	Did the decedent, at the time of death, own any interest in a partnership or unincorporated business or any stock in an inactive or closely held corporation?		
11	Did the decedent make any transfer described in section 2035, 2036, 2037, or 2038 (see the instructions for Schedule G beginning on page 11 of the separate instructions)? If "Yes," you must complete and attach Schedule G		
12	Were there in existence at the time of the decedent's death:		
a	Any trusts created by the decedent during his or her lifetime?		
b	Any trusts not created by the decedent under which the decedent possessed any power, beneficial interest, or trusteeship?		
13	Did the decedent ever possess, exercise, or release any general power of appointment? If "Yes," you must complete and attach Schedule H		
14	Was the marital deduction computed under the transitional rule of Public Law 97-34, section 403(e)(3) (Economic Recovery Tax Act of 1981)? If "Yes," attach a separate computation of the marital deduction, enter the amount on item 18 of the Recapitulation, and note on item 18 "computation attached."		
15	Was the decedent, immediately before death, receiving an annuity described in the "General" paragraph of the instructions for Schedule I? If "Yes," you must complete and attach Schedule I		
16	Did the decedent have a total "excess retirement accumulation" (as defined in section 4980A(d)) in qualified employer plans and individual retirement plans? If "Yes," you must complete and attach Schedule S		

Part 5.—Recapitulation

Item number	Gross estate	Alternate value	Value at date of death
1	Schedule A—Real Estate		
2	Schedule B—Stocks and Bonds		
3	Schedule C—Mortgages, Notes, and Cash		
4	Schedule D—Insurance on the Decedent's Life (attach Form(s) 712)		
5	Schedule E—Jointly Owned Property (attach Form(s) 712 for life insurance) .		
6	Schedule F—Other Miscellaneous Property (attach Form(s) 712 for life insurance) .		
7	Schedule G—Transfers During Decedent's Life (attach Form(s) 712 for life insurance)		
8	Schedule H—Powers of Appointment		
9	Schedule I—Annuities		
10	Total gross estate (add items 1 through 9). Enter here and on line 1 of the Tax Computation		

Item number	Deductions		Amount
11	Schedule J—Funeral Expenses and Expenses Incurred in Administering Property Subject to Claims		
12	Schedule K—Debts of the Decedent		
13	Schedule K—Mortgages and Liens		
14	Total of items 11 through 13		
15	Allowable amount of deductions from item 14 (see the instructions for item 15 of the Recapitulation) . . .		
16	Schedule L—Net Losses During Administration		
17	Schedule L—Expenses Incurred in Administering Property Not Subject to Claims		
18	Schedule M—Bequests, etc., to Surviving Spouse		
19	Schedule O—Charitable, Public, and Similar Gifts and Bequests		
20	Total allowable deductions (add items 15 through 19). Enter here and on line 2 of the Tax Computation . . .		

Page 3

Form 709 – Gift Tax Return

Form **709**	United States Gift (and Generation-Skipping Transfer) Tax Return			
(Rev. December 1996)	(Section 6019 of the Internal Revenue Code) (For gifts made after December 31, 1991)			OMB No. 1545-0020
Department of the Treasury Internal Revenue Service	Calendar year 19 .... ► **See separate Instructions. For Privacy Act Notice, see the Instructions for Form 1040.**			

Part 1—General Information

1 Donor's first name and middle initial	2 Donor's last name	3 Donor's social security number
4 Address (number, street, and apartment number)		5 Legal residence (domicile) (county and state)
6 City, state, and ZIP code		7 Citizenship

		Yes	No
8	If the donor died during the year, check here ► ☐ and enter date of death.........................		
9	If you received an extension of time to file this Form 709, check here ► ☐ and attach the Form 4868, 2688, 2350, or extension letter		
10	Enter the total number of separate donees listed on Schedule A—count each person only once. ►		
11a	Have you (the donor) previously filed a Form 709 (or 709-A) for any other year? If the answer is "No," do not complete line 11b		
11b	If the answer to line 11a is "Yes," has your address changed since you last filed Form 709 or 709-A?		
12	Gifts by husband or wife to third parties.—Do you consent to have the gifts (including generation-skipping transfers) made by you and by your spouse to third parties during the calendar year considered as made one-half by each of you? (See instructions.) (If the answer is "Yes," the following information must be furnished and your spouse must sign the consent shown below. If the answer is "No," skip lines 13–18 and go to Schedule A.)		
13	Name of consenting spouse	14 SSN	
15	Were you married to one another during the entire calendar year? (see instructions)		
16	If the answer to 15 is "No," check whether ☐ married ☐ divorced or ☐ widowed, and give date (see instructions) ►		
17	Will a gift tax return for this calendar year be filed by your spouse?		
18	Consent of Spouse—I consent to have the gifts (and generation-skipping transfers) made by me and by my spouse to third parties during the calendar year considered as made one-half by each of us. We are both aware of the joint and several liability for tax created by the execution of this consent.		

Consenting spouse's signature ►   Date ►

Part 2—Tax Computation

1	Enter the amount from Schedule A, Part 3, line 15	1	
2	Enter the amount from Schedule B, line 3	2	
3	Total taxable gifts (add lines 1 and 2)	3	
4	Tax computed on amount on line 3 (see Table for Computing Tax in separate instructions)	4	
5	Tax computed on amount on line 2 (see Table for Computing Tax in separate instructions) . . .	5	
6	Balance (subtract line 5 from line 4)	6	
7	Maximum unified credit (nonresident aliens, see instructions)	7	192,800 | 00
8	Enter the unified credit against tax allowable for all prior periods (from Sch. B, line 1, col. C) . .	8	
9	Balance (subtract line 8 from line 7)	9	
10	Enter 20% (.20) of the amount allowed as a specific exemption for gifts made after September 8, 1976, and before January 1, 1977 (see instructions)	10	
11	Balance (subtract line 10 from line 9)	11	
12	Unified credit (enter the smaller of line 6 or line 11)	12	
13	Credit for foreign gift taxes (see instructions)	13	
14	Total credits (add lines 12 and 13)	14	
15	Balance (subtract line 14 from line 6) (do not enter less than zero)	15	
16	Generation-skipping transfer taxes (from Schedule C, Part 3, col. H, Total)	16	
17	Total tax (add lines 15 and 16)	17	
18	Gift and generation-skipping transfer taxes prepaid with extension of time to file	18	
19	If line 18 is less than line 17, enter BALANCE DUE (see instructions)	19	
20	If line 18 is greater than line 17, enter AMOUNT TO BE REFUNDED	20	

Under penalties of perjury, I declare that I have examined this return, including any accompanying schedules and statements, and to the best of my knowledge and belief it is true, correct, and complete. Declaration of preparer (other than donor) is based on all information of which preparer has any knowledge.

Donor's signature ►   Date ►

Preparer's signature
(other than donor) ►   Date ►

Preparer's address
(other than donor) ►

(left margin, vertical: Attach check or money order here.)

For Paperwork Reduction Act Notice, see page 1 of the separate instructions for this form.   Cat. No. 16783M   Form **709** (Rev. 12-96)

Form 709 *(Continued)*

Form 709 (Rev. 12-96)   Page **2**

SCHEDULE A   **Computation of Taxable Gifts**

Does the value of any item listed on Schedule A reflect any valuation discount? If the answer is "Yes," see instructions . . . Yes ☐ No ☐

Part 1—Gifts Subject Only to Gift Tax. *Gifts less political organization, medical, and educational exclusions—see instructions*

A Item number	B • Donee's name and address • Relationship to donor (if any) • Description of gift • If the gift was made by means of a trust, enter trust's identifying number and attach a copy of the trust instrument • If the gift was of securities, give CUSIP number	C Donor's adjusted basis of gift	D Date of gift	E Value at date of gift
1				

Total of Part 1 (add amounts from Part 1, column E) . . . . ▶

Part 2—Gifts That are Direct Skips and are Subject to Both Gift Tax and Generation-Skipping Transfer Tax. You must list the gifts in chronological order. *Gifts less political organization, medical, and educational exclusions—see instructions. (Also list here direct skips that are subject only to the GST tax at this time as the result of the termination of an "estate tax inclusion period." See instructions.)*

A Item number	B • Donee's name and address • Relationship to donor (if any) • Description of gift • If the gift was made by means of a trust, enter trust's identifying number and attach a copy of the trust instrument • If the gift was of securities, give CUSIP number	C Donor's adjusted basis of gift	D Date of gift	E Value at date of gift
1				

Total of Part 2 (add amounts from Part 2, column E) . . . . ▶

Part 3—Taxable Gift Reconciliation

1	Total value of gifts of donor (add totals from column E of Parts 1 and 2)	1
2	One-half of items ....attributable to spouse (see instructions)	2
3	Balance (subtract line 2 from line 1)	3
4	Gifts of spouse to be included (from Schedule A, Part 3, line 2 of spouse's return—see instructions) . .	4
	If any of the gifts included on this line are also subject to the generation-skipping transfer tax, check here ▶ ☐ and enter those gifts also on Schedule C, Part 1.	
5	Total gifts (add lines 3 and 4)	5
6	Total annual exclusions for gifts listed on Schedule A (including line 4, above) (see instructions) . . .	6
7	Total included amount of gifts (subtract line 6 from line 5)	7
Deductions (see instructions)		
8	Gifts of interests to spouse for which a marital deduction will be claimed, based on items .... of Schedule A	8
9	Exclusions attributable to gifts on line 8	9
10	Marital deduction—subtract line 9 from line 8	10
11	Charitable deduction, based on items ....less exclusions . .	11
12	Total deductions—add lines 10 and 11	12
13	Subtract line 12 from line 7	13
14	Generation-skipping transfer taxes payable with this Form 709 (from Schedule C, Part 1, col H, Total)	14
15	Taxable gifts (add lines 13 and 14). Enter here and on line 1 of the Tax Computation on page 1 . . .	15

(If more space is needed, attach additional sheets of same size.)

Form 709 *(Continued)*

Form 709 (Rev. 12-96)   Page **3**

SCHEDULE A   **Computation of Taxable Gifts** *(continued)*

16 Terminable Interest (QTIP) Marital Deduction. (See instructions for line 8 of Schedule A.)

If a trust (or other property) meets the requirements of qualified terminable interest property under section 2523(f), and

   a. The trust (or other property) is listed on Schedule A, and

   b. The value of the trust (or other property) is entered in whole or in part as a deduction on line 8, Part 1 of Schedule A,

then the donor shall be deemed to have made an election to such trust (or other property) treated as qualified terminable interest property under section 2523(f).

If less than the entire value of the trust (or other property) that the donor has included in Part 1 of Schedule A is entered as a deduction on line 8, the donor shall be considered to have made an election only as to a fraction of the trust (or other property). The numerator of this fraction is equal to the amount of the trust (or other property) deducted on line 10 of Part 1, Schedule A. The denominator is equal to the total value of the trust (or other property) listed in Part 1 of Schedule A.

If you make the QTIP election (see instructions for line 8 of Schedule A), the terminable interest property involved will be included in your spouse's gross estate upon his or her death (section 2044). If your spouse disposes (by gift or otherwise) of all or part of the qualifying life income interest, he or she will be considered to have made a transfer of the entire property that is subject to the gift tax (see Transfer of Certain Life Estates on page 3 of the instructions).

17 Election Out of QTIP Treatment of Annuities

☐ ◄ Check here if you elect under section 2523(f)(6) **NOT** to treat as qualified terminable interest property any joint and survivor annuities that are reported on Schedule A and would otherwise be treated as qualified terminable interest property under section 2523(f). (See instructions.) Enter the item numbers (from Schedule A) for the annuities for which you are making this election ►

SCHEDULE B   **Gifts From Prior Periods**

If you answered "Yes" on line 11a of page 1, Part 1, see the instructions for completing Schedule B. If you answered "No," skip to the Tax Computation on page 1 (or Schedule C, if applicable).

A Calendar year or calendar quarter (see instructions)	B Internal Revenue office where prior return was filed	C Amount of unified credit against gift tax for periods after December 31, 1976	D Amount of specific exemption for prior periods ending before January 1, 1977	E Amount of taxable gifts

1 Totals for prior periods (without adjustment for reduced specific exemption)	**1**	
2 Amount, if any, by which total specific exemption, line 1, column D, is more than $30,000		**2**
3 Total amount of taxable gifts for prior periods (add amount, column E, line 1, and amount, if any, on line 2). (Enter here and on line 2 of the Tax Computation on page 1.)		**3**

(If more space is needed, attach additional sheets of same size.)

Form 709 *(Continued)*

Form 709 (Rev. 12-96)   Page **4**

SCHEDULE C	Computation of Generation-Skipping Transfer Tax

Note: *Inter vivos direct skips that are completely excluded by the GST exemption must still be fully reported (including value and exemptions claimed) on Schedule C.*

Part 1—Generation-Skipping Transfers

A Item No. (from Schedule A, Part 2, col. A)	B Value (from Schedule A, Part 2, col. E)	C Split Gifts (enter ½ of col. B) (see instructions)	D Subtract col. C from col. B	E Nontaxable portion of transfer	F Net Transfer (subtract col. E from col. D)
1					
2					
3					
4					
5					
6					

If you elected gift splitting and your spouse was required to file a separate Form 709 (see the instructions for "Split Gifts"), you must enter all of the gifts shown on Schedule A, Part 2, of your spouse's Form 709 here. In column C, enter the item number of each gift in the order it appears in column A of your spouse's Schedule A, Part 2. We have preprinted the prefix "S-" to distinguish your spouse's item numbers from your own when you complete column A of Schedule C, Part 3. In column D, for each gift, enter the amount reported in column C, Schedule C, Part 1, of your spouse's Form 709.	Split gifts from spouse's Form 709 (enter item number) S- S- S- S- S- S- S- S-	Value included from spouse's Form 709	Nontaxable portion of transfer	Net transfer (subtract col. E from col. D)

Part 2—GST Exemption Reconciliation (Section 2631) and Section 2652(a)(3) Election

Check box ► ☐ if you are making a section 2652(a)(3) (special QTIP) election (see instructions)

Enter the item numbers (from Schedule A) of the gifts for which you are making this election ► ....

1	Maximum allowable exemption	1	$1,000,000
2	Total exemption used for periods before filing this return	2	
3	Exemption available for this return (subtract line 2 from line 1)	3	
4	Exemption claimed on this return (from Part 3, col. C total, below)	4	
5	Exemption allocated to transfers not shown on Part 3, below. **You must attach a Notice of Allocation.** (See instructions.)	5	
6	Add lines 4 and 5	6	
7	Exemption available for future transfers (subtract line 6 from line 3)	7	

Part 3—Tax Computation

A Item No. (from Schedule C, Part 1)	B Net transfer (from Schedule C, Part 1, col. F)	C GST Exemption Allocated	D Divide col. C by col. B	E Inclusion Ratio (subtract col. D from 1.000)	F Maximum Estate Tax Rate	G Applicable Rate (multiply col. E by col. F)	H Generation-Skipping Transfer Tax (multiply col. B by col. G)
1					55% (.55)		
2					55% (.55)		
3					55% (.55)		
4					55% (.55)		
5					55% (.55)		
6					55% (.55)		
					55% (.55)		
					55% (.55)		
					55% (.55)		
					55% (.55)		

Total exemption claimed. Enter here and on line 4, Part 2, above. May not exceed line 3, Part 2, above	**Total generation-skipping transfer tax.** Enter here, on line 14 of Schedule A, Part 3, and on line 16 of the Tax Computation on page 1	

(If more space is needed, attach additional sheets of same size.)

APPENDIX D

Form 5305 – Individual Retirement Trust Account

Form 5305-SEP – Simplified Employee Pension-Individual Retirement Accounts Contribution Agreement

Form 5305A-SEP – Salary Reduction and Other Elective Simplified Employee Pension-Individual Retirement Accounts Contribution Agreement

Form 5305-SIMPLE – Savings Incentive Match Plan for Employees of Small Employers (SIMPLE)

Form 5305 – Individual Retirement Account

Form 5305
(Rev. January 1998)
Department of the Treasury
Internal Revenue Service

Individual Retirement Trust Account
(Under section 408(a) of the Internal Revenue Code)

DO NOT File
With the Internal
Revenue Service

Name of grantor	Date of birth of grantor	Identifying number (see instructions)

Address of grantor		
		Check if Amendment ▸ ☐

Name of trustee	Address or principal place of business of trustee

The grantor whose name appears above is establishing an individual retirement account under section 408(a) to provide for his or her retirement and for the support of his or her beneficiaries after death.

The trustee named above has given the grantor the disclosure statement required under Regulations section 1.408-6.

The grantor has assigned the trust .... dollars ($ ....) in cash.

The grantor and the trustee make the following agreement:

Article I

The trustee may accept additional cash contributions on behalf of the grantor for a tax year of the grantor. The total cash contributions are limited to $2,000 for the tax year unless the contribution is a rollover contribution described in section 402(c), 403(a)(4), 403(b)(8), 408(d)(3), or an employer contribution to a simplified employee pension plan as described in section 408(k).

Article II

The grantor's interest in the balance in the trust account is nonforfeitable.

Article III

1. No part of the trust funds may be invested in life insurance contracts, nor may the assets of the trust account be commingled with other property except in a common trust fund or common investment fund (within the meaning of section 408(a)(5)).

2. No part of the trust funds may be invested in collectibles (within the meaning of section 408(m)) except as otherwise permitted by section 408(m)(3), which provides an exception for certain gold, silver, and platinum coins, coins issued under the laws of any state, and certain bullion.

Article IV

1. Notwithstanding any provision of this agreement to the contrary, the distribution of the grantor's interest in the trust account shall be made in accordance with the following requirements and shall otherwise comply with section 408(a)(6) and Proposed Regulations section 1.408-8, including the incidental death benefit provisions of Proposed Regulations section 1.401(a)(9)-2, the provisions of which are herein incorporated by reference.

2. Unless otherwise elected by the time distributions are required to begin to the grantor under paragraph 3, or to the surviving spouse under paragraph 4, other than in the case of a life annuity, life expectancies shall be recalculated annually. Such election shall be irrevocable as to the grantor and the surviving spouse and shall apply to all subsequent years. The life expectancy of a nonspouse beneficiary may not be recalculated.

3. The grantor's entire interest in the trust account must be, or begin to be, distributed by the grantor's required beginning date, April 1 following the calendar year end in which the grantor reaches age 70½. By that date, the grantor may elect, in a manner acceptable to the trustee, to have the balance in the trust account distributed in:

(a) A single sum payment.

(b) An annuity contract that provides equal or substantially equal monthly, quarterly, or annual payments over the life of the grantor.

(c) An annuity contract that provides equal or substantially equal monthly, quarterly, or annual payments over the joint and last survivor lives of the grantor and his or her designated beneficiary.

(d) Equal or substantially equal annual payments over a specified period that may not be longer than the grantor's life expectancy.

(e) Equal or substantially equal annual payments over a specified period that may not be longer than the joint life and last survivor expectancy of the grantor and his or her designated beneficiary.

4. If the grantor dies before his or her entire interest is distributed to him or her, the entire remaining interest will be distributed as follows:

(a) If the grantor dies on or after distribution of his or her interest has begun, distribution must continue to be made in accordance with paragraph 3.

(b) If the grantor dies before distribution of his or her interest has begun, the entire remaining interest will, at the election of the grantor or, if the grantor has not so elected, at the election of the beneficiary or beneficiaries, either

(i) Be distributed by the December 31 of the year containing the fifth anniversary of the grantor's death, or

(ii) Be distributed in equal or substantially equal payments over the life or life expectancy of the designated beneficiary or beneficiaries starting by December 31 of the year following the year of the grantor's death. If, however, the beneficiary is the grantor's surviving spouse, then this distribution is not required to begin before December 31 of the year in which the grantor would have reached age 70½.

(c) Except where distribution in the form of an annuity meeting the requirements of section 408(b)(3) and its related regulations has irrevocably commenced, distributions are treated as having begun on the grantor's required beginning date, even though payments may actually have been made before that date.

(d) If the grantor dies before his or her entire interest has been distributed and if the beneficiary is other than the surviving spouse, no additional cash contributions or rollover contributions may be accepted in the account.

Cat. No. 11810K   Form **5305** (Rev. 1-98)

Form 5305 *(continued)*

Form 5305 (Rev. 1-98)   Page 2

5. In the case of a distribution over life expectancy in equal or substantially equal annual payments, to determine the minimum annual payment for each year, divide the grantor's entire interest in the trust as of the close of business on December 31 of the preceding year by the life expectancy of the grantor (or the joint life and last survivor expectancy of the grantor and the grantor's designated beneficiary, or the life expectancy of the designated beneficiary, whichever applies). In the case of distributions under paragraph 3, determine the initial life expectancy (or joint life and last survivor expectancy) using the attained ages of the grantor and designated beneficiary as of their birthdays in the year the grantor reaches age 70½. In the case of a distribution in accordance with paragraph 4(b)(ii), determine life expectancy using the attained age of the designated beneficiary as of the beneficiary's birthday in the year distributions are required to commence.

6. The owner of two or more individual retirement accounts may use the "alternative method" described in Notice 88-38, 1988-1 C.B. 524, to satisfy the minimum distribution requirements described above. This method permits an individual to satisfy these requirements by taking from one individual retirement account the amount required to satisfy the requirement for another.

Article V

1. The grantor agrees to provide the trustee with information necessary for the trustee to prepare any reports required under section 408(i) and Regulations section 1.408-5 and 1.408-6.

2. The trustee agrees to submit reports to the Internal Revenue Service and the grantor as prescribed by the Internal Revenue Service.

Article VI

Notwithstanding any other articles which may be added or incorporated, the provisions of Articles I through III and this sentence will be controlling. Any additional articles that are not consistent with section 408(a) and related regulations will be invalid.

Article VII

This agreement will be amended from time to time to comply with the provisions of the Code and related regulations. Other amendments may be made with the consent of the persons whose signatures appear below.

Note: *The following space (Article VIII) may be used for any other provisions you want to add. If you do not want to add any other provisions, draw a line through this space. If you do add provisions, they must comply with applicable requirements of state law and the Internal Revenue Code.*

Article VIII

Grantor's signature ....   Date ....

Trustee's signature ....   Date ....

Witness' signature ....
                                                    (Use only if signature of the grantor or the trustee is required to be witnessed.)

General Instructions

Section references are to the Internal Revenue Code unless otherwise noted.

Purpose of Form

Note: *Users of the October 1992 revision of Form 5305 are not required to use the January 1998 revision of the form.*

Form 5305 is a model trust account agreement that meets the requirements of section 408(a) and has been automatically approved by the IRS. An individual retirement account (IRA) is established after the form is fully executed by both the individual (grantor) and the trustee and must be completed no later than the due date of the individual's income tax return for the tax year (without regard to extensions). This account must be created in the United States for the exclusive benefit of the grantor or his or her beneficiaries.

Individuals may rely on regulations for the Tax Reform Act of 1986 to the extent specified in those regulations.

Do not file Form 5305 with the IRS. Instead, keep it for your records.

For more information on IRAs, including the required disclosures the trustee must give the grantor, see **Pub. 590**, Individual Retirement Arrangements (IRAs).

Definitions

Trustee. The trustee must be a bank or savings and loan association, as defined in section 408(n), or any person who has the approval of the IRS to act as trustee.

Grantor. The grantor is the person who establishes the trust account.

Identifying Number

The grantor's social security number will serve as the identifying number of his or her IRA. An employer identification number (EIN) is required only for an IRA for which a return is filed to report unrelated business taxable income. An EIN is required for a common fund created for IRAs.

IRA for Nonworking Spouse

Form 5305 may be used to establish the IRA trust for a nonworking spouse.

Contributions to an IRA trust account for a nonworking spouse must be made to a

separate IRA trust account established by the nonworking spouse.

Specific Instructions

Article IV. Distributions made under this article may be made in a single sum, periodic payment, or a combination of both. The distribution option should be reviewed in the year the grantor reaches age 70½ to ensure that the requirements of section 408(a)(6) have been met.

Article VIII. Article VIII and any that follow it may incorporate additional provisions that are agreed to by the grantor and trustee to complete the agreement. They may include, for example, definitions, investment powers, voting rights, exculpatory provisions, amendment and termination, removal of the trustee, trustee's fees, state law requirements, beginning date of distributions, accepting only cash, treatment of excess contributions, prohibited transactions with the grantor, etc. Use additional pages if necessary and attach them to this form.

Note: *Form 5305 may be reproduced and reduced in size.*

Form 5305-SEP – Simplified Employee Pension-Individual Retirement Accounts Contribution Agreement

Form **5305-SEP** (Rev. January 1997) Department of the Treasury Internal Revenue Service	**Simplified Employee Pension-Individual** **Retirement Accounts Contribution Agreement** (Under section 408(k) of the Internal Revenue Code)	OMB No. 1545-0499 **DO NOT File With** **the Internal** **Revenue Service**

_____ makes the following agreement under section 408(k) of the
(Name of employer)
Internal Revenue Code and the instructions to this form.

Article I — Eligibility Requirements (Check appropriate boxes — see **Instructions**.)

The employer agrees to provide for discretionary contributions in each calendar year to the individual retirement account or individual retirement annuity (IRA) of all employees who are at least _____ years old (not to exceed 21 years old) and have performed services for the employer in at least _____ years (not to exceed 3 years) of the immediately preceding 5 years. This simplified employee pension (SEP) ☐ includes ☐ does not include employees covered under a collective bargaining agreement, ☐ includes ☐ does not include certain nonresident aliens, and ☐ includes ☐ does not include employees whose total compensation during the year is less than $400*.

Article II — SEP Requirements (See **Instructions**.)

The employer agrees that contributions made on behalf of each eligible employee will be:

A. Based only on the first $160,000* of compensation.
B. Made in an amount that is the same percentage of compensation for every employee.
C. Limited annually to the smaller of $30,000* or 15% of compensation.
D. Paid to the employee's IRA trustee, custodian, or insurance company (for an annuity contract).

_____   _____
Employer's signature and date   Name and title

Paperwork Reduction Act Notice

You are not required to provide the information requested on a form that is subject to the Paperwork Reduction Act unless the form displays a valid OMB control number. Books or records relating to a form or its instructions must be retained as long as their contents may become material in the administration of any Internal Revenue law. Generally, tax returns and return information are confidential, as required by Code section 6103.

The time needed to complete this form will vary depending on individual circumstances. The estimated average time is:

Recordkeeping . . . . 1 hr., 40 min.
Learning about the
law or the form . . . . 1 hr., 35 min.
Preparing the form . . . . 1 hr., 41 min.

If you have comments concerning the accuracy of these time estimates or suggestions for making this form simpler, we would be happy to hear from you. You can write to the Tax Forms Committee, Western Area Distribution Center, Rancho Cordova, CA 95743-0001. DO NOT send this form to this address. Instead, keep it for your records.

Instructions

Section references are to the Internal Revenue Code unless otherwise noted.

Purpose of Form

Form 5305-SEP (Model SEP) is used by an employer to make an agreement to provide benefits to all eligible employees under a SEP described in section 408(k). Do not file this form with the IRS. See Pub. 560, Retirement Plans for the Self-Employed, and Pub. 590, Individual Retirement Arrangements (IRAs).

Instructions to the Employer

Simplified Employee Pension. — A SEP is a written arrangement (a plan) that provides you with a simplified way to make contributions toward your employees' retirement income. Under a SEP, you can contribute to an employee's individual retirement account or annuity (IRA). You make contributions directly to an IRA set up by or for each employee with a bank, insurance company, or other qualified financial institution. When using Form 5305-SEP to establish a SEP, the IRA must be a Model IRA established on an IRS form or a master or prototype IRA for which the IRS has issued a favorable opinion letter. Making the agreement on Form 5305-SEP does not establish an employer IRA described in section 408(c).

When Not To Use Form 5305-SEP. — Do not use this form if you:

1. Currently maintain any other qualified retirement plan. This does not prevent you from maintaining another SEP.

2. Previously maintained a defined benefit plan that is now terminated.

3. Have any eligible employees for whom IRAs have not been established.

4. Use the services of leased employees (described in section 414(n)).

5. Are a member of an affiliated service group (described in section 414(m)), a controlled group of corporations (described in section 414(b)), or trades or businesses under common control (described in sections 414(c) and 414(o)), unless all eligible employees of all the members of such groups, trades, or businesses, participate in the SEP.

6. Will not pay the cost of the SEP contributions. Do not use Form 5305-SEP for a SEP that provides for elective employee

contributions even if the contributions are made under a salary reduction agreement.

Use Form 5305A-SEP, or a nonmodel SEP if you permit elective deferrals to a SEP.

Note: SEPs permitting elective deferrals cannot be established after 1996.

Eligible Employees. — All eligible employees must be allowed to participate in the SEP. An eligible employee is any employee who: (1) is at least 21 years old, and (2) has performed "service" for you in at least 3 of the immediately preceding 5 years.

Note: You can establish less restrictive eligibility requirements, but not more restrictive ones.

Service is any work performed for you for any period of time, however short. If you are a member of an affiliated service group, a controlled group of corporations, or trades or businesses under common control, service includes any work performed for any period of time for any other member of such group, trades, or businesses.

Excludable Employees. — The following employees do not have to be covered by the SEP: (1) employees covered by a collective bargaining agreement whose retirement benefits were bargained for in good faith by you and their union, (2) nonresident alien employees who did not earn U.S. source income from you, and (**) employees who received less than $400* in compensation during the year.

Contribution Limits. — The SEP rules permit you to make an annual contribution of up to 15% of the employee's compensation or $30,000*, whichever is less. Compensation, for this purpose, does not include employer contributions to the SEP or the employee's compensation in excess of $160,000.* If you also maintain a Model Elective SEP or any

* This amount reflects the cost-of-living increase effective January 1, 1997. The amount is adjusted annually.
The IRS announces the increase, if any, in a news release and in the Internal Revenue Bulletin.

ISA
STF FED5478F.1

Form **5305-SEP** (Rev. 1-97)

Form 5305-SEP (continued)

other SEP that permits employees to make elective deferrals, contributions to the two SEPs together may not exceed the smaller of $30,000* or 15% of compensation for any employee.

Contributions cannot discriminate in favor of highly compensated employees. You are not required to make contributions every year. But you must contribute to the SEP-IRAs of all of the eligible employees who actually performed services during the year of the contribution. This includes eligible employees who die or quit working before the contribution is made.

You may also not integrate your SEP contributions with, or offset them by, contributions made under the Federal Insurance Contributions Act (FICA).

If this SEP is intended to meet the top-heavy minimum contribution rules of section 416, but it does not cover all your employees who participate in your elective SEP, then you must make minimum contributions to IRAs established on behalf of those employees.

Deducting Contributions. — You may deduct contributions to a SEP subject to the limits of section 404(h). This SEP is maintained on a calendar year basis and contributions to the SEP are deductible for your tax year with or within which the calendar year ends. Contributions made for a particular tax year must be made by the due date of your income tax return (including extensions) for that tax year.

Completing the Agreement. — This agreement is considered adopted when:

• IRAs have been established for all your eligible employees;

• You have completed all blanks on the agreement form without modification; and

• You have given all your eligible employees the following information:

1. A copy of Form 5305-SEP.

2. A statement that IRAs other than the IRAs into which employer SEP contributions will be made may provide different rates of return and different terms concerning, among other things, transfers and withdrawals of funds from the IRAs.

3. A statement that, in addition to the information provided to an employee at the time the employee becomes eligible to participate, the administrator of the SEP must furnish each participant within 30 days of the effective date of any amendment to the SEP, a copy of the amendment and a written explanation of its effects.

4. A statement that the administrator will give written notification to each participant of any employer contributions made under the SEP to that participant's IRA by the later of January 31 of the year following the year for which a contribution is made or 30 days after the contribution is made.

Employers who have established a SEP using Form 5305-SEP and have furnished each eligible employee with a copy of the completed Form 5305-SEP and provided the other documents and disclosures described in Instructions to the Employer and Information for the Employee, are not required to file the annual information returns, Forms 5500, 5500-C/R, or 5500-EZ for the SEP. However, under Title I of ERISA, this relief from the annual reporting requirements may not be available to an employer who selects, recommends, or influences its employees to choose IRAs into which contributions will be made

under the SEP, if those IRAs are subject to provisions that impose any limits on a participant's ability to withdraw funds (other than restrictions imposed by the Code that apply to all IRAs). For additional information on Title I requirements, see the Department of Labor regulation at 29 CFR 2520.104-48.

Information for the Employee

The information below explains what a SEP is, how contributions are made, and how to treat your employer's contributions for tax purposes. For more information, see Pub. 590.

Simplified Employee Pension. — A SEP is a written arrangement (a plan) that allows an employer to make contributions toward your retirement. Contributions are made to an individual retirement account/annuity (IRA). Contributions must be made to either a Model IRA executed on an IRS form or a master or prototype IRA for which the IRS has issued a favorable opinion letter.

An employer is not required to make SEP contributions. If a contribution is made, it must be allocated to all the eligible employees according to the SEP agreement. The Model SEP (Form 5305-SEP) specifies that the contribution for each eligible employee will be the same percentage of compensation (excluding compensation higher than $160,000*) for all employees.

Your employer will provide you with a copy of the agreement containing participation rules and a description of how employer contributions may be made to your IRA. Your employer must also provide you with a copy of the completed Form 5305-SEP and a yearly statement showing any contributions to your IRA.

All amounts contributed to your IRA by your employer belong to you even after you stop working for that employer.

Contribution Limits. — Your employer will determine the amount to be contributed to your IRA each year. However, the amount for any year is limited to the smaller of $30,000* or 15% of your compensation for that year. Compensation does not include any amount that is contributed by your employer to your IRA under this SEP. Your employer is not required to make contributions every year or to maintain a particular level of contributions.

Tax Treatment of Contributions. — Employer contributions to your SEP-IRA are excluded from your income unless there are contributions in excess of the applicable limit. Employer contributions within these limits will not be included on your Form W-2.

Employee Contributions. — You may contribute the smaller of $2,000 or 100% of your compensation to an IRA. However, the amount you can deduct may be reduced or eliminated because, as a participant in a SEP, you are covered by an employer retirement plan.

SEP Participation. — If your employer does not require you to participate in a SEP as a condition of employment, and you elect not to participate, all other employees of your employer may be prohibited from participating. If one or more eligible employees do not participate and the employer tries to establish a SEP for the remaining employees, it could cause adverse tax consequences for the participating employees.

An employer may not adopt this IRS Model SEP if the employer maintains another qualified retirement plan or has ever maintained a qualified defined benefit plan. This does not prevent your employer from adopting this IRS Model SEP and also maintaining an IRS Model Elective SEP or other SEP. However, if you work for several employers, you may be covered by a SEP of one employer and a different SEP or pension or profit-sharing plan of another employer.

SEP-IRA Amounts — Rollover or Transfer to Another IRA. — You can withdraw or receive funds from your SEP-IRA if within 60 days of receipt, you place those funds in another IRA or SEP-IRA. This is called a "rollover" and can be done without penalty only once in any 1-year period. However, there are no restrictions on the number of times you may make "transfers" if you arrange to have these funds transferred between the trustees or the custodians so that you never have possession of the funds.

Withdrawals. — You may withdraw your employer's contribution at any time, but any amount withdrawn is includible in your income unless rolled over. Also, if withdrawals occur before you reach age 59½, you may be subject to a tax on early withdrawal.

Excess SEP Contributions. — Contributions exceeding the yearly limitations may be withdrawn without penalty by the due date (plus extensions) for filing your tax return (normally April 15), but any excess contribution left in your SEP-IRA account after that time may have adverse tax consequences. Withdrawals of those contributions may be taxed as premature withdrawals.

Financial Institution Requirements. — The financial institution where your IRA is maintained must provide you with a disclosure statement that contains the following information in plain, nontechnical language:

1. The law that relates to your IRA.

2. The tax consequences of various options concerning your IRA.

3. Participation eligibility rules, and rules on the deductibility of retirement savings.

4. Situations and procedures for revoking your IRA, including the name, address, and telephone number of the person designated to receive notice of revocation. (This information must be clearly displayed at the beginning of the disclosure statement.)

5. A discussion of the penalties that may be assessed because of prohibited activities concerning your IRA.

6. Financial disclosure that provides the following information:

a. Projects value growth rates of your IRA under various contribution and retirement schedules, or describes the method of determining annual earnings and charges that may be assessed.

b. Describes whether, and for when, the growth projections are guaranteed, or a statement of the earnings rate and the terms on which the projections are based.

c. States the sales commission for each year expressed as a percentage of $1,000.

In addition, the financial institution must provide you with a financial statement each year. You may want to keep these statements to evaluate your IRA's investment performance.

* This amount reflects the cost-of-living increase effective January 1, 1997. The amount is adjusted annually. The IRS announces the increase, if any, in a news release and in the Internal Revenue Bulletin.

STF FED5478F 2

Form 5305A-SEP – Salary Reduction and Other Elective Simplified Employee Pension-Individual Retirement Accounts Contribution Agreement

Form **5305A-SEP** (Rev. December 1997) Department of the Treasury Internal Revenue Service	**Salary Reduction and Other Elective Simplified Employee Pension-Individual Retirement Accounts Contribution Agreement** (Under section 408(k) of the Internal Revenue Code)	OMB No. 1545-1012 **DO NOT File with the Internal Revenue Service**

_____ amends its elective SEP by adopting the following Model Elective SEP under
Name of employer

section 408(k) of the Internal Revenue Code and the instructions to this form. (Important: *An employer may not establish an elective SEP after 1996.*)

Article I — Eligibility Requirements (Check appropriate boxes — see instructions.)

Provided the requirements of Article III are met, the employer agrees to permit elective deferrals to be made in each calendar year to the individual retirement accounts or individual retirement annuities (IRAs), established by or for all employees who are at least _____ years old (not to exceed 21 years) and have performed services for the employer in at least _____ years (not to exceed 3 years) of the immediately preceding 5 years. This simplified employee pension (SEP) ☐ includes ☐ does not include employees covered under a collective bargaining agreement, ☐ includes ☐ does not include certain nonresident aliens, and ☐ includes ☐ does not include employees whose total compensation during the year is less than $400*.

Article II — Elective Deferrals (See instructions.)

A. **Salary Reduction Option.** An eligible employee may elect to have his or her compensation reduced by the following percentage or amount per pay period, as designated in writing to the employer. Check appropriate box(es) and fill in the blanks.

   1. ☐ An amount not in excess of _____ % (not to exceed 15%) of an eligible employee's compensation.

   2. ☐ An amount not in excess of $ _____ .

B. **Cash Bonus Option.** An eligible employee may base elective deferrals on bonuses that, at the employee's election, may be contributed to the SEP or received in cash during the calendar year. Check if elective deferrals on bonuses may be made to this SEP .... ▶ ☐

C. **Timing of Elective Deferrals.** No deferral election may be based on compensation an eligible employee received, or had a right to receive, before execution of the deferral election.

Article III — SEP Requirements (See instructions.)

The employer agrees that each employee's elective deferrals to the SEP will be:

A. Based only on the first $160,000* of compensation.

B. Limited annually to the smaller of: (1) 15% of compensation; or (2) $9,500* for 1997 ($10,000* for 1998).

C. Limited further, under section 415, if the employer also maintains another SEP.

D. Paid to the employee's IRA trustee, custodian, or insurance company (for an annuity contract) or, if necessary, an IRA established for an employee by the employer.

E. Made only if at least 50% of the employer's employees eligible to participate elect to have amounts contributed to the SEP. If the 50% requirement is not satisfied as of the end of any calendar year, then all of the elective deferrals made by the employees for that calendar year will be considered "disallowed deferrals," i.e., IRA contributions that are not SEP-IRA contributions.

F. Made only if the employer had 25 or fewer employees eligible to participate at all times during the prior calendar year.

G. Adjusted only if deferrals to this SEP for any calendar year do not meet the "deferral percentage limitation" described on page 3.

Article IV — Excess SEP Contributions (See instructions.)

Elective deferrals by a "highly compensated employee" must satisfy the deferral percentage limitation under section 408(k)(6)(A)(iii). Amounts in excess of this limitation will be deemed excess SEP contributions for the affected highly compensated employee or employees.

Article V — Notice Requirements (See instructions.)

A. The employer will notify each highly compensated employee, by March 15 following the end of the calendar year to which any excess SEP contributions relate, of the excess SEP contributions to the highly compensated employee's SEP-IRA for the applicable year. The notification will specify the amount of the excess SEP, the calendar year in which the contributions are includible in income, and must provide an explanation of applicable penalties if the excess contributions are not withdrawn on time.

B. The employer will notify each employee who makes an elective deferral to a SEP that, until March 15 after the year of the deferral, any transfer or distribution from that employee's SEP-IRA of SEP contributions (or income on these contributions) attributable to elective deferrals made that year will be includible in income for purposes of sections 72(t) and 408(d)(1).

C. The employer will notify each employee by March 15 of each year of any disallowed deferrals to the employee's SEP-IRA for the preceding calendar year. Such notification will specify the amount of the disallowed deferrals and the calendar year in which those deferrals are includible in income and must provide an explanation of applicable penalties if the disallowed deferrals are not withdrawn on time.

Article VI — Top-Heavy Requirements (See instructions.)

A. Unless paragraph B below is checked, the employer will satisfy the top-heavy requirements of section 416 by making a minimum contribution each year to the SEP-IRA of each employee eligible to participate in this SEP (other than a key employee as defined in section 416(i)). This contribution, in combination with other nonelective contributions, if any, is equal to the smaller of 3% of each eligible nonkey employee's compensation or a percentage of such compensation equal to the percentage of compensation at which elective and nonelective contributions are made under this SEP (and any other SEP maintained by the employer) for the year for the key employee for whom such percentage is the highest for the year.

B. ☐ The top-heavy requirements of section 416 will be satisfied through contributions to nonkey employees' SEP-IRAs under this employer's nonelective SEP.

* Except where stated otherwise, this amount reflects the cost-of-living increase in effect for 1997 and 1998. The amount is adjusted annually. The IRS announces the increase, if any, in a news release, in the Internal Revenue Bulletin, and on the IRS's Internet Web Site at www.irs.ustreas.gov.

For Paperwork Reduction Act Notice, see page 7.   Form **5305A-SEP** (Rev. 12-97)
ISA
STF FED5470F.1

Form 5305A-SEP *(continued)*

Form 5305A-SEP (Rev. 12-97)   Page **2**

Article VI — Top-Heavy Requirements *(Continued)*

C. To satisfy the minimum contribution requirement under section 416, all nonelective SEP contributions will be taken into account but elective deferrals will not be taken into account.

Article VII — Effective Date (See instructions.)
This SEP will be effective upon adoption and establishment of IRAs for all eligible employees.

Employer's signature	Date	Name and title

Changes To Note

The Small Business Job Protection Act of 1996 ("The Act") made several changes to the laws affecting simplified employee pensions (SEPs). Most importantly, it prohibited the establishment of new elective SEPs after 1996. The Act also repealed the family aggregation rules, under which the compensation and elective deferrals of certain "highly compensated employees" was combined with the compensation and elective deferrals of family members for purposes of determining the compensation and deferral percentages of participants. The definition of "highly compensated employee" was also changed beginning in 1997.

Instructions

Section references are to the Internal Revenue Code unless otherwise noted.

Purpose of Form

Form 5305A-SEP is a model elective simplified employee pension (SEP) used by an employer to permit employees to make elective deferrals to a SEP described in section 408(k). DO NOT file this form with the IRS.

Important. *SEPs permitting elective deferrals cannot be established after 1996. If you established a SEP before 1997 that permitted elective deferrals, under current law you may continue to maintain such SEP for years after 1996.*

If you wish to continue using a model elective SEP, this version of Form 5305A-SEP must be adopted by December 31, 1998.

What Is A SEP?

A SEP is a written arrangement (a plan) that provides you with a simplified way to make contributions toward your employees' retirement income. Under an elective SEP, employees may choose whether or not to make elective deferrals to the SEP or to receive the amounts in cash. If elective deferrals are made, you contribute the amounts deferred by your employees directly into an individual retirement arrangement (IRA) set up by or for each employee (a bank, insurance company, or other qualified financial institution). The IRA, established by or for an employee, must be one for which the IRS has issued a favorable opinion letter or a model IRA published by the Service as Form 5305, Individual Retirement Trust Account, or Form 5305-A, Individual Retirement Custodial Account. It cannot be a SIMPLE IRA (an IRA designed to accept contributions made under a SIMPLE IRA Plan

5TF FED5470F.2

described in section 408(p)). Adopting Form 5305A-SEP does not establish an employer IRA described in section 408(c).

The information provided below is intended to help you understand and administer the elective deferral rules of your SEP.

When To Use Form 5305A-SEP

Use this form only if you intend to permit elective deferrals to a SEP. If you want to establish a SEP to which nonelective employer contributions may be made, use Form 5305-SEP, Simplified Employee Pension — Individual Retirement Accounts Contribution Agreement, or a nonmodel SEP instead of, or in addition to, this form.

Do not use Form 5305A-SEP if you:

1. Have any leased employees as defined in section 414(n)(2).

2. Previously maintained or have maintained a defined benefit plan that is now terminated.

3. Currently maintain any other qualified retirement plan. This does not prevent you from also maintaining a Model SEP (Form 5305-SEP) or other SEP to which either elective or nonelective contributions are made.

4. Have more than 25 employees eligible to participate in the SEP at any time during the prior calendar year. (If you are a member of one of the groups described in paragraph 2 under **Excess SEP Contributions — Deferral Percentage Limitation** on page 3, you may use this SEP only if in the prior year there were never more than 25 employees eligible to participate in this SEP, in total, of all the members of such groups, trades, or businesses. In addition, all eligible employees of all the members of such groups, trades, or businesses must be eligible to make elective deferrals to this SEP.)

5. Are a state or local government or a tax-exempt organization.

Completing the Agreement

This SEP agreement is considered adopted when:

1. You have completed all blanks on the form.

2. You have given all eligible employees the following information:

a. A copy of Form 5305A-SEP. (Any individual who in the future becomes eligible to participate in this SEP must be given Form 5305A-SEP, upon becoming an eligible employee.)

b. A statement that IRAs other than the IRAs into which employer SEP contributions will be made may provide different rates of return and different terms concerning, among other things, transfers and withdrawals of funds from the IRAs.

c. A statement that, in addition to the information provided to an employee at the time the employee becomes eligible to participate, the administrator of the SEP must furnish each participant within 30 days of the effective date of any amendment to the SEP, a copy of the amendment and a written explanation of its effects.

d. A statement that the administrator will give written notification to each participant of any employer contributions made under the SEP to that participant's IRA by the later of January 31 of the year following the year for which a contribution is made or 30 days after the contribution is made.

Employers who have established an elective SEP using Form 5305A-SEP and have provided each participant a copy of the completed Form 5305A-SEP and the other documents and disclosures described in Instructions for the Employer and Instructions for the Employee, are not required to file the annual information returns, Forms 5500, 5500-C/R, or 5500-EZ, for the SEP. However, under Title I of ERISA, this relief from the annual reporting requirements may not be available to an employer who selects, recommends, or influences its employees to choose IRAs into which contributions will be made under the SEP, if those IRAs are subject to provisions that impose any limits on a participant's ability to withdraw funds (other than restrictions imposed by the Code that apply to all IRAs). For additional information on Title I requirements, see the Department of Labor regulations at 29 CFR 2520.104-49.

Forms and Publications You May Use

An employer may need to use any of the following forms or publications:

- Form W-2, Wage and Tax Statement.

- Form 5330, Return of Excise Taxes Related to Employee Benefit Plans. Employers who are liable for the 10% tax on excess contributions use this form to pay the excise tax.

- Pub. 560, Retirement Plans for the Self-Employed.

- Pub. 590, Individual Retirement Arrangements (IRAs).

Deducting Contributions

You may deduct, subject to any applicable limits, contributions made to a SEP. This SEP is maintained on a calendar year basis, and contributions to the SEP are deductible for your tax year with or within which the particular calendar year ends. See section 404(h). Contributions made for a particular tax

Form 5305A-SEP *(continued)*

Form 5305A-SEP (Rev. 12-97)   Page 3

year and contributed by the due date of your income tax return, including extensions, are deemed made in that tax year and the contributions are deductible if they would otherwise be deductible had they actually been contributed by the end of that tax year. See Rev. Rul. 90-105, 1990-2 C.B. 69. However, the deductibility of your contributions may be limited if the contributions are excess contributions. See **Excess SEP Contributions — Deferral Percentage Limitation** below and the Deferral Percentage Limitation Worksheet on page 8.

Effective Date

Insert the date the provisions of this agreement are effective. This date will be January 1, 1997, the first time you adopt this version of Form 5305A-SEP to continue to use a model elective SEP.

Eligible Employees

All eligible employees must be allowed to participate in the SEP. An eligible employee is an employee who: (1) is at least 21 years old, and (2) has performed "service" for you in at least 3 of the immediately preceding 5 years.

Note: *You can establish less restrictive eligibility requirements, but not more restrictive ones.*

Service means any work performed for you for any period of time, however short. If you are a member of an affiliated service group, a controlled group of corporations, or trades or businesses under common control, service includes any work performed for any period of time for any other member of such group, trades, or businesses.

Excludable Employees

The following employees do not have to be covered by the SEP: (1) employees covered by a collective bargaining agreement whose retirement benefits were bargained for in good faith by you and their union, (2) nonresident alien employees who did not earn U.S. source income from you, and (3) employees who received less than $400* in compensation during the year.

Elective Deferrals

You may permit your employees to make elective deferrals through salary reduction or on the basis of bonuses that, at the employee's option, may be contributed to the SEP or received by the employee in cash during the year.

You must inform your employees how they may make, change, or terminate elective deferrals based on either salary reduction or cash bonuses. You must also provide a form on which they may make their deferral elections. You may use the Model Elective SEP Deferral Form (elective form) on page 5, or a form that explains the information contained in this form in a way that is written to be understood by the average plan participant.

SEP Requirements

● Elective deferrals may not be based on more than $160,000* of compensation. Compensation, for purposes other than the $400* rule (see Excludable Employees above), is defined as wages under section 3401(a) for income tax withholding at the source but without regard to any rules that limit the remuneration included in wages

based on the nature or location of the employment or the services performed (such as the exception for agricultural labor in section 3401(a)(2)). Compensation also includes earned income under section 401(c)(2). Compensation does not include any employer SEP contributions. Compensation, for purposes of the $400* rule, is the same, except it includes deferrals made to this SEP or under a "cafeteria plan" described in section 125.

● The maximum limit on the amount an employee may elect to defer under this SEP for a year is the smaller of 15% of the employee's compensation or the limitation under section 402(g), as explained below.

Note: *The deferral limit is 15% of compensation (minus any employer SEP contributions). Compute this amount using the following formula: Compensation (before subtracting employer SEP contributions) × 13.0435%.*

● If you make nonelective contributions to this SEP for a calendar year, or maintain any other SEP to which contributions are made for that calendar year, then contributions to all such SEPs may not exceed the smaller of $30,000* or 15% of compensation for any employee.

Excess Elective Deferrals

Section 402(g) limits the maximum amount of compensation an employee may elect to defer under a SEP (and certain other arrangements) during the calendar year. This limit is $9,500* for 1997 ($10,000* for 1998). Amounts deferred for a year in excess of this limit are considered "excess elective deferrals" and are subject to the rules described below.

The limit applies to the total elective deferrals the employee makes for the calendar year, from all employers, under the following arrangements:

● Elective SEPs under section 408(k)(6);

● Cash or deferred arrangements under section 401(k);

● Salary reduction arrangements under section 403(b); and

● SIMPLE IRA Plans under section 408(p).

Thus, an employee may have excess elective deferrals even if the amount deferred under this SEP alone does not exceed the section 402(g) limit.

If an employee who elects to defer compensation under this SEP and any other SEP or arrangement has made excess elective deferrals for a calendar year, the employee must withdraw those deferrals by April 15 following the calendar year to which the deferrals relate. Deferrals not withdrawn by April 15 will be subject to the IRA contribution limits of sections 219 and 408 and are considered excess contributions to the employee's IRA. For the employee, these excess elective deferrals are subject to a 6% tax on excess contributions under section 4973.

Income on excess elective deferrals is includible in the employee's income in the year it is withdrawn from the IRA. The income must be withdrawn by April 15 following the calendar year for which the deferrals were made. If the income is withdrawn after that date and the recipient is not 59½ years of age, it may be subject to the 10% tax on early distributions under section 72(t)

Excess SEP Contributions — Deferral Percentage Limitation

The amount each of your "highly compensated employees" may contribute to an elective deferral SEP is also limited by the "deferral percentage limitation." This is based on the amount of money deferred, on average, by your nonhighly compensated employees. Deferrals made by a highly compensated employee that exceed this deferral percentage limitation for a calendar year are considered "excess SEP contributions" and must be removed from the employee's SEP-IRA, as discussed below.

The deferral percentage limitation for your highly compensated employees is computed by first averaging the "deferral percentages" (defined below) for the eligible nonhighly compensated employees for the year and then multiplying this result by 1.25. The deferral percentage for a calendar year of any highly compensated employee eligible to participate in this SEP may not be more than the resulting product, the "deferral percentage limitation."

Only elective deferrals are included in this computation. Nonelective SEP contributions may not be included. The determination of the deferral percentage for any employee is made under section 408(k)(6).

For purposes of this computation, the calculation of the number and identity of highly compensated employees, and their deferral percentages, is made on the basis of the entire "affiliated employer" (defined below).

A worksheet is provided on page 8 to assist in figuring the deferral percentage. You may want to photocopy it for yearly use.

The following definitions apply for purposes of computing the deferral percentage limitation under this SEP:

1. **Deferral percentage** is the ratio (expressed as a percentage to 2 decimal places) of an employee's elective deferrals to a calendar year to the employee's compensation for that year. No more than $160,000* per individual is taken into account. The deferral percentage of an employee who is eligible to make an elective deferral, but who does not make a deferral during the year, is zero. If a highly compensated employee also makes elective deferrals under another elective SEP maintained by the employer, then the deferral percentage of that highly compensated employee includes elective deferrals made under the other SEP

2. **Affiliated employer** includes (a) any corporation that is a member of a controlled group of corporations, described in section 414(b) that includes the employer, (b) any trade or business that is under common control, defined in section 414(c) with the employer, (c) any organization that is a member of an affiliated service group, defined in section 414(m) that includes the employer, and (d) any other entity required to be aggregated with the employer under regulations under section 414(o).

3. A **highly compensated employee** is an individual described in section 414(q) who:

Except where stated otherwise, this amount reflects the cost-of-living increase in effect for 1997 and 1998. The amount is adjusted annually. The IRS announces the increase, if any, in a news release, in the Internal Revenue Bulletin, and on the IRS's Internet Web Site at www.irs.ustreas.gov.

STF FED5470F.3

Form 5305A-SEP *(continued)*

Form 5305A-SEP (Rev. 12-97) Page 4

a. Was a 5% owner defined in section 416(i)(1)(B)(i) during the current or preceding year; or

b. For the preceding year had compensation in excess of $80,000* and was in the top-paid group (the top 20% of employees, by compensation).

Excess SEP Contributions — Notification

You must notify each affected employee, if any, by March 15 of the amount of any excess SEP contributions made to that employee's SEP-IRA for the preceding calendar year. (If needed, use the model form on page 5 of these instructions.) These excess SEP contributions are includible in the employee's gross income in the preceding calendar year. However, if the excess SEP contributions (not including allocable income) total less than $100, then the excess contributions are includible in the employee's gross income in the calendar year of notification. Income allocable to the excess SEP contributions is includible in gross income in the year of withdrawal from the IRA.

If you do not notify any of your employees by March 15 of an excess SEP contribution, you must pay a 10% tax on the excess SEP contribution for the preceding calendar year. The tax is reported in Part XII of Form 5330. If you do not notify your employees by December 31 of the calendar year following the calendar year in which the excess SEP contributions arose, the SEP no longer will be treated as meeting the rules of section 408(k)(6). In this case, any contribution to an employee's IRA will be subject to the IRA contribution limits of sections 219 and 408 and thus may be considered an excess contribution to the employee's IRA.

Your notification to each affected employee of the excess SEP contributions must specifically state in a manner written to be understood by the average employee:

• The amount of the excess SEP contributions attributable to that employee's elective deferrals;

• The calendar year in which the excess SEP contributions are includible in gross income; and

• Information stating that the employee must withdraw the excess SEP contributions (and allocable income) from the SEP-IRA by April 15 following the calendar year of notification by the employer. Excess contributions not withdrawn by April 15 following the year of notification will be subject to the IRA contribution limits of sections 219 and 408 for the preceding calendar year and

may be considered excess contributions to the employee's IRA. For the employee, the excess contributions may be subject to the 6% tax on excess contributions under section 4973. If income allocable to an excess SEP contribution is not withdrawn by April 15 following the calendar year of notification by the employer, the employee may be subject to the 10% tax on early distributions under section 72(t) when withdrawn.

For information on reporting excess SEP contributions, see Notice 87-77, 1987-2 C.B. 385, Notice 88-33, 1988-1 C.B. 513, Notice 89-32, 1989-1 C.B. 671, and Rev. Proc. 91-44, 1991-2 C.B. 733.

To avoid the complications caused by excess SEP contributions, you may want to monitor elective deferrals on a continuing basis throughout the calendar year to insure that the deferrals comply with the limits as they are paid into each employee's SEP-IRA.

Disallowed Deferrals

If you determine at the end of any calendar year that more than half of your eligible employees have chosen not to make elective deferrals for that year, then all elective deferrals made by your employees for that year will be considered disallowed deferrals, i.e., IRA contributions that are not SEP-IRA contributions.

You must notify each affected employee by March 15 that the employee's deferrals for the previous calendar year are no longer considered SEP-IRA contributions. Such disallowed deferrals are includible in the employee's gross income in that preceding calendar year. Income allocable to the disallowed deferrals is includible in the employee's gross income in the year of withdrawal from the IRA.

Your notification of the disallowed deferrals must clearly state:

• The amount of the disallowed deferrals;

• The calendar year in which the disallowed deferrals and earnings are includible in gross income; and

• That the employee must withdraw the disallowed deferrals (and allocable income) from the IRA by April 15 following the calendar year of notification by the employer. Those disallowed deferrals not withdrawn by April 15 following the year of notification will be subject to the IRA contribution limits of sections 219 and 408 and thus may be considered an excess contribution to the employee's IRA. For the employee, these disallowed deferrals may be subject to the 6% tax

on excess contributions under section 4973. If income allocable to a disallowed deferral is not withdrawn by April 15 following the calendar year of notification by the employer, the employee may be subject to the 10% tax on early distributions under section 72(t) when withdrawn.

Disallowed deferrals should be reported the same way excess SEP contributions are reported.

Restrictions on Withdrawals

Your highly compensated employees may not withdraw or transfer from their SEP-IRAs any SEP contributions (or income on these contributions) attributable to elective deferrals made for a particular calendar year until March 15 of the following year. Before that date, however, you may notify your employees when the deferral percentage limitation test has been completed for a particular calendar year and that this withdrawal restriction no longer applies. In general, any transfer or distribution made before March 15 of the following year (or notification, if sooner) will be includible in the employee's gross income and the employee may also be subject to a 10% tax on early withdrawal. This restriction does not apply to an employee's excess elective deferrals.

Top-Heavy Requirements

Elective deferrals may not be used to satisfy the minimum contribution requirement under section 416. In any year in which a key employee makes an elective deferral, this SEP is deemed top-heavy for purposes of section 416, and you are required to make a minimum top-heavy contribution under either this SEP or another SEP for each nonkey employee eligible to participate in this SEP.

A key employee under section 416(i)(1) is any employee or former employee (and the beneficiaries of these employees) who, at any time during the determination period, was:

• An officer of the employer (if the employee's compensation exceeds 50% of the section 415(b)(1)(A) limit, which was $125,000* for 1997 (130,000* for 1998);

• An owner of one of the 10 largest interests in the employer (if the employee's compensation exceeds 100% of the section 415(c)(1)(A) limit, which is $30,000*;

• A 5% owner of the employer, as defined in section 416(i)(1)(B)(i); or

• A 1% owner of the employer (if the employee has compensation in excess of $150,000).

The determination period is the current calendar year and the 4 preceding years.

*Except where stated otherwise, this amount reflects the cost-of-living increase in effect for 1997 and 1998. The amount is adjusted annually. The IRS announces the increase, if any, in a news release, in the Internal Revenue Bulletin, and on the IRS's internet Web Site at www.irs.ustreas.gov.

STF FED5470F 4

Form 5305A-SEP *(continued)*

Model Elective SEP Deferral Form

I. Salary reduction deferral

Subject to the requirements of the Model Elective SEP of _____ , I authorize the following amount

(name of employer)

or percentage to be withheld from each of my paychecks and contributed to my SEP-IRA:

(a) _____ % (not to exceed 15%) of my salary; or **(b)** $ _____ .

This salary reduction authorization shall remain in effect until I provide written modification or termination of its terms to my employer.

II. Cash bonus deferral

Subject to the requirements of the Model Elective SEP of _____ , I authorize the following amount

(name of employer)

to be contributed to my SEP-IRA rather than being paid to me in cash: $ _____ .

III. Amount of deferral

I understand that the total amount I defer in any calendar year may not exceed the smaller of:
(a) 15% of my compensation (determined without including any SEP-IRA contributions); or (b) $9,500* for 1997 ($10,000* for 1998).

IV. Commencement of deferral

The deferral election specified in either I or II, above, shall not become effective before _____

(Month, day, year)

(Specify a date no earlier than the first day of the first pay period beginning after this authorization.)

V. Distributions from SEP-IRAs

I understand that I should not withdraw or transfer any amounts from my SEP-IRA that are attributable to elective deferrals and income on elective deferrals for
a particular calendar year (except for excess elective deferrals) until March 15 of the subsequent year or, if sooner, when my employer notifies me that the
deferral percentage limitation test for that plan year has been completed. Any such amounts that I withdraw or transfer before this time will be includible in
income for purposes of sections 72(t) and 408(d)(1).

Signature of employee ▶ _____   Date ▶ _____

*This amount is adjusted annually. The IRS announces the increase, if any, in a news release, in the Internal Revenue Bulletin, and on the IRS's Internet Web Site at
www.irs.ustreas.gov.

Notification of Excess SEP Contributions

To: _____

(name of employee)

Our calculations indicate that the elective deferrals you made to your SEP-IRA for calendar year _____ exceed the maximum

permissible limits under section 408(k)(6). You made excess SEP contributions of $ _____ for that year.

These excess SEP contributions are includible in your gross income for the _____ (insert the year identified above, or if less than $100,
the following year) calendar year.

These excess SEP contributions must be distributed from your SEP-IRA by April 15, 19 _____ (insert year after the calendar year in which
this notice is given) in order to avoid possible penalties. Income allocable to the excess amounts must be withdrawn at the same time and is includible in
income in the year of withdrawal. Excess SEP contributions remaining in your SEP-IRA account after that time are subject to a 6% excise tax, and the income
on these excess SEP contributions may be subject to a 10% penalty when finally withdrawn.

Signature of employer ▶ _____   Date ▶ _____

STF FED5470F.5

Form 5305A-SEP *(continued)*

Instructions for the Employee

The following instructions explain what a simplified employee pension plan (SEP) is, how contributions to a SEP are made, and how to treat these contributions for tax purposes. For more information, see the SEP agreement on pages 1 and 2 and the Instructions for the Employer beginning on page 2.

What Is A SEP?

A SEP is a written arrangement (a plan) that allows an employer to make contributions toward your retirement without becoming involved in more complex retirement plans. A SEP may include a salary reduction arrangement, like the one provided on this form. Under this arrangement, you can elect to have your employer contribute part of your pay to your own individual retirement account or annuity (IRA), set up by you or on your behalf with a bank, insurance company, or other qualified financial institution. The part contributed is tax deferred. Only the remaining part of your pay is currently taxable. This type of SEP is available only to an employer with 25 or fewer eligible employees.

The IRA must be one for which the IRS has issued a favorable opinion letter or a model IRA published by the IRS as Form 5305, Individual Retirement Trust Account, or Form 5305-A, Individual Retirement Custodial Account. It cannot be a SIMPLE IRA (an IRA designed to accept contributions made under a SIMPLE IRA Plan described in section 408(p)).

Your employer must provide you with a copy of the SEP agreement containing eligibility requirements and a description of the basis upon which contributions may be made.

All amounts contributed to your IRA belong to you, even after you quit working for your employer.

Forms and Publications You May Use

An employee may use either of the two forms and the publication listed below.

• Form 5329, Return for Additional Taxes Attributable to Qualified Retirement Plans (including IRAs), Annuities, and Modified Endowment Contracts. Use Form 5329 to pay tax on excess contributions and/or tax on early distributions.

• Form 8606, Nondeductible IRAs (Contributions, Distributions, and Basis). Use Form 8606 to report nondeductible IRA contributions.

• Pub. 590, Individual Retirement Arrangements (IRAs).

Elective Deferrals

Annual Limitation

The maximum amount that you may defer to a SEP for any calendar year is limited to the smaller of 15% of compensation or $9,500* for 1997 ($10,000* for 1998).

The 15% limit may be reduced if your employer also maintains a SEP to which nonelective contributions are made for a year. In this case, total contributions on your behalf to all such SEPs may not exceed the smaller of $30,000* or 15% of your compensation. If these

limits are exceeded, the amount you may elect to contribute to this SEP for the year will be reduced.

The $9,500* limit for 1997 ($10,000* for 1998), imposed under section 402(g), is an overall limit on the maximum amount that you may defer in each calendar year to all elective SEPs, SIMPLE IRA Plans under section 408(p), and cash or deferred arrangements under section 401(k), regardless of how many employers you may have worked for during the calendar year.

For a highly compensated employee, there may be a further limit on the amount you can defer. Figured by your employer and known as the deferral percentage limitation, it limits the percentage of pay that a highly compensated employee can elect to defer to a SEP-IRA. Your employer will notify any highly compensated employee who has exceeded the limitation.

Tax Treatment

Elective deferrals that do not exceed the limits discussed above are excluded from your gross income in the year of the deferral. They are not included as taxable wages on Form W-2, Wage and Tax Statement. However, elective deferrals are treated as wages for social security, Medicare, and unemployment (FUTA) tax purposes.

Excess Amounts

There are three ways in which you may have excess amounts in an elective SEP-IRA.

1. Making excess elective deferrals (i.e., amounts in excess of the section 402(g) limit). You must determine whether you have exceeded the limit in the calendar year. For 1997, the section 402(g) limit for contributions made to an elective SEP is $9,500* ($10,000* for 1998).

2. Highly compensated employees who make excess SEP contributions (i.e., amounts in excess of the deferral percentage limitation referred to above). The employer must determine if an employee has made excess SEP contributions.

3. Having disallowed deferrals (i.e., more than half of your employer's eligible employees choose not to make elective deferrals for a year). All elective deferrals made by employees for that year are considered disallowed deferrals, as discussed below. Your employer must also determine if there are disallowed deferrals.

Excess Elective Deferrals

Excess elective deferrals are includible in your gross income in the calendar year of deferral. Income earned on the excess elective deferrals is includible in the year of withdrawal from the IRA. You should withdraw excess elective deferrals and any allocable income by April 15 following the year to which the deferrals relate. These amounts may not be transferred or rolled over tax-free to another SEP-IRA.

If you do not withdraw excess elective deferrals and any allocable income by April 15, the excess elective deferrals will be subject to the IRA contribution limits of sections 219 and 408 and will be considered excess contributions to your IRA. Such excess deferrals are subject to a 6% excise tax for each year they remain in the SEP-IRA. The excise tax is reported in Part II of Form 5329.

Income earned on excess elective deferrals is includible in your gross income in the year you withdraw it from your IRA. This income should be withdrawn by April 15 following the calendar year in which the deferrals were made. If the income is withdrawn after that date and you are not 59½ years of age, it may be subject to the 10% tax on early distributions. Report the tax in Part I of Form 5329. Also see Pub. 590 for a discussion of exceptions to the age 59½ rule.

Excess SEP Contributions

If you are a highly compensated employee, your employer must notify you of any excess SEP contributions you made to this SEP. The notification should show the amount of the excess SEP contributions, the calendar year of the contributions, and the penalties that may be assessed if the contributions are not withdrawn from your IRA within the applicable time period.

Your employer must notify you of the excess SEP contributions by March 15 following the calendar year for which you made the excess SEP contributions. Generally, you include the excess SEP contributions in income for the calendar year in which you made the original deferrals. This may require you to file an amended individual income tax return. However, any excess SEP contribution less than $100 (not including allocable income) must be included in income in the calendar year of notification. Income earned on these excess contributions must be included in your gross income when you withdraw it from your IRA.

You must withdraw these excess SEP contributions (and allocable income) from your IRA. You may withdraw these amounts without penalty, until April 15 following the calendar year in which you were notified by your employer of the excess SEP contributions. Otherwise, the excess SEP contributions are subject to the IRA contribution limits of sections 219 and 408 and will be considered an excess contribution to your IRA. Thus, the excess SEP contributions are subject to a 6% excise tax reportable in Part II of Form 5329 for each year the contributions remain in your IRA.

If you do not withdraw the income earned on the excess SEP contributions by April 15 following the calendar year of notification by your employer, the income may be subject to a 10% tax on early distributions if you are not 59½ years of age when you withdraw it. Report the tax in Part I of Form 5329. Also see Pub. 590.

If you have both excess elective deferrals and excess SEP contributions, the amount of excess elective deferrals that you withdraw by April 15 will reduce any excess SEP contributions that must be withdrawn for the corresponding calendar year.

Disallowed Deferrals

You are not required to make elective deferrals to a SEP-IRA. However, if more than 50% of your employer's eligible employees choose not to make elective deferrals in a calendar year, then no employee may participate for that calendar year. If you make elective deferrals during a year in which this happens, then your deferrals for that year will be "disallowed," and the deferrals will be treated as ordinary IRA contributions (which may be excess IRA contributions) rather than SEP-IRA contributions.

*Except where stated otherwise, this amount reflects the cost-of-living increase in effect for 1997 and 1998. The amount is adjusted annually. The IRS announces the increase, if any, in a news release, in the Internal Revenue Bulletin, and on the IRS's internet Web Site at www.irs.ustreas.gov.

STF FED5470F 6

Form 5305A-SEP *(continued)*

Disallowed deferrals and any income the deferrals have earned may be withdrawn, without penalty until April 15 following the calendar year in which you are notified of the disallowed deferrals. Amounts left in the IRA after that date will be subject to the same penalties discussed in Excess SEP Contributions above.

Income Allocable To Excess Amounts

The rules for determining and allocating income to excess elective deferrals, excess SEP contributions, and disallowed deferrals are the same as those governing regular IRA contributions. The trustee or custodian of your SEP-IRA will inform you of the income allocable to these amounts.

Additional Top-Heavy Contributions

If you are not a key employee, your employer must make an additional contribution to your SEP-IRA for a year in which the SEP is considered "top heavy." (Your employer can tell you if you are a key employee. Also, see Top-Heavy Requirements on page 4 for the definition of a key employee.) This additional contribution will not exceed 3% of your compensation. It may be less if your employer has already made a contribution to your SEP-IRA, and for certain other reasons.

IRA Contribution for SEP Participants

In addition to any SEP amounts, you may contribute the smaller of $2,000 or 100% of your compensation to an IRA. However, the amount of your contribution that you may deduct on your income tax return is subject to various income limits. Get Form 8606. Also, you may want to get Pub. 590.

SEP-IRA Amounts — Rollover or Transfer To Another IRA

If you are a highly compensated employee, you may not withdraw or transfer from your SEP-IRA any SEP contributions (or income on these contributions) attributable to elective deferrals made during the year until March 15 of the following year or, if sooner, at the time your employer notifies you that the deferral percentage limitation (discussed under Annual Limitation on page 6) has been completed for that year. In general, any transfer or distribution made before this time is includible in your gross income and may also be subject to a 10% tax on early distribution. Report this tax in Part I of Form 5329. You may, however, remove excess elective deferrals from your SEP-IRA before this time but you may not roll over or transfer these deferrals to another IRA.

If the restrictions above do not apply, you may withdraw funds from your SEP-IRA and no more than 60 days later place those funds in another IRA, but not in a SIMPLE IRA. This is called a "rollover" and can be done without penalty only once in any 1-year period. However, there are no restrictions on the number of times that you may make "transfers" if you arrange to have these funds transferred between the trustees or the custodians so that you never have possession of the funds.

You may not, however, roll over or transfer excess elective deferrals, excess SEP contributions, or disallowed deferrals from your SEP-IRA to another IRA. These amounts may be reduced only by a distribution to you.

Employer To Provide Information on SEP-IRAs and Form 5305A-SEP

Your employer must give you a copy of the following information:

1. A copy of a completed Form 5305A-SEP, the Model Elective SEP Deferral Form (used to defer amounts to the SEP), and, if applicable, a copy of the Notice of Excess SEP Contributions. Your employer should also provide you with a statement of any contributions made during the calendar year to your SEP-IRA. Highly compensated employees must also be notified at the time the deferral percentage limitation test is completed.

2. A statement that IRAs other than SEP-IRAs receiving contributions under this SEP may have different rates of return and different terms (e.g., transfers and withdrawals from the IRAs).

3. A statement that the administrator of an amended SEP must furnish to each participant within 30 days of the amendment, a copy of the amendment and an explanation of its effects.

4. A statement that the administrator must notify each participant in writing of any employer contributions to the SEP-IRA. The notification must be made by the later of January 31 following the year of the contribution or 30 days after the contribution is made.

Financial Institution Requirements

The financial institution where your IRA is maintained must provide you with a disclosure statement that contains the following information in plain, nontechnical language:

1. The law that relates to your IRA.

2. The tax consequences of various options concerning your IRA.

3. Participation eligibility rules, and rules on the deductibility of retirement savings.

4. Situations and procedures for revoking your IRA, including the name, address, and telephone number of the person designated to receive notice of revocation. (This information must be clearly displayed at the beginning of the disclosure statement.)

5. A discussion of the penalties that may be assessed because of prohibited activities concerning the IRA.

6. Financial disclosure that provides the following information.

a. Projects value growth rates of the IRA under various contribution and retirement schedules, or describes the method of computing and allocating annual earnings and charges that may be assessed.

b. Describes whether, and for what period, the growth projections are guaranteed, or a statement of earnings rate and the terms on which these projections are based.

c. States the sales commission to be charged in each year expressed as a percentage of $1,000.

In addition, the financial institution must provide you with a financial statement each year. You may want to keep these statements to evaluate your IRA's investment performance and to report IRA distributions for tax purposes.

Paperwork Reduction Act Notice. You are not required to provide the information requested on a form that is subject to the Paperwork Reduction Act unless the form displays a valid OMB control number. Books or records relating to a form or its instructions must be retained as long as their contents may become material in the administration of any Internal Revenue law. Generally, tax returns and return information are confidential, as required by Code section 6103.

The time needed to complete this form will vary depending on individual circumstances. The estimated average time is:

Recordkeeping . . . . 3 hr., 52 min.

Learning about the
law or the form . . . . 3 hr., 57 min.

Preparing the form . . . . 50 min.

If you have comments concerning the accuracy of these time estimates or suggestions for making this form simpler, we would be happy to hear from you. You can write to the Tax Forms Committee, Western Area Distribution Center, Rancho Cordova, CA 95743-0001. DO NOT send this form to this address. Instead, keep it for your records.

Form 5305A-SEP *(continued)*

Form 5305A-SEP (Rev. 12-97)							Page 8
Deferral Percentage Limitation Worksheet (See instructions on page 3.)							
(a) Employee Name	(b) Status H = HCE* O = Other	(c) Compensation (see below)	(d) Deferrals (see below)	(e) Ratio (d) ÷ (c)	(f) Permitted ratio (for HCE* only, see below)	(g) Permitted amount (for HCE* only) (c) × (f)	(h) Excess (for HCE* only) (d) minus (g)
1							
2							
3							
4							
5							
6							
7							
8							
9							
10							
11							
12							
13							
14							
15							
16							
17							
18							
19							
20							
21							
22							
23							
24							
25							

* **Highly compensated employee.** — See the definition beginning on page 3.

Column (c). Compensation. — Enter compensation from this employer and any related employers.

Column (d). Deferrals. — Enter all SEP elective deferrals.

Column (f). Permitted ratio. —

A Enter the total of the ratios in column (e) for the employees marked as "O" in column (b) _____

B Divide line A by the number of employees marked as "O" in column (b) _____

C Permitted ratio. — Multiply line B by 1.25 and enter the permitted ratio here _____

STF FED5470F 9

Form 5305-SIMPLE – Savings Incentive Match Plan for Employees of Small Employers (SIMPLE)

Form **5305-SIMPLE** (October 1996) Department of the Treasury Internal Revenue Service	**Savings Incentive Match Plan for Employees of Small Employers (SIMPLE)** (for Use With a Designated Financial Institution)	OMB No. 1545-1502 **DO NOT File with the Internal Revenue Service**

_____ establishes the following SIMPLE

Name of Employer

plan under section 408(p) of the Internal Revenue Code and pursuant to the instructions contained in this form.

Article I — Employee Eligibility Requirements *(Complete appropriate box(es) and blanks — see instructions.)*

1 General Eligibility Requirements. The Employer agrees to permit salary reduction contributions to be made in each calendar year to the SIMPLE individual retirement account or annuity established at the designated financial institution (SIMPLE IRA) for each employee who meets the following requirements (select either 1a or 1b):

a ☐ **Full Eligibility.** All employees are eligible.

b ☐ **Limited Eligibility.** Eligibility is limited to employees who are described in both (i) and (ii) below:

    (i) Current compensation. Employees who are reasonably expected to receive at least $_____ in compensation *(not to exceed $5,000)* for the calendar year.

    (ii) Prior compensation. Employees who have received at least $_____ in compensation *(not to exceed $5,000)* during any _____ calendar year(s) *(insert 0, 1,or 2)* preceding the calendar year.

2 Excludable Employees (OPTIONAL)

☐ The Employer elects to exclude employees covered under a collective bargaining agreement for which retirement benefits were the subject of good faith bargaining.

Article II — Salary Reduction Agreements *(Complete the box and blank, if appropriate — see instructions.)*

1 Salary Reduction Election. An eligible employee may make a salary reduction election to have his or her compensation for each pay period reduced by a percentage. The total amount of the reduction in the employee's compensation cannot exceed $6,000* for any calendar year.

2 Timing of Salary Reduction Elections

a For a calendar year, an eligible employee may make or modify a salary reduction election during the 60-day period immediately preceding January 1 of that year. However, for the year in which the employee becomes eligible to make salary reduction contributions, the period during which the employee may make or modify the election is a 60-day period that includes either the date the employee becomes eligible or the day before.

b In addition to the election periods in 2a, eligible employees may make salary reduction elections or modify prior elections _____ *(If the Employer chooses this option, insert a period or periods (e.g. semi-annually, quarterly, monthly, or daily) that will apply uniformly to all eligible employees.)*

c No salary reduction election may apply to compensation that an employee received, or had a right to immediately receive, before execution of the salary reduction election.

d An employee may terminate a salary reduction election at any time during the calendar year. ☐ If this box is checked, an employee who terminates a salary reduction election not in accordance with 2b may not resume salary reduction contributions during the calendar year.

Article III — Contributions *(Complete the blank, if appropriate — see instructions.)*

1 Salary Reduction Contributions. The amount by which the employee agrees to reduce his or her compensation will be contributed by the Employer to the employee's SIMPLE IRA.

2 Other Contributions

a **Matching Contributions**

    (i) For each calendar year, the Employer will contribute a matching contribution to each eligible employee's SIMPLE IRA equal to the employee's salary reduction contributions up to a limit of 3% of the employee's compensation for the calendar year.

    (ii) The Employer may reduce the 3% limit for the calendar year in (i) only if: (1) The limit is not reduced below 1%; (2) The limit is not reduced for more than 2 calendar years during the 5-year period ending with the calendar year the reduction is effective; and (3) Each employee is notified of the reduced limit within a reasonable period of time before the employees' 60-day election period for the calendar year *(described in Article II, item 2a)*.

b **Nonelective Contributions**

    (i) For any calendar year, instead of making matching contributions, the Employer may make nonelective contributions equal to 2% of compensation for the calendar year to the SIMPLE IRA of each eligible employee who has at least $_____ *(not more than $5,000)* in compensation for the calendar year. No more than $160,000* in compensation can be taken into account in determining the nonelective contribution for each eligible employee.

    (ii) For any calendar year, the Employer may make 2% nonelective contributions instead of matching contributions only if: (1) Each eligible employee is notified that a 2% nonelective contribution will be made instead of a matching contribution; and (2) This notification is provided within a reasonable period of time before the employees' 60-day election period for the calendar year *(described in Article II, item 2a)*.

3 Time and Manner of Contributions

a The Employer will make the salary reduction contributions (described in 1 above) to the designated financial institution for the IRAs established under this SIMPLE plan no later than 30 days after the end of the month in which the money is withheld from the employee's pay. See instructions.

b The Employer will make the matching or nonelective contributions (described in 2a and 2b above) to the designated financial institution for the IRAs established under this SIMPLE plan no later than the due date for filing the Employer's tax return, including extensions, for the taxable year that includes the last day of the calendar year for which the contributions are made.

For Paperwork Reduction Act Notice, see Instructions.

ISA

STF FED9011F.1

Form **5305-SIMPLE** (10-96)

Form 5305-SIMPLE *(continued)*

Form 5305-SIMPLE (10-96)   Page **2**

Article IV — Other Requirements and Provisions

1 **Contributions in General.** The Employer will make no contributions to the SIMPLE IRAs other than salary reduction contributions *(described in Article III, item 1)* and matching or nonelective contributions *(described in Article III, items 2a and 2b)* .

2 **Vesting Requirements.** All contributions made under this SIMPLE plan are fully vested and nonforfeitable.

3 **No Withdrawal Restrictions.** The Employer may not require the employee to retain any portion of the contributions in his or her SIMPLE IRA or otherwise impose any withdrawal restrictions.

4 **No Cost Or Penalty For Transfers.** The Employer will not impose any cost or penalty on a participant for the transfer of the participant's SIMPLE IRA balance to another IRA.

5 **Amendments To This SIMPLE Plan.** This SIMPLE plan may not be amended except to modify the entries inserted in the blanks or boxes provided in Articles I, II, III, VI, and VII.

6 **Effects Of Withdrawals and Rollovers**

a An amount withdrawn from the SIMPLE IRA is generally includible in gross income. However, a SIMPLE IRA balance may be rolled over or transferred on a tax-free basis to another IRA designed solely to hold funds under a SIMPLE plan. In addition, an individual may roll over or transfer his or her SIMPLE IRA balance to any IRA on a tax-free basis after a 2-year period has expired since the individual first participated in a SIMPLE plan. Any rollover or transfer must comply with the requirements under section 408.

b If an individual withdraws an amount from a SIMPLE IRA during the 2-year period beginning when the individual first participated in a SIMPLE plan and the amount is subject to the additional tax on early distributions under section 72(t), this additional tax is increased from 10% to 25%.

Article V — Definitions

1 **Compensation**

a **General Definition of Compensation.** Compensation means the sum of the wages, tips, and other compensation from the Employer subject to federal income tax withholding (as described in section 6051(a)(3)) and the employee's salary reduction contributions made under this plan, and, if applicable, elective deferrals under a section 401(k) plan, a SARSEP, or a section 403(b) annuity contract and compensation deferred under a section 457 plan required to be reported by the Employer on Form W-2 (as described in section 6058(a)(8)).

b **Compensation for Self-Employed Individuals.** For self-employed individuals, compensation means the net earnings from self-employment determined under section 1402(a) prior to subtracting any contributions made pursuant to this plan on behalf of the individual.

2 **Employee.** Employee means a common-law employee of the Employer. The term employee also includes a self-employed individual and a leased employee described in section 414(n) but does not include a nonresident alien who received no earned income from the Employer that constitutes income from sources within the United States.

3 **Eligible Employee.** An eligible employee means an employee who satisfies the conditions in Article I, item 1 and is not excluded under Article I, item 2.

4 **Designated Financial Institution.** A designated financial institution is a trustee, custodian or insurance company (that issues annuity contracts) for the SIMPLE plan that receives all contributions made pursuant to the SIMPLE plan and deposits those contributions to the SIMPLE IRA of each eligible employee.

Article VI — Procedures for Withdrawal *(The designated financial institution will provide the instructions (to be attached or inserted in the space below) on the procedures for withdrawals of contributions by employees.)*

Article VII — Effective Date

This SIMPLE plan is effective _____ .(See instructions.)

Name of Employer

By: Signature   Date

Address of Employer

Name and title

The undersigned agrees to serve as designated financial institution, receiving all contributions made pursuant to this SIMPLE plan and depositing those contributions to the SIMPLE IRA of each eligible employee as soon as practicable. Upon the request of any participant, the undersigned also agrees to transfer the participant's balance in a SIMPLE IRA established under this SIMPLE plan to another IRA without cost or penalty to the participant.

Name of designated financial institution

By: Signature   Date

Address

Name and title

This amount will be adjusted to reflect any annual cost-of-living increases announced by the IRS.

STF FED9011F.2

Form 5305-SIMPLE *(continued)*

Form 5305-SIMPLE (10-96)   Page 3

Model Notification to Eligible Employees

I. Opportunity to Participate in the SIMPLE Plan

You are eligible to make salary reduction contributions to the _____
SIMPLE plan. This notice and the attached summary description provide you with information that you should consider before you decide whether to start, continue, or change your salary reduction agreement.

II. Employer Contribution Election

For the _____ calendar year, the employer elects to contribute to your SIMPLE IRA *(employer must select either (1), (2), or (3)):*

☐ (1) A matching contribution equal to your salary reduction contributions up to a limit of 3% of your compensation for the year;

☐ (2) A matching contribution equal to your salary reduction contributions up to limit of _____ % *(employer must insert a number from 1 to 3 and is subject to certain restrictions)* of your compensation for the year; or

☐ (3) A nonelective contribution equal to 2% of your compensation for the year (limited to $160,000*) if you are an employee who makes at least $ _____ *(employer must insert an amount that is $5,000 or less)* in compensation for the year.

III. Administrative Procedures

If you decide to start or change your salary reduction agreement, you must complete the salary reduction agreement and return it to _____ *(employer should designate a place or individual)* by _____ *(employer should insert a date that is not less than 60 days after notice is given).*

Model Salary Reduction Agreement

I. Salary Reduction Election

Subject to the requirements of the SIMPLE plan of _____ *(name of employer)* I authorize _____ % or
$_____ % *(which equals_____ % of my current rate of pay)*
to be withheld from my pay for each pay period and contributed to my SIMPLE IRA as a salary reduction contribution.

II. Maximum Salary Reduction

I understand that the total amount of my salary reduction contributions in any calendar year cannot exceed $6,000.*

III. Date Salary Reduction Begins

I understand that my salary reduction contributions will start as soon as permitted under the SIMPLE plan and as soon as administratively feasible or, if later, _____ . *(Fill in the date you want the salary reduction contributions to begin. The date must be after you sign this agreement.)*

IV. Duration of Election

This salary reduction agreement replaces any earlier agreement and will remain in effect as long as I remain an eligible employee under the SIMPLE plan or until I provide my employer with a request to end my salary reduction contributions or provide a new salary reduction agreement as permitted under this SIMPLE plan.

Signature of employee   _____

Date   _____

This amount will be adjusted to reflect any annual cost-of-living increases announced by the IRS.

STF FED9011F.3

Form 5305-SIMPLE *(continued)*

Section references are to the Internal Revenue Code unless otherwise noted.

Paperwork Reduction Act Notice

You are not required to provide the information requested on a form that is subject to the Paperwork Reduction Act unless the form displays a valid OMB control number. Books or records relating to a form or its instructions must be retained as long as their contents may become material in the administration of any Internal Revenue law. Generally, tax returns and return information are confidential, as required by section 6103.

The time needed to complete this form will vary depending on individual circumstances. The estimated average time is:

Recordkeeping . . . . 3 hr., 38 min.
Learning about the
law or the form . . . . 2 hr., 26 min.
Preparing the form . . . . 47 min.

If you have comments concerning the accuracy of these time estimates or suggestions for making this form simpler, we would be happy to hear from you. You can write to the Tax Forms Committee, Western Area Distribution Center, Rancho Cordova, CA 95743-0001. DO NOT send this form to this address. Instead, keep it for your records.

General Instructions

Note: *The instructions for this form are designed to assist in the establishment and administration of the SIMPLE plan; they are not intended to supersede any provisions in the SIMPLE plan.*

Purpose of Form

Form 5305-SIMPLE is a model Savings Incentive Match Plan for Employees of Small Employers (SIMPLE) plan document that an employer may use in combination with SIMPLE IRAs to establish a SIMPLE plan described in section 408(p). It is important that you keep this form for your records. DO NOT file this form with the IRS. For more information, see Pub. 560, Retirement Plans for the Self-Employed, and Pub. 590, Individual Retirement Arrangements (IRAs).

Instructions for the Employer

Which Employers May Establish and Maintain a SIMPLE plan?

You are eligible to establish and maintain a SIMPLE plan only if you meet both of the following requirements:

1. Last calendar year, you had no more than 100 employees (including self-employed individuals) who earned $5,000 or more in compensation from you during the year. If you have a SIMPLE plan but later exceed this 100-employee limit, you will be treated as meeting the limit for the two years following the calendar year in which you last satisfied the limit. If the failure to continue to satisfy the 100-employee limit is due to an acquisition or similar transaction involving your business, special rules apply. Consult your tax advisor to find out if you can still maintain the plan after the transaction.

2. You do not maintain during any part of the calendar year another qualified plan with respect to which contributions are made, or benefits are accrued, for service in the calendar year. For this purpose, a qualified plan (defined in section 219(g)(5)) includes a qualified pension plan, a profit-sharing plan, a stock bonus plan, a qualified annuity plan, a tax-sheltered annuity plan, and a simplified employee pension (SEP) plan.

Certain related employers (trades or businesses under common control) must be treated as a single employer for purposes of the SIMPLE requirements. These are: (1) a controlled group of corporations under section 414(b); (2) a partnership or sole proprietorship under common control under section 414(c); or (3) an affiliated service group under section 414(m). In addition, if you have leased employees required to be treated as your own employees under the rules of section 414(n), then you must count all such leased employees for the requirements listed above.

What is a SIMPLE plan?

A SIMPLE plan is a written arrangement that provides you and your employees with a simplified way to make contributions to provide retirement income for your employees. Under a SIMPLE plan, employees may choose whether to make salary reduction contributions to the SIMPLE plan rather than receiving these amounts as part of their regular compensation. In addition, you will contribute matching or nonelective contributions on behalf of eligible employees (see **Employee Eligibility Requirements** below and **Contributions** on page 5). All contributions under this plan will be deposited into a SIMPLE individual retirement account or annuity established for each eligible employee with the designated financial institution named in Article VII (SIMPLE IRA).

The information provided below is intended to help you understand and administer the rules of your SIMPLE plan.

When to Use Form 5305-SIMPLE

A SIMPLE plan may be established by using this Model Form or any other document that satisfies the statutory requirements. Thus, you are not required to use Form 5305-SIMPLE to establish and maintain a SIMPLE plan. Further, do not use Form 5305-SIMPLE if:

1. You do not want to require that all SIMPLE plan contributions initially go to a financial institution designated by you. (e.g., you want to permit each of your eligible employees to choose a financial institution that will initially receive contributions.);

2. You want employees who are nonresident aliens receiving no earned income from you that constitutes income from sources within the United States to be eligible under this plan; or

3. You want to establish a SIMPLE 401(k) plan.

Completing Form 5305-SIMPLE

Pages 1 and 2 of Form 5305-SIMPLE contain the operative provisions of your SIMPLE plan. This SIMPLE plan is considered adopted when you have completed all appropriate boxes and blanks and it has been executed by you and the designated financial institution.

The SIMPLE plan is a legal document with important tax consequences for you and your employees. You may want to consult with your attorney or tax advisor before adopting this plan.

Employee Eligibility Requirements (Article I)

Each year for which this SIMPLE plan is effective, you must permit salary reduction contributions to be made by all of your employees who are reasonably expected to receive at least $5,000 in compensation from you during the year, and who received at least $5,000 in compensation from you in any 2 preceding years. However, you can expand the group of employees who are eligible to participate in the SIMPLE plan by completing the options provided in Article I, items 1a and 1b. To choose full eligibility, check the box in Article I, item 1a. Alternatively, to choose limited eligibility, check the box in Article I, item 1b, and then insert $5,000 or a lower compensation amount (including zero) and 2 or a lower number of years of service in the blanks in (i) and (ii) of Article I, item 1b.

In addition, you can exclude from participation those employees covered under a collective bargaining agreement for which retirement benefits were the subject of good faith bargaining. You may do this by checking the box in Article I, item 2.

Form 5305-SIMPLE *(continued)*

Salary Reduction Agreements (Article II)

As indicated in Article II, item 1, a salary reduction agreement permits an eligible employee to make a salary reduction election to have his or her compensation for each pay period reduced by a percentage (expressed as a percentage or dollar amount). The total amount of the reduction in the employee's compensation cannot exceed $6,000* for any calendar year.

Timing of Salary Reduction Elections

For a calendar year, an eligible employee may make or modify a salary reduction election during the 60-day period immediately preceding January 1 of that year. However, for the year in which the employee becomes eligible to make salary reduction contributions, the period during which the employee may make or modify the election is a 60-day period that includes either the date the employee becomes eligible or the day before.

You can extend the 60-day election periods to provide additional opportunities for eligible employees to make or modify salary reduction elections using the blank in Article II, item 2b. For example, you can provide that eligible employees may make new salary reduction elections or modify prior elections for any calendar quarter during the 30 days before that quarter.

You may use (but are not required to) the Model Salary Reduction Agreement on page 3 to enable eligible employees to make or modify salary reduction elections.

Employees must be permitted to terminate their salary reduction elections at any time. They may resume salary reduction contributions if permitted under Article II, item 2b. However, by checking the box in Article II, item 2d, you may prohibit an employee who terminates a salary reduction election outside the normal election cycle from resuming salary reduction contributions during the remainder of the calendar year.

Contributions (Article III)

Only contributions described below may be made to this SIMPLE plan. No additional contributions may be made.

Salary Reduction Contributions

As indicated in Article III, item 1, salary reduction contributions consist of the amount by which the employee agrees to reduce his or her compensation. You must contribute the salary reduction contributions to the designated financial institution for the employee's SIMPLE IRA.

Other Contributions

Matching Contributions

In general, you must contribute a matching contribution to each eligible employee's SIMPLE IRA equal to the employee's salary reduction contributions. This matching contribution cannot exceed 3% of the employee's compensation. See Definition of Compensation, below.

You may reduce this 3% limit to a lower percentage, but not lower than 1%. You cannot lower the 3% limit for more than 2 calendar years out of the 5-year period ending with the calendar year the reduction is effective.

Note: *If any year in the 5-year period described above is a year before you first established any SIMPLE plan, you will be treated as making a 3% matching contribution for that year for purposes of determining when you may reduce the employer matching contribution.*

In order to elect this option, you must notify the employees of the reduced limit within a reasonable period of time before the applicable 60-day election periods for the year. See Timing of Salary Reduction Elections above.

Nonelective contributions. — Instead of making a matching contribution, you may, for any year, make a nonelective contribution equal to 2% of compensation for each eligible employee who has at least $5,000 in compensation for the year. Nonelective contributions may not be based on more than $160,000* of compensation.

In order to elect to make nonelective contributions, you must notify employees within a reasonable period of time before the applicable 60-day election periods for such year. See Timing of Salary Reduction Elections above.

Note: *Insert $5,000 in Article III, item 2b(i) to impose the $5,000 compensation requirement. You may expand the group of employees who are eligible for nonelective contributions by inserting a compensation amount lower than $5,000.*

Effective Date (Article VII)

Insert in Article VII, the date you want the provisions of the SIMPLE plan to become effective. You must insert January 1 of the applicable year unless this is the first year for which you are adopting any SIMPLE plan. If this is the first year for which you are adopting a SIMPLE plan, you may insert any date between January 1 and October 1, inclusive of the applicable year. Do not insert any date before January 1, 1997.

Other Important Information About Your SIMPLE Plan

Timing of Salary Reduction Contributions

Under the Internal Revenue Code, for all SIMPLE plans, the employer must make the salary reduction contributions to the SIMPLE IRAs of all eligible employees no later than the 30th day of the month following the month in which the amounts would otherwise have been payable to the employee in cash. The Department of Labor has indicated that most SIMPLE plans are also subject to Title I of the Employee Retirement Income Security Act of 1974 (ERISA). The Department of Labor has informed the IRS that, as a matter of enforcement policy, for these plans, salary reduction contributions must be made to the SIMPLE IRA at the designated financial institution as of the earliest date on which those contributions can reasonably be segregated from the employer's general assets, but in no event later than the 30-day deadline described above.

Definition of Compensation

"Compensation" means the amount described in section 6051(a)(3) (wages, tips, and other compensation from the employer subject to federal income tax withholding under section 3401(a)). Usually, this is the amount shown in box 1 of Form W-2, Wage and Tax Statement. For further information, see **Pub. 15** (Circular E), Employer's Tax Guide. Compensation also includes the salary reduction contributions made under this plan, and, if applicable, compensation deferred under a section 457 plan. In determining an employee's compensation for prior years, the employee's elective deferrals under a section 401(k) plan, a SARSEP, or a section 403(b) annuity contract are also included in the employee's compensation.

For self-employed individuals, compensation means the net earnings from self-employment determined under section 1402(a) prior to subtracting any contributions made pursuant to this SIMPLE plan on behalf of the individual.

Employee Notification

You must notify eligible employees prior to the employees' 60-day election period described above that they can make or change salary reduction elections. In this notification, you must indicate whether you will provide:

This amount will be adjusted to reflect any annual cost-of-living increases announced by the IRS.

STF FED90111.2

Form 5305-SIMPLE *(continued)*

Form 5305-SIMPLE (10-96)   Page 6

1. A matching contribution equal to your employees' salary reduction contributions up to a limit of 3% of their compensation;

2. A matching contribution equal to your employees' salary reduction contributions subject to a percentage limit that is between 1 and 3% of their compensation; or

3. A nonelective contribution equal to 2% of your employees' compensation.

You can use the **Model Notification** to **Eligible Employees** on page 3 to satisfy these employee notification requirements for this SIMPLE plan. A **Summary Description** must also be provided to eligible employees at this time. This summary description requirement may be satisfied by providing a completed copy of pages 1 and 2 of Form 5305-SIMPLE (including the Article IV Procedures for Withdrawals and transfers from the SIMPLE IRAs established under this SIMPLE plan).

If you fail to provide the employee notification (including the summary description) described above, you will be liable for a penalty of $50 per day until the notification is provided. If you can show that the failure was due to reasonable cause, the penalty will not be imposed.

Reporting Requirements

You are not required to file any annual information returns for your SIMPLE plan, such as Forms 5500, 5500-C/R, or 5500-EZ. However, you must report to the IRS which eligible employees are active participants in the SIMPLE plan and the amount of your employees' salary reduction contributions to the SIMPLE plan on Form W-2. These contributions are subject to social security, medicare, railroad retirement, and federal unemployment tax.

Deducting Contributions

Contributions to this SIMPLE plan are deductible in your tax year containing the end of the calendar year for which the contributions are made.

Contributions will be treated as made for a particular tax year if they are made for that year and are made by the due date (including extensions) of your income tax return for that year.

Choosing the Designated Financial Institution

As indicated in Article V, item 4, a designated financial institution is a trustee, custodian, or insurance company (that issues annuity contracts) for the SIMPLE plan that would receive all contributions made pursuant to the SIMPLE plan and deposit the contributions to the SIMPLE IRA of each eligible employee.

Only certain financial institutions, such as banks, savings & loan associations, insured credit unions, insurance companies (that issue annuity contracts), or IRS-approved nonbank trustees may serve as a designated financial institution under a SIMPLE plan.

You are not required to choose a designated financial institution for your SIMPLE plan. However, if you do not want to choose a designated financial institution, you cannot use this form (See **When to Use Form 5305-SIMPLE** on page 4).

Instructions for the Designated Financial Institution

Completing Form 5305-SIMPLE

By completing Article VII, you have agreed to be the designated financial institution for this SIMPLE plan. You agree to maintain IRAs on behalf of all individuals receiving contributions under the plan and to receive all contributions made pursuant to this plan and to deposit those contributions to the SIMPLE IRAs of each eligible employee as soon as practicable. You also agree that upon the request of a participant, you will transfer the participant's balance in a SIMPLE IRA to another IRA without cost or penalty to the participant.

Summary Description

Each year the SIMPLE plan is in effect, you must provide the employer the information described in section 408(l)(2)(B). This requirement may be satisfied by providing the employer a current copy of Form 5305-SIMPLE (including instructions) together with your procedures for withdrawals and transfers from the SIMPLE IRAs established under this SIMPLE plan. The summary description must be received by the employer in sufficient time to comply with the **Employee Notification** requirements on page 5.

If you fail to provide the summary description described above, you will be liable for a penalty of $50 per day until the notification is provided. If you can show that the failure was due to reasonable cause, the penalty will not be imposed.

STF FED9011L3

INDEX

T

ESTABLISH A FRAMEWORK
FOR EXCELLENCE
WITH THE OASIS PRESS ®

Fastbreaking changes in technology and the global marketplace continue to create unprecedented opportunities for businesses in the new millennium. However, with these opportunities will also come many new challenges. Today, more than ever, small businesses need to excel in all areas of operation to compete and suceed in an ever-changing world.

The Successful Business Library takes you through the '90s and beyond, helping you solve the day-to-day problems you face now, and prepares you for the unexpected problems you may be facing down the road. With any of our products, you will receive up-to-date and practical business solutions, which are easy to use and easy to understand. No jargon or theories, just solid, nuts-and-bolts information.

Whether you are an entrepreneur going into business for the first time or an experienced consultant trying to keep up with the latest rules and regulations, The Successful Business Library provides you with the step-by-step guidance, and action-oriented plans you need to succeed in today's world. As an added benefit, PSI Research/The Oasis Press® unconditionally guarantees your satisfaction with the purchase of any book or software application in our catalog.

For more information about The Oasis Press®
contact us at:
1-800-228-2275

or visit us online at http://www.psi-research.com
email: info@psi-research.com

Buyer's Guide to Business Insurance

by Don Bury and Larry Heischman

Straightforward advice on shopping for insurance, understanding types of coverage, and comparing proposals and premium rates. Worksheets help you identify and weigh the risks any business is likely to face, then helps determine if any of those might be safely self-insured or eliminated.

Paperback Price: $19.95
ISBN: 1-55571-162-6
Pages: 312

The Small Business Insider's Guide to Bankers

by Suzanne Caplan and Thomas M. Nunnally

In business, the banker and the institution they represent are often perceived as opponents to your business' success. Shows why business owners should take a leading role in developing and nurturing a worthwhile and lasting partnership with their banker. This inside look will help new, as well as seasoned business owners develop a functional understanding of how the banking industry operates, how to speak their language, and how to turn your banker into an advocate for the growth and success of your business.

Paperback Price: $18.95
ISBN: 1-55571-305-X
Pages: 160

BOOKS THAT SAVE YOU TIME & MONEY
FROM THE OASIS PRESS ®

SmartStart Your (State) Business

by The Editors at The Oasis Press®

This all-in-one, easy-to-understand guide will help you get started on the right foot. Packed with valuable startup information, SmartStart Your (State) Business will prepare you to deal with federal, state, and local regulations imposed on small businesses. This concise, friendly, and up-to-date sourcebook is an affordable investment that details each critical step of starting your own business — from choosing a business structure that fits your company's needs to writing a top-notch business plan; to the latest financing options available in your state to handling your business' financial statements.

SmartStart paves the way for your business' success and includes:

- All the necessary filing requirements and their corresponding forms, phone numbers, addresses, and Internet addresses.

- Up-to-date demographic and economic influences and offers insights into how these statistics will impact your business.

- Critical tax issues to help you understand what you'll have to pay — as well as strategies to save you money.

- Tips on major employment, environmental, and safety and health issues facing small business owners.

Be sure to specify which state you want when ordering

CALL 1·800·228·2275 TO ORDER

ORDER DIRECTLY
FROM THE OASIS PRESS ®

Order Form

Check the titles you want and how many;

✔	QUANTITY	
☐		Secure Your Future **($19.95)**
☐		Surviving Success **($19.95)**
☐		Buyer's Guide to Business Insurance **($19.95)**
☐		The Small Business Insider's Guide to Bankers **($18.95)**
☐		SmartStart Your (State) Business **($19.95)** Please specify which state(s) you would prefer:

* *Note: because this is a new series, you may want to call for availability.*

	If your purchase is:	shipping in the U.S. is:
SUBTOTAL	**$0 - $25**	**$5.00**
SHIPPING	**$25.01 - $50**	**$6.00**
	$50.01 - $100	**$7.00**
TOTAL	**$100.01 - $175**	**$9.00**

For orders more than $175.00 or if you are living outside the United States, please call.

SHIPPING & BILLING INFORMATION

Name:

Address:

City, State, Zip:

Phone:

Check: *enclosed to PSI Research* Charge: ☐ VISA ☐ MC ☐ AMEX ☐ DCVR

Card Number: Expires:

Signature: Name on Card:

QUESTIONS? CALL 1-800-228-2275